The OSINT Search Mastery: Hacking Search Engines for Intelligence

Algoryth Ryker

<u>Uncover Hidden Data, Expose Secrets, and Master Search for Open-Source Intelligence</u>

Every Search Holds a Secret—If You Know Where to Look

Search engines are the gateway to the world's information. Every day, billions of queries are processed by Google, Bing, Yandex, and other search platforms. But what if I told you that most people—including professionals—only scratch the surface of what these search engines can truly reveal?

Beneath the simple search bar lies an intricate web of algorithms, hidden databases, advanced operators, and powerful pivoting techniques that can transform ordinary searches into high-powered intelligence-gathering missions. Are you ready to go beyond the basics and unlock the full potential of search for OSINT investigations?

In "**<u>The OSINT Search Mastery</u>**," you will learn how to think like an intelligence analyst, navigate search algorithms, uncover hidden information, and extract valuable data that most people overlook. Whether you're a cybersecurity professional, law enforcement officer, private investigator, journalist, researcher, or simply an inquisitive mind, this book will teach you how to hack search engines for intelligence gathering.

What You Will Learn

1. Understanding Search Engine Algorithms – The Science Behind Search

To master OSINT search techniques, you must first understand how search engines work—and how they can be manipulated.

- **How Search Engines Work**: Crawlers, indexing, and ranking algorithms
- **SEO & OSINT**: How search engine optimization influences results
- **Surface Web, Deep Web & Dark Web**: What search engines index—and what they don't
- **Personalized Search Results**: How search engines track users & how to avoid bias
- **Search Engine Limitations**: Why search engines can hide, filter, or manipulate data

2. Google Hacking & Advanced Operators – The Secrets Behind Search Queries

Google is the most powerful OSINT tool—if you know how to use it correctly.

- **Google Dorking**: How to exploit Google's advanced search capabilities
- **Mastering Google Operators**: Filetype, site:, intitle:, inurl:, and more
- **Finding Hidden Documents**: Exposed PDFs, spreadsheets, and private reports
- **Locating Publicly Exposed Databases**: Unprotected logins, passwords, and records
- **Metadata Extraction**: How to pull data from indexed files
- **Case Study**: Real-world investigations using Google Dorking

3. Search Engine Pivoting – Following the Digital Trail

A single data point can lead to a web of connections—if you know how to pivot.

- **The Art of Search Pivoting**: Using one data piece to find more
- **Reverse Searching** Usernames, Emails & Phone Numbers
- **Pivoting** Through Social Media & Forum Mentions
- **Finding Hidden Connections** Using Search Techniques
- **Practical Exercises**: Real-world pivoting challenges

4. Alternative Search Engines – When Google Isn't Enough

Google isn't the only player in the game—and sometimes, it's not the best tool for the job.

- Why Google is Limited & When to Use Alternatives
- Exploring Bing, Yandex, and Baidu for OSINT
- **Privacy-Focused Search Engines**: DuckDuckGo, Startpage, and more
- **Academic & Government Databases**: Google Scholar, legal records, and business filings
- **Cybercrime-Specific Search Engines**: Tracking malicious actors through alternative search methods
- **Real-World Search Engine** Effectiveness Test

5. Metadata & Filetype Searches – Extracting Hidden Clues

Every file contains hidden data—if you know where to look.

- What is Metadata & Why is it Important in OSINT?
- Extracting Metadata from PDFs, Word Docs & Images
- Finding Publicly Exposed Metadata in Search Engines
- Using Filetype Search Operators to Locate Specific Documents

- Reverse Searching Metadata for Clues & Connections
- **Case Study**: Tracing a target through metadata

6. People Search Engines & Public Records – Finding Digital Footprints

People leave more information online than they realize—and you can find it.

- How People Search Engines Work & Where They Get Their Data
- Free vs. Paid People Search Services
- Finding Social Media Profiles, Phone Numbers & Addresses
- Verifying Identities Using Public Records & Data Leaks
- Cross-Referencing Data for Accuracy & Reducing False Positives
- Ethical & Legal Considerations in People Searching

7. Academic & Government Database Searches – Unlocking Open Data

The government and academia store vast amounts of valuable information—if you know where to look.

- What Information is Available in Public Databases?
- Using Google Scholar & Research Papers for OSINT
- Searching Legal & Government Databases for Intelligence
- Extracting Information from Business & Corporate Filings
- Historical Records & Archives: Finding past data online
- Case Study: Using government data in OSINT investigations

8. Deep & Dark Web Search Techniques – Going Beyond the Surface

Not all information is indexed—but that doesn't mean it's invisible.

- **Deep Web vs. Dark Web**: Understanding the unindexed internet
- How to Search Unindexed Pages on the Deep Web
- **Tor & Onion Search Engines**: Finding hidden sites
- **Dark Web Marketplaces & Forums**: How to investigate illicit activities
- **Monitoring** Dark Web Leaks & Data Breaches
- **Case Study**: Investigating cybercrime using deep & dark web searches

9. Social Media Search Strategies – Finding the Truth Behind Digital Personas

Social media isn't just for entertainment—it's an intelligence goldmine.

- Using Social Media as a Search Engine for OSINT
- Advanced Facebook Search Techniques
- Twitter Hashtag & Mention Tracking for Intelligence
- Instagram & TikTok Search Tricks
- Finding Deleted & Archived Social Media Content
- **Case Study**: Identifying Fake Social Media Accounts Through Search

10. Automation & Scripting for Search – Scaling OSINT Investigations

When manual search isn't enough, automation is the key.

- Introduction to Search Automation for OSINT
- Using Google Custom Search for Advanced Queries
- Python & APIs for Automating OSINT Searches
- Scraping Search Results for Large-Scale Investigations
- Real-Time Intelligence Monitoring with Automated Search
- Ethical & Legal Issues in Automated Search OSINT

11. Anonymity & Safe Searching – Protecting Your Digital Footprint

OSINT investigations can expose your digital identity—unless you know how to stay hidden.

- The Risks of Search Engine Tracking in OSINT Investigations
- How to Avoid Fingerprinting & Search Bias
- Using VPNs, Proxies & Tor for Anonymous Searching
- Private Browsers & Search Engines for Secure OSINT
- Best Practices for Protecting Your Digital Footprint
- **Case Study**: Conducting OSINT While Maintaining OPSEC

12. Real-World OSINT Search Challenges – Putting Your Skills to the Test

You've learned the techniques—now apply them in real-world investigations.

- Finding a Missing Person Using Search Techniques
- Tracking a Cybercriminal Through Search Engine Data
- Investigating a Disinformation Campaign via Google Dorking
- Exposing Fake News & Fraudulent Websites Through Search
- Extracting Intelligence from a Public Data Breach

- Final OSINT Search Challenge: Combining All Techniques

Become an OSINT Search Master

This book isn't just about finding information—it's about uncovering the truth hidden beneath layers of digital noise. Whether you're investigating a person, a cyber threat, or a misinformation campaign, search mastery is the foundation of OSINT success.

Are you ready to go beyond surface-level searching and unlock the hidden power of search engines?

Let's begin.

1. Understanding Search Engine Algorithms

Search engines are the gatekeepers of the internet, using complex algorithms to crawl, index, and rank vast amounts of data. To master OSINT (Open-Source Intelligence), understanding how these algorithms work is crucial. Search engines like Google, Bing, and others rely on ranking factors such as relevance, backlinks, and user behavior to determine which results appear first. However, these algorithms are not static—they evolve constantly to combat spam, improve accuracy, and refine search experiences. By dissecting their mechanics, leveraging advanced operators, and anticipating algorithmic changes, OSINT analysts can manipulate queries to uncover hidden or obscure information that remains invisible to the average user.

1.1 How Search Engines Work: Crawlers, Indexing & Ranking

Search engines are the backbone of modern information retrieval, allowing users to navigate the vast expanse of the internet efficiently. Understanding how they work is crucial for OSINT professionals looking to refine their search techniques and uncover hidden data. At their core, search engines function through three primary processes: crawling, indexing, and ranking. Each of these steps determines how and where information appears in search results, and knowing how to manipulate them can significantly enhance an analyst's ability to extract intelligence.

Crawling: The Web's Digital Spiders

Crawling is the first step in a search engine's process of discovering new and updated content on the web. Search engines deploy automated bots, commonly referred to as web crawlers or spiders, to systematically browse the internet and collect data from web pages. These bots start from a known set of URLs and follow hyperlinks, mapping out the web by continuously discovering new pages.

How Crawlers Work

- **Starting Point (Seed URLs):** Search engines begin their crawl with a predefined list of websites, often including popular and frequently updated sites.
- **Following Links**: As crawlers visit web pages, they analyze the content and extract links, which are added to their queue for future crawling.
- **Revisiting & Updating**: Crawlers revisit pages periodically to detect updates, changes, or new content, ensuring the index remains current.

However, not all pages are easily accessible to crawlers. Certain areas of the web, known as the Deep Web, contain content hidden behind logins, dynamic scripts, or robot exclusion protocols (robots.txt files), which instruct search engines not to index specific parts of a site.

OSINT Implications

For OSINT analysts, understanding how crawlers work can reveal why certain information appears in search results while other data remains hidden. Analysts can use this knowledge to:

- **Identify Unindexed Data**: Some pages may not be crawled due to robots.txt restrictions, meaning valuable intelligence could be located by accessing databases directly or through alternative search engines.
- **Manipulate Crawling Behavior**: Webmasters can control how their site is indexed using directives like noindex tags, which can help analysts determine what organizations are deliberately hiding.
- **Leverage Site-Specific Searches**: Using Google's site: operator can help analysts determine what portions of a website have been indexed.

Indexing: Storing & Organizing the Web

Once a page is crawled, the next step is indexing, where the search engine processes and stores the collected data in a massive database known as the search index. This index acts as a structured repository of web content, allowing search engines to retrieve relevant results quickly when a query is entered.

How Indexing Works

- **Content Processing**: The search engine extracts key elements from the page, including text, metadata, images, and links.
- **Keyword Analysis**: Words and phrases are analyzed to determine the primary topics of the page.
- **Metadata & Structured Data**: Additional information, such as title tags, descriptions, and schema markup, helps categorize the content more effectively.
- **Duplicate Content Detection**: Search engines filter out identical or near-duplicate pages to avoid redundancy in results.
- **Storage in the Index**: The processed data is stored in the search engine's index, which allows for fast retrieval during searches.

Why Some Pages Are Not Indexed

- Blocked by robots.txt or meta tags (e.g., meta name="robots" content="noindex").
- Low-quality or duplicate content, which search engines may de-prioritize.
- Restricted access, such as password-protected pages or dynamically generated content.

OSINT Implications

For OSINT analysts, indexing determines what data is readily available through search queries and what requires alternative retrieval methods. Key strategies include:

- **Using Cached Versions**: If a page has been indexed but later removed, the cache: operator in Google can retrieve its last stored version.
- **Extracting Metadata**: Information from indexed metadata (e.g., title: and description: fields) can provide clues about a page's content without needing direct access.
- **Accessing Unindexed Content**: Combining traditional search techniques with deep web resources (such as academic databases or government archives) can reveal non-indexed data.

Ranking: The Search Algorithm at Work

The final and most crucial step in how search engines operate is ranking, which determines the order in which results appear. Search engines use complex algorithms to assess and prioritize web pages based on relevance, authority, and user intent.

Key Ranking Factors

- **Relevance**: How well a page matches the user's query based on keywords, topic relevance, and semantic search principles.
- **Authority**: Websites with strong backlinks, high domain authority, and reputable sources rank higher.
- **User Experience (UX):** Search engines consider page speed, mobile-friendliness, and user engagement metrics (e.g., click-through rate, bounce rate).
- **Freshness**: Recently updated content often gets priority, especially for time-sensitive topics.
- **Context & Personalization**: Search results are tailored based on user location, search history, and previous interactions.

Google's Core Algorithm Components

- **PageRank**: Google's original algorithm that evaluates the importance of a page based on the number and quality of inbound links.
- **BERT & NLP**: Advanced natural language processing (NLP) models help Google understand search intent beyond exact keyword matching.
- **RankBrain**: A machine-learning system that refines search results based on user behavior.

OSINT Implications

Understanding ranking mechanisms allows OSINT professionals to optimize searches and bypass common obstacles:

- **Avoiding Filter Bubbles**: Search personalization can limit the diversity of results. Using private browsing or VPNs can help access more neutral search results.
- **Targeting High-Authority Sources**: Government, academic, and reputable news sites are often prioritized in rankings, making them ideal for verified intelligence.
- **Leveraging Alternative Search Engines**: Google's ranking system filters out certain content; using Bing, Yandex, or specialized databases can yield different results.

Search engines operate through a sophisticated system of crawling, indexing, and ranking, determining what information is accessible and how it appears in search results. For OSINT professionals, mastering these mechanics is key to refining search strategies, uncovering hidden intelligence, and bypassing algorithmic limitations. By leveraging site operators, analyzing metadata, and understanding ranking biases, analysts can enhance their ability to retrieve critical data efficiently and effectively.

1.2 The Role of SEO & Its Impact on OSINT

Search Engine Optimization (SEO) is the practice of optimizing web content to rank higher in search engine results. While SEO is primarily used for marketing and online visibility, its influence on search rankings directly affects OSINT (Open-Source Intelligence) investigations. Understanding SEO techniques helps analysts navigate search result biases, uncover hidden information, and refine search strategies to bypass obstacles created by digital marketing efforts. This chapter explores how SEO impacts OSINT, the techniques websites use to manipulate rankings, and how analysts can work around these tactics to extract more accurate and comprehensive intelligence.

What is SEO?

SEO is the process of improving a website's visibility on search engines like Google, Bing, and Yandex. It involves technical and content-based strategies to influence ranking algorithms, making certain pages more discoverable than others.

SEO consists of three main components:

- **On-Page SEO** – Optimizing individual web pages through keyword placement, metadata, content quality, and user experience.
- **Off-Page SEO** – Building backlinks, social media engagement, and external signals to boost a website's authority.
- **Technical SEO** – Improving website speed, security, mobile-friendliness, and structured data to enhance crawlability and indexing.

For OSINT analysts, understanding these components is crucial because SEO shapes the information that appears first in search results, potentially obscuring more valuable intelligence.

How SEO Affects OSINT Investigations

SEO techniques impact OSINT efforts by influencing what information is easily accessible versus what gets buried under layers of optimized content. Here's how:

1. Search Engine Bias & Manipulated Rankings

Companies, governments, and individuals use SEO to control narratives by pushing favorable content to the top and burying negative or sensitive information. This means that:

- Reputation Management Services use aggressive SEO tactics to flood search results with positive stories while pushing down negative ones.
- Crisis Management SEO is used by organizations to overshadow scandals or controversies by publishing high-ranking press releases and blogs.

Keyword Hijacking occurs when websites target popular search queries to rank higher, even if the content isn't truly relevant.

OSINT Strategy: To bypass manipulated results, analysts can use:

- Time filters to find older, less optimized content.
- Alternative search engines like Bing, Yandex, or DuckDuckGo, which may rank pages differently.
- Advanced Google operators like inurl:, intitle:, or filetype: to directly access unfiltered content.

2. Content Farms & Misinformation

Many websites use SEO to mass-produce content that ranks well but lacks depth or accuracy. These "content farms" generate thousands of articles targeting trending keywords, drowning out factual or investigative content.

OSINT Strategy:

- Use fact-checking sources (Snopes, FactCheck.org) to verify information.
- Cross-reference multiple sources before drawing conclusions.
- Rely on official and academic databases for authoritative intelligence.

3. Dark & Hidden SEO Techniques (Black Hat SEO)

While most SEO practices follow ethical guidelines, some entities use black hat SEO techniques to manipulate search engines aggressively. These tactics can obscure or distort OSINT research.

Common Black Hat SEO Tactics:

- **Keyword Stuffing**: Overloading pages with keywords to manipulate rankings.
- **Cloaking**: Showing different content to users versus search engines.
- **PBNs (Private Blog Networks):** A network of fake websites linking to each other to boost rankings artificially.
- **Negative SEO**: Attacking competitor sites to de-rank them, making OSINT sources harder to find.

OSINT Strategy:

Analyze backlink profiles using tools like Ahrefs or OpenLinkProfiler to identify fake networks.

Use cached pages or archived content (Wayback Machine) to view previous versions of manipulated pages.
Look beyond the first page of results, where less-optimized but potentially valuable content may exist.

Bypassing SEO Barriers in OSINT Investigations

To overcome SEO-driven biases and ranking manipulations, OSINT analysts can employ the following techniques:

1. Use Search Operators to Cut Through SEO Clutter

Search operators help refine queries and locate precise information:

- **site:[domain]** – Searches within a specific website (e.g., site:example.com).
- **intitle:[keyword]** – Finds pages with specific words in the title.
- **inurl:[keyword]** – Locates URLs containing certain words.
- **filetype:[extension]** – Searches for specific document types (e.g., PDFs, XLSX).
- **before:[YYYY-MM-DD] / after:[YYYY-MM-DD]** – Filters results by date.

2. Use Alternative Search Engines

Google's dominance means its ranking algorithm is heavily influenced by SEO tactics. Other search engines may return different results:

- **Bing/Yandex**: Often index different parts of the web and rank results differently.
- **DuckDuckGo**: Prioritizes privacy and doesn't personalize results.
- **Shodan/Censys**: Specialized search engines for internet-connected devices.
- **Academic & Government Databases**: Less influenced by SEO, offering authoritative sources.

3. Leverage the Deep & Dark Web

Since traditional search engines prioritize optimized content, some valuable intelligence may reside beyond the surface web:

- **Wayback Machine (Archive.org)** – Retrieves past versions of altered or deleted content.
- **Onion Search Engines (Ahmia, OnionLand)** – Uncover dark web discussions and leaked databases.

- **FOIA & Government Archives** – Less likely to be SEO-optimized but contain official records.

4. Analyze Backlinks & Web Relationships

SEO often relies on backlink strategies to boost rankings. By analyzing backlinks, OSINT analysts can:

- Identify hidden connections between websites and organizations.
- Uncover satellite sites that serve as SEO buffers for reputation management.
- Track down deleted pages that were previously linked but have since been removed.
- Tools like Ahrefs, Majestic SEO, and Google Search Console can be useful for backlink analysis.

SEO plays a major role in shaping the information landscape of search engines, often influencing what OSINT analysts can access. While SEO can be used to manipulate, filter, or obscure intelligence, understanding its mechanics allows analysts to bypass these barriers effectively. By using advanced search operators, alternative search engines, backlink analysis, and deep web tools, OSINT practitioners can extract high-quality intelligence beyond the reach of traditional SEO-driven results. Mastering the interplay between SEO and OSINT ensures that analysts can navigate an increasingly manipulated digital environment while maintaining the integrity and accuracy of their findings.

1.3 Differences Between Surface Web, Deep Web & Dark Web Searches

The internet is vast, but not all of it is accessible through standard search engines. OSINT analysts must understand the different layers of the web to effectively gather intelligence. The internet can be categorized into three main segments:

- **Surface Web** – The publicly accessible portion of the internet indexed by search engines.
- **Deep Web** – Content that is not indexed by search engines, including databases, private networks, and password-protected sites.
- **Dark Web** – An encrypted, anonymous part of the internet that requires special tools like Tor or I2P to access.

Each layer presents unique challenges and opportunities for OSINT investigations. This chapter explores how these segments differ, their relevance to intelligence gathering, and how to conduct effective searches across them.

1. Surface Web: The Indexed & Searchable Internet

What is the Surface Web?

The surface web consists of web pages that search engines like Google, Bing, and Yandex can index and display in search results. This includes news sites, blogs, social media profiles, business directories, and publicly accessible government records.

How to Search the Surface Web for OSINT

Search engines use crawlers to index surface web content, making it easily searchable. However, OSINT analysts can refine their searches using advanced techniques:

Google Dorking (Advanced Search Operators):

- **site:example.com** – Search within a specific domain.
- **intitle:"confidential" filetype:pdf** – Find documents with "confidential" in the title.
- **inurl:admin login** – Locate admin login pages.

Alternative Search Engines:

- **Yandex & Bing** – May index different content than Google.
- **DuckDuckGo** – Prioritizes privacy and avoids tracking-based personalization.
- **Wayback Machine (Archive.org)** – Retrieves historical versions of websites.

Limitations of the Surface Web for OSINT

While useful, the surface web has significant limitations:

- **SEO Manipulation**: Many results are influenced by SEO, making it harder to find unbiased information.
- **Data Removal**: Websites can delete or alter content, making historical research difficult.
- **Limited Scope**: Most valuable intelligence lies beyond search engine reach, requiring deeper investigation.

2. Deep Web: The Hidden but Accessible Internet

What is the Deep Web?

The deep web refers to any content not indexed by traditional search engines. Contrary to popular belief, it is not inherently illicit—most of it consists of everyday online services requiring authentication. Examples include:

- **Private databases** (academic research, financial records, medical records).
- **Government archives** (FOIA requests, legal filings, court records).
- **Subscription-based content** (news paywalls, premium reports).
- **Internal company portals** (corporate intranets, SaaS dashboards).

How to Search the Deep Web for OSINT

Since search engines do not index deep web content, OSINT analysts must use alternative tools and techniques:

Specialized Search Engines:

- **Google Scholar** (scholar.google.com) – Access academic papers and research.
- **WorldCat** (worldcat.org) – Search global library catalogs.
- **SEC EDGAR Database** (sec.gov/edgar.shtml) – Find corporate financial filings.

Government & Legal Databases:

- **PACER** (pacer.uscourts.gov) – U.S. federal court records.
- **FOIA.gov** – Freedom of Information Act (FOIA) requests.
- **Business Registries** – Many countries provide corporate ownership records.

Deep Web People Search Tools:

- **Pipl, Spokeo, and BeenVerified** – Aggregate public records, social media, and professional history.
- **LinkedIn & Facebook Graph Search Techniques** – Identify connections between individuals and organizations.

Challenges of Deep Web OSINT Investigations

- **Authentication Barriers**: Many deep web resources require logins or subscriptions.
- **Legal & Ethical Concerns**: Accessing restricted data without permission may violate laws.
- **Verification Issues:** Unlike indexed content, deep web information may lack search engine-backed credibility signals.

3. Dark Web: The Encrypted & Anonymous Internet

What is the Dark Web?

The dark web is a small portion of the deep web that is intentionally hidden and accessible only through specialized software like Tor (The Onion Router) or I2P (Invisible Internet Project). Unlike the deep web, which includes private but legal content, the dark web often hosts anonymous marketplaces, forums, and whistleblower platforms.

Common uses of the dark web include:

Legitimate Activities:

- Secure communication for journalists, activists, and dissidents.
- Privacy-focused services like ProtonMail's onion site.
- Open-source intelligence on cyber threats.

Illicit Activities:

- Black markets for drugs, weapons, and stolen data.
- Hacking forums and cybercrime networks.
- Fraudulent financial services, including money laundering.

How to Search the Dark Web for OSINT

Since traditional search engines do not index dark web content, specialized tools are required:

Tor Search Engines:

- **Ahmia (ahmia.fi)** – Indexes some Tor sites.
- **OnionLand Search** – Searches dark web marketplaces and forums.
- **DarkSearch.io** – Claims to be a "Google for the dark web."

Dark Web Monitoring Tools:

- **IntelX (intelx.io)** – Searches leaked databases, breach information, and hidden web pages.
- **DarkTracer** – Monitors dark web activity related to cybercrime.
- **Have I Been Pwned? (haveibeenpwned.com)** – Checks if an email appears in leaked data breaches.

Tracking Dark Web Forums & Marketplaces:

- Use OSINT Telegram channels for updates on darknet markets.
- Monitor cybercrime groups on forums like RaidForums (before it was taken down).
- Look for leaked credentials, stolen data, or discussions on hacking operations.

Risks & Ethical Considerations

- **Legal Implications**: Accessing dark web marketplaces, hacking forums, or illicit services can violate laws in many countries.
- **Cybersecurity Risks**: Many dark web sites contain malware, phishing attempts, or tracking mechanisms.
- **Attribution Concerns**: Analysts should use VPNs, sandboxed environments, and burner identities to protect their anonymity.

Key Differences Between Surface Web, Deep Web & Dark Web

Feature	Surface Web	Deep Web	Dark Web
Accessibility	Public, indexed by search engines	Requires login, databases, or subscriptions	Requires Tor/I2P, anonymous access
Search Engines	Google, Bing, DuckDuckGo	Internal search tools, database queries	Ahmia, DarkSearch.io
Content	Websites, blogs, news, public records	Academic journals, court filings, subscription-based data	Anonymous forums, marketplaces, leaked data
Risk Level	Low	Medium (authentication required)	High (cybercrime, malware, legal risks)
OSINT Uses	General research, social media tracking	Investigating companies, finding hidden information	Tracking cyber threats, monitoring illicit activity

Understanding the differences between the surface web, deep web, and dark web is essential for OSINT professionals. While the surface web is the most accessible, much of the valuable intelligence lies within the deep web, requiring specialized search techniques. Meanwhile, the dark web presents opportunities for gathering intelligence on cybercrime and emerging threats but comes with significant risks. Mastering search strategies across all three layers ensures analysts can extract critical information while maintaining security and ethical standards.

1.4 How Search Engines Personalize Results (And How to Avoid It)

Search engines like Google, Bing, and Yandex personalize search results based on user data, tailoring what each person sees to their browsing habits, location, and preferences. While this improves user experience, it also introduces biases that can hinder OSINT (Open-Source Intelligence) investigations. OSINT analysts must be aware of how personalization works and how to bypass it to obtain neutral, unfiltered results.

This chapter explores how search engines personalize results, the implications for intelligence gathering, and practical techniques to avoid personalized filtering.

How Search Engines Personalize Results

Search engines collect vast amounts of user data to customize search rankings. The primary factors influencing personalized results include:

1. Search History & Click Behavior

- Search engines track past queries and clicked links to predict what a user might find relevant.
- Frequently visited sites and topics influence the ranking of future search results.
- **Example**: If an analyst frequently searches for cybersecurity topics, Google may prioritize tech blogs and security-related sites in their results.

2. Location & IP Address

- Search engines use geolocation (based on IP addresses, GPS, or Wi-Fi networks) to serve region-specific results.
- Local businesses, news, and government websites appear higher for users in certain locations.
- **Example**: A search for "data breach laws" in the U.S. will prioritize U.S. legal sources, while the same query in the EU may return GDPR-related results.

3. Device & Browser Information

- The device type (mobile, desktop, tablet) and browser (Chrome, Firefox, Edge) can affect search rankings.
- Mobile users may see mobile-optimized results first, while desktop users may get more complex websites.

4. Cookies & Logged-In Accounts

- If a user is logged into a Google, Microsoft, or social media account, the search engine can tailor results based on their activity across different platforms.
- Google's ecosystem (Gmail, YouTube, Google Maps) shares data across services to refine search results.
- **Example**: If an analyst frequently watches cybersecurity videos on YouTube, Google may suggest related articles in search results.

5. Social Media & Network Influence

- Google and Bing may incorporate social media signals (likes, shares, and follows) to adjust search rankings.
- Personalized search results may reflect what people in a user's network find important.

6. AI & Machine Learning Algorithms

- Search engines continuously refine personalization using artificial intelligence (AI) and machine learning (ML).
- AI-powered systems analyze user intent, query context, and behavioral data to modify search rankings dynamically.

Why Personalization is a Problem for OSINT

While personalization improves convenience, it poses several issues for OSINT analysts:

1. Filter Bubbles & Echo Chambers

- Analysts may only see results that align with their past searches, limiting exposure to diverse perspectives.
- Opposing viewpoints or lesser-known sources may be hidden from results.

2. Inconsistent Search Results

- The same search query can yield different results based on the user's location, device, or browsing history.
- Two analysts searching for the same term may get entirely different information.

3. SEO & Manipulation Risks

- Search engine optimization (SEO) strategies exploit personalization to push specific content higher in rankings.
- Reputation management firms use personalization to bury negative content about individuals or companies.

4. Privacy & Tracking Concerns

- OSINT analysts researching sensitive topics risk exposing their interests to search engines and third parties.

- Repeatedly searching for specific topics may trigger tracking mechanisms, increasing the risk of surveillance.

How to Avoid Search Engine Personalization

OSINT analysts must take proactive steps to ensure neutral, unfiltered search results. Below are effective techniques to bypass personalization:

1. Use Private Browsing & Incognito Mode

- Browsers like Chrome, Firefox, and Edge offer incognito or private mode, preventing cookies from storing session data.
- **Limitations**: This does not prevent IP tracking or fingerprinting.

2. Clear Cookies & Browser Cache

- Regularly delete cookies, cache, and site data to reset search preferences.
- Tools like CCleaner or BleachBit can automate cookie removal.
- **Limitation**: Some tracking methods persist even after clearing cookies.

3. Use a VPN or Proxy Server

- Virtual Private Networks (VPNs) hide the real IP address, preventing location-based personalization.
- Proxies can route searches through different geographic locations.
- **Example**: Using a European VPN server can reveal search results from a European perspective.
- **Limitations**: Some search engines detect and block VPN-based searches.

4. Log Out of Google & Other Accounts

- Ensure you are logged out of Google, Bing, Yahoo, and social media accounts before conducting OSINT searches.
- Use a separate browser profile for intelligence gathering.

5. Change Search Engine Preferences

- Google allows users to disable Web & App Activity and Personalized Search in account settings.
- Go to: Google Account > Data & Privacy > Web & App Activity > Turn Off.

6. Use Anonymous Search Engines

- Search engines like DuckDuckGo, Startpage, and SearX do not track searches or personalize results.
- SearX allows users to query multiple search engines while masking their identity.

7. Use Alternative Search Engines for Diversity

- Bing & Yandex may provide different perspectives from Google.
- Brave Search offers an independent, privacy-focused alternative.
- Metasearch engines (like Dogpile and Swisscows) aggregate results from multiple sources.

8. Modify URL Parameters to Disable Personalization

Append &pws=0 to Google search URLs to disable personalized search.

Example:

https://www.google.com/search?q=cybersecurity&pws=0

Limitation: Google may still apply some ranking filters based on IP.

9. Use TOR for Completely Anonymous Searching

- The Onion Router (Tor) anonymizes searches by routing traffic through multiple servers.
- Ideal for investigating sensitive topics without revealing analyst identity.
- **Limitation**: Some search engines block Tor users or present captchas.

10. Compare Results Across Different Devices & Locations

- Conduct searches on different devices (mobile vs. desktop) and using different network connections.
- Use public Wi-Fi or a different ISP to compare search result variations.
- Testing Personalization: How to Verify Unbiased Search Results
- Run the same search query using different browsers and devices.
- Compare results using a VPN or Tor to simulate different locations.

- Use a non-tracking search engine (DuckDuckGo) alongside Google to spot ranking biases.
- Check Google's cached version of a webpage to see how content changes over time.

Search engines tailor results using sophisticated personalization techniques, but OSINT analysts must work around these filters to obtain neutral, unmanipulated intelligence. By using private browsing, VPNs, anonymous search engines, and advanced search techniques, investigators can break free from search engine biases and access a broader, more accurate pool of information. Mastering these methods is essential for conducting reliable, objective OSINT research.

1.5 The Limitations of Search Engines for OSINT Investigations

Search engines like Google, Bing, and Yandex are powerful tools for OSINT (Open-Source Intelligence) investigations, but they have significant limitations. While they provide access to a vast amount of publicly available information, they are not all-encompassing and often fail to retrieve the most critical intelligence. OSINT analysts must understand these limitations and explore alternative methods to obtain complete and accurate data.

This chapter discusses the key constraints of search engines in OSINT investigations and strategies to overcome them.

1. Search Engines Do Not Index the Entire Web

The Surface Web vs. The Deep Web

Search engines only index a fraction of the internet, known as the surface web. A vast amount of information resides in the deep web—data that is hidden from search engine crawlers and requires login credentials, database queries, or direct access.

Why Search Engines Cannot Index Everything:

1. **Database-Driven Content** – Government records, legal documents, academic research, and business registries often reside in databases that require internal searches.

2. **Paywalled or Subscription-Based Content** – Premium news articles, industry reports, and scientific journals are often behind paywalls.
3. **Dynamic & Session-Based Content** – Some websites generate content dynamically in response to user input, making it invisible to search engine bots.

How to Overcome This Limitation:

- Use specialized deep web search engines (e.g., Google Scholar, WorldCat, PACER).
- Access government and corporate databases directly.
- Utilize FOIA (Freedom of Information Act) requests for restricted public records.

2. Search Engines Prioritize SEO & Paid Results

Search Engine Optimization (SEO) Manipulates Results

Search engines rank pages based on algorithms that favor well-optimized content. This often leads to biased, commercial, or low-quality information appearing at the top, while valuable intelligence remains buried.

Problems with SEO for OSINT:

- Reputation Management Firms manipulate search results to hide negative information about individuals and companies.
- Fake News & Disinformation websites exploit SEO tactics to spread propaganda.
- Corporate & Political Biases influence ranking algorithms, altering the visibility of certain topics.

How to Overcome This Limitation:

- Use advanced search operators (-site:, inurl:, intitle:) to bypass SEO manipulation.
- Cross-check information across multiple sources to detect biases.
- Investigate alternative search engines (DuckDuckGo, SearX, Brave Search) for neutral results.

3. Search Engines Filter & Censor Results

Geopolitical & Legal Censorship

Many countries enforce strict internet regulations, leading to search engine censorship. For example:

- China (Great Firewall) blocks Google and restricts access to foreign news.
- Russia censors politically sensitive content.
- European Union enforces the "Right to Be Forgotten," allowing individuals to request content removal.

Additionally, search engines comply with legal takedown requests, removing content under copyright laws (DMCA), defamation claims, or law enforcement orders.

How to Overcome This Limitation:

- Use VPNs or Tor to bypass regional restrictions.
- Explore country-specific search engines (e.g., Baidu, Yandex) for alternative perspectives.
- Monitor archived content using the Wayback Machine (archive.org).

4. Search Engines Struggle with Real-Time & Hidden Data

Real-Time Information is Limited

Search engines are not ideal for tracking breaking news, emerging cyber threats, or live events because their indexing processes take time. Many OSINT investigations require real-time monitoring, which search engines cannot provide.

How to Overcome This Limitation:

- Use social media monitoring tools like TweetDeck, CrowdTangle, and Hootsuite.
- Track news aggregators (Google News, Bing News) and real-time data feeds.
- Utilize dark web monitoring services for cyber threat intelligence.

Hidden & Private Social Media Data

Most social media platforms limit search engine access to their content. Facebook, LinkedIn, and Instagram heavily restrict external indexing, preventing OSINT analysts from retrieving valuable information via search engines.

How to Overcome This Limitation:

- Use platform-specific search techniques (e.g., LinkedIn Boolean searches).
- Leverage OSINT tools like Maltego, Pipl, and Social-Searcher to extract social media data.
- Conduct manual reconnaissance using fake profiles and engagement techniques (while staying within ethical and legal boundaries).

5. Personalization & Bias Affect Search Results

Algorithmic Bias & Filter Bubbles

Search engines personalize results based on past behavior, location, and browsing history. This creates filter bubbles, reinforcing existing biases and limiting exposure to diverse perspectives.

How to Overcome This Limitation:

- Disable personalized search by adding &pws=0 to Google searches.
- Use private browsing modes, VPNs, or anonymous search engines like Startpage.
- Compare multiple search engines to detect ranking differences.

6. Cybersecurity Risks & Privacy Concerns

Tracking & Data Collection

Search engines log queries, track user behavior, and store search histories. For OSINT analysts, this poses privacy risks and potential exposure to adversaries.

How to Overcome This Limitation:

- Use privacy-focused search engines (DuckDuckGo, Qwant, Brave Search).
- Avoid searching for sensitive topics on personal devices.
- Utilize sandboxed environments (e.g., virtual machines) for research.

Malicious Search Results

Hackers and threat actors use SEO poisoning to spread malware through search engine results. Clicking on malicious links can lead to:

- Drive-by downloads that install malware automatically.
- Phishing pages disguised as legitimate sites.

- Fake research papers designed to spread misinformation.

How to Overcome This Limitation:

- Use sandboxed browsers (or virtual machines) when clicking on unknown links.
- Check URLs carefully before visiting unfamiliar sites.
- Utilize URL reputation checkers (VirusTotal, URLVoid) to verify links.

Key Takeaways: Why OSINT Analysts Cannot Rely Solely on Search Engines

Limitation	Impact on OSINT	Solution
Not indexing the deep web	Critical data remains hidden	Use specialized databases & direct searches
SEO manipulation	Biased, commercial, or misleading results	Use advanced search operators & verify sources
Censorship & legal restrictions	Some content is removed or hidden	Use VPNs, Tor, and alternative search engines
Lack of real-time data	Cannot track breaking events or live threats	Use social media monitoring & news aggregators
Algorithmic bias & personalization	Creates filter bubbles & skews intelligence	Use incognito mode, disable personalization, & compare sources
Privacy & security risks	OSINT analysts can be tracked or exposed	Use anonymous search engines & VPNs

While search engines are valuable OSINT tools, they are far from perfect. Their inability to access deep web content, reliance on SEO rankings, censorship policies, and lack of real-time intelligence limit their effectiveness in investigations. OSINT analysts must combine search engine techniques with specialized tools, alternative data sources, and privacy measures to ensure thorough, unbiased, and secure intelligence gathering.

1.6 Search Engine Manipulation: How Information Is Hidden

Search engines are powerful tools for information discovery, but they are also vulnerable to manipulation. Various entities—governments, corporations, hackers, and individuals—use Search Engine Manipulation (SEM) techniques to hide, suppress, or distort information. Whether it's for reputation management, censorship, or disinformation campaigns, understanding how search engines can be manipulated is critical for OSINT analysts who need unbiased, unfiltered intelligence.

This chapter explores the different methods used to manipulate search engine results, the risks associated with these tactics, and techniques OSINT analysts can use to detect and bypass such manipulation.

1. What is Search Engine Manipulation (SEM)?

Search Engine Manipulation (SEM) refers to tactics used to alter the visibility, ranking, or discoverability of information on search engines like Google, Bing, and Yandex. Manipulation can take different forms, including hiding negative information, amplifying propaganda, censoring content, or flooding search results with distractions.

Why is SEM Used?

- **Reputation management** – Hiding negative articles, reviews, or reports about individuals or companies.
- **Censorship** – Governments suppressing politically sensitive content.
- **Disinformation & propaganda** – Spreading fake news, misleading narratives, or biased viewpoints.
- **SEO exploitation** – Boosting specific content through aggressive Search Engine Optimization (SEO) tactics.

Corporate interests – Burying competitors' content or legal cases.

For OSINT analysts, SEM presents a challenge: how to uncover the truth behind search results that are intentionally manipulated.

2. Techniques Used to Manipulate Search Engine Results

1. Search Engine Optimization (SEO) for Suppression & Promotion

SEO is typically used to improve visibility, but it can also be weaponized to hide or promote specific content artificially.

How SEO Manipulation Works:

- **Flooding the web with positive content** – Reputation management firms create large amounts of SEO-optimized content to bury negative search results.

- **Keyword manipulation** – Websites use keyword stuffing to rank for irrelevant or misleading terms.
- **Backlink schemes** – Buying or exchanging high-authority backlinks to boost rankings.
- **Content farming** – Creating low-quality blog posts, fake news, or automated articles to push legitimate information lower.

🔍 Example:

- A politician facing corruption allegations hires a PR firm to publish hundreds of positive articles about their achievements.
- These articles are optimized with the politician's name and outrank negative reports about the corruption scandal.

☐ How to Counter:

- Use advanced search operators (-site:, inurl:, intitle:) to filter out promotional content.
- Check Google's cached pages to see how content has changed over time.
- Analyze backlink structures using tools like Ahrefs or Majestic.

2. The Right to Be Forgotten (RTBF) & Legal Content Removal

Some individuals or companies request search engines to remove or deindex certain results under privacy laws or defamation claims.

How RTBF Works:

- The EU's General Data Protection Regulation (GDPR) allows people to request the removal of outdated, irrelevant, or defamatory content from search engines.
- Google DMCA Takedowns allow companies to request removal of copyright-infringing content.
- Defamation lawsuits can force web hosts or search engines to deindex content.

🔍 Example:

A businessman with a criminal past successfully requests Google to remove old news articles about his fraud case, making it harder for journalists and OSINT analysts to uncover his history.

- Check alternative search engines like Bing, Yandex, and DuckDuckGo (they may not honor takedown requests).
- Use archived versions from the Wayback Machine (archive.org) or Google Cache.
- Search for court records, public databases, or investigative reports that may contain the same information.

3. Shadow Banning & Content Deprioritization

Some content is not deleted but is deprioritized—making it harder to find. This is common in social media platforms but also happens in search engines.

How Shadow Banning Works:

- Google's quality algorithms penalize certain content (e.g., misinformation, controversial topics) and push it lower in rankings.
- Some search engines demonetize or blacklist websites based on political, medical, or controversial content.
- Social media sites use algorithmic suppression to make specific posts harder to find.

🔍 **Example:**

A whistleblower's website exposing government corruption is technically still online but appears on page 15 of Google search results due to ranking suppression.

☐ **How to Counter:**

- Search using multiple search engines (Google, Bing, Yandex, DuckDuckGo).
- Look for direct website links instead of relying solely on search rankings.
- Use social media OSINT tools to track engagement metrics and hidden posts.

4. Geoblocking & Censorship

Search engines may block or alter results based on the user's location. This is especially common in authoritarian regimes.

How Geoblocking Works:

- Some government-controlled search engines (e.g., China's Baidu) filter out foreign or politically sensitive content.
- Google customizes results based on country-specific laws and requests.
- Some websites restrict access based on IP address location.

🔍 Example:

A journalist in China searches for "Tiananmen Square Massacre" on Baidu and finds zero critical reports, only government-approved content.

☐ How to Counter:

- Use VPNs, proxies, or Tor to simulate searches from different locations.
- Search on country-specific search engines (e.g., Yandex for Russian content, Baidu for Chinese).
- Check Google Transparency Reports for censorship requests.

5. Disinformation & Fake News Flooding

Malicious actors deliberately flood search engines with false or misleading information to obscure the truth.

How Fake News Manipulates Search Engines:

- **Bot-driven content generation** – Automated blogs publish large volumes of misleading articles.
- **Clickbait & sensationalism** – Misleading headlines are designed to game search engine algorithms.
- **Fake social media engagement** – Likes, shares, and comments amplify misleading content.

🔍 Example:

A disinformation campaign creates thousands of AI-generated fake news articles about a geopolitical event, making it harder to find credible sources.

☐ How to Counter:

- Verify content using fact-checking websites (Snopes, Politifact, Bellingcat).
- Investigate who owns or funds the source of the information.

- Cross-reference information across trusted sources and multiple languages.

Conclusion: How OSINT Analysts Can Overcome Search Engine Manipulation

Manipulation Method	Impact	Countermeasure
SEO Suppression	Buries negative or sensitive content	Use search operators, cached pages, and backlink analysis
RTBF & Legal Removals	Content is deindexed	Check alternative engines, archives, and public records
Shadow Banning	Content is deprioritized, not deleted	Use multiple search engines, direct links, and social media analysis
Geoblocking	Certain results are hidden by region	Use VPNs, proxies, and localized search engines
Fake News Flooding	False information obscures real data	Fact-check, verify sources, and use trusted investigative tools

For OSINT analysts, understanding how search engines are manipulated is just as important as knowing how to search effectively. By using advanced techniques, alternative tools, and critical thinking, investigators can uncover hidden truths that search engines try to suppress.

2. Google Hacking & Advanced Operators

Google is more than just a search engine—it's a powerful OSINT tool when used with precision. Google Hacking, also known as Google Dorking, involves using advanced search operators to uncover hidden information, misconfigured databases, exposed login portals, and sensitive documents that are unintentionally indexed. By mastering operators like site: for domain-specific searches, intitle: and inurl: for targeted page results, and filetype: for specific document retrieval, OSINT analysts can extract intelligence efficiently. Understanding how to combine these operators creatively allows for deep, granular searches that bypass conventional limitations, turning Google into a high-powered intelligence-gathering machine. However, ethical considerations and legal boundaries must always be kept in mind when navigating this gray area of open-source research.

2.1 What is Google Dorking? A Powerful OSINT Tool

Google is often seen as a simple search engine, but for OSINT (Open-Source Intelligence) investigators, it is a powerful tool for uncovering hidden information. One of the most effective techniques used in OSINT is Google Dorking, also known as Google Hacking. This method leverages advanced search operators to extract sensitive, overlooked, or unintentionally exposed data from the internet.

In this chapter, we will explore what Google Dorking is, how it works, and how OSINT analysts can use it to find exposed files, hidden databases, login credentials, and more.

1. Understanding Google Dorking

Google Dorking refers to the use of advanced search queries and operators to refine searches and locate specific types of information. By using these special commands, analysts can bypass standard search filters and reveal data that is not intended for public access.

Google's web crawlers index vast amounts of content, including improperly secured files, misconfigured websites, and forgotten databases. OSINT investigators use Google Dorking to retrieve:

✅ **Exposed login pages** (admin portals, webcams, sensitive dashboards)

☑ **Publicly accessible files** (PDFs, DOCs, XLS files with sensitive data)

☑ **Database records** (SQL dumps, passwords, customer data)

☑ **Website vulnerabilities** (server misconfigurations, outdated software)

☑ **Emails & personal data** (employee directories, leaked contact details)

💡 **Example: Searching for login pages**

inurl:admin login

This command searches for URLs containing "admin" and "login," often revealing admin panels for various websites.

While Google Dorking is a legitimate OSINT technique, it can also be misused by cybercriminals. Ethical investigators must always stay within legal and ethical boundaries when conducting searches.

2. How Google Dorking Works: Using Search Operators

Google's search engine recognizes specific operators and parameters that allow users to fine-tune searches. Below are some of the most useful Google Dorks for OSINT investigations.

A. Finding Specific File Types

Search for documents, spreadsheets, or text files that may contain sensitive data.

🔍 **Examples:**

- filetype:pdf confidential
- filetype:xls "username" "password"
- filetype:txt site:example.com

- filetype:pdf confidential → Searches for PDFs containing the word "confidential."

- filetype:xls "username" "password" → Looks for spreadsheets containing potential

  login details.

- filetype:txt site:example.com → Finds text files on a specific website.

B. Searching for Exposed Directories

Some websites have unprotected directories that reveal internal files.

🔍 **Examples:**

- intitle:"index of" "backup"
- intitle:"index of" "database"
- "index of" "backup" → Finds open directory listings containing backups.
- "index of" "database" → May expose databases with sensitive information.

C. Finding Login Pages & Admin Panels

Login pages are often exposed due to poor security configurations.

🔍 **Examples:**

1. inurl:admin login
2. inurl:login site:gov
3. inurl:admin login → Finds login pages for administrator accounts.
4. inurl:login site:gov → Searches for government-related login portals.

D. Discovering Exposed Cameras & IoT Devices

Some security cameras and IoT devices are accessible via Google due to misconfigured settings.

🔍 **Examples:**

- inurl:"viewerframe?mode=motion"
- intitle:"webcamXP 5"
- inurl:"viewerframe?mode=motion" → Finds live security cameras.
- intitle:"webcamXP 5" → Detects cameras running webcamXP software.

E. Identifying Vulnerable Websites

OSINT analysts can check for outdated software or security flaws.

🔍 Examples:

- inurl:php?id= site:.edu
- inurl:/wp-content/plugins/ site:.com
- inurl:php?id= site:.edu → Finds university websites that might be vulnerable to SQL injection.
- inurl:/wp-content/plugins/ site:.com → Detects WordPress plugin directories, which can reveal outdated software.

3. Practical OSINT Use Cases for Google Dorking

1. Investigating Corporate Exposures

Google Dorking can uncover sensitive business information, including financial reports, internal memos, and customer databases.

Example Dork:

- filetype:xls "employee salaries" site:company.com

🔎 **Potential Findings**: An exposed Excel file listing employee salary data.

2. Uncovering Government & Law Enforcement Documents

Many government databases, police reports, and legal documents are indexed by Google.

Example Dork:

- filetype:pdf site:.gov "confidential"

🔎 **Potential Findings**: Publicly accessible government reports labeled "confidential."

3. Tracking Down Email Addresses & Contact Information

Attackers and OSINT analysts alike use Google Dorking to find employee email addresses, phone numbers, and internal directories.

Example Dork:

- site:linkedin.com "@company.com"

🔎 **Potential Findings**: Employee email addresses associated with a company.

4. Searching for Exposed Security Cameras

Some organizations fail to secure their surveillance cameras, making them viewable through Google.

Example Dork:

- inurl:"/view.shtml"

🔎 **Potential Findings**: Live video feeds from unsecured IP cameras.

5. Detecting Data Breaches & Leaked Credentials

If login credentials are leaked in a publicly accessible document, they might appear in search results.

Example Dork:

- filetype:txt "password" site:pastebin.com

🔎 **Potential Findings**: Plaintext password lists from data breaches.

4. Ethical & Legal Considerations

While Google Dorking is a powerful OSINT tool, it comes with ethical and legal responsibilities.

🚨 What You Should NOT Do:

✗ Access unauthorized or password-protected content.

✗ Use Dorks to find and exploit website vulnerabilities.

✗ Retrieve personally identifiable information (PII) for malicious purposes.

💡 What You CAN Do (Legally & Ethically):

✅ Use Google Dorking for publicly available data.

✅ Perform security audits (with permission).

✅ Use Dorking to assess your own organization's security.

⚠️ **Warning**: Many companies monitor search activity for security threats. Running certain dorks may trigger intrusion detection systems (IDS) or even result in legal consequences. Always research local cybersecurity laws before using advanced search techniques.

5. Conclusion: Why Google Dorking is Essential for OSINT

Google Dorking is one of the most powerful OSINT techniques for extracting information that is hidden in plain sight. Whether analyzing corporate leaks, government documents, or security vulnerabilities, advanced search operators provide a deeper level of intelligence gathering.

However, with great power comes great responsibility. Ethical use of Google Dorking ensures that OSINT investigators stay within legal boundaries while maximizing their ability to uncover valuable intelligence.

2.2 Mastering Google Search Operators: Filetype, Site, Intitle & More

Google is the world's most powerful search engine, but most users barely scratch the surface of its capabilities. For OSINT (Open-Source Intelligence) analysts, mastering Google search operators is essential for uncovering hidden, sensitive, or overlooked information. By refining queries with advanced commands, analysts can locate specific files, websites, databases, login pages, leaked documents, and more—all while bypassing standard search limitations.

This chapter will dive deep into the most effective Google search operators, how they work, and how to combine them for precision OSINT investigations.

1. What Are Google Search Operators?

Search operators are special commands that refine Google searches by specifying conditions, filtering results, or targeting certain types of content. These commands allow OSINT investigators to:

✅ Find specific file types (PDFs, Excel sheets, text files)

✅ Search within a specific website or domain

✅ Locate publicly accessible admin panels, cameras, and login pages

✅ Discover cached or archived pages

✅ Identify intentionally hidden information

With the right combination of operators, OSINT analysts can turn Google into an intelligence-gathering weapon.

2. Essential Google Search Operators for OSINT

Below are the most important search operators and their practical OSINT applications.

1. site: – Search Within a Specific Website

This operator restricts results to a single domain.

🔍 **Example Searches:**

- site:gov "confidential"
- site:example.com filetype:pdf
- site:linkedin.com "cybersecurity analyst"

✅ Find sensitive documents on government websites.

✅ Search for employee information on corporate sites.

✅ Locate hidden pages and reports within an organization's domain.

□ **OSINT Use Case:**

If you're investigating a company's leaked reports, try:

- site:company.com filetype:xls "budget"

This may uncover Excel spreadsheets with budget data.

2. filetype: – Search for Specific File Formats

Google indexes documents, spreadsheets, presentations, and more—often containing sensitive data.

🔍 Example Searches:

- filetype:pdf "confidential"
- filetype:xls "password"
- filetype:txt site:pastebin.com

✅ Locate internal reports, memos, and classified PDFs.

✅ Find plain-text credentials, API keys, or password lists.

✅ Discover exposed databases or configuration files.

☐ OSINT Use Case:

If you suspect a company has leaked financial reports, try:

- site:company.com filetype:xls "revenue"

This may expose spreadsheets containing financial data.

3. intitle: – Search for Specific Words in Page Titles

This operator finds pages where the title contains specific keywords.

🔍 Example Searches:

- intitle:"index of" "backup"
- intitle:"admin login"
- intitle:"webcamXP 5"

✅ Locate open directory listings containing backups and databases.

✅ Find exposed admin panels that lack proper authentication.

✅ Discover unsecured webcams and surveillance feeds.

☐ OSINT Use Case:

To find open directories with downloadable files, try:

- intitle:"index of" "documents"

This often reveals files that were never meant to be public.

4. inurl: – Search for Keywords in URLs

This operator restricts results to URLs containing specific words.

🔍 Example Searches:

- inurl:admin login
- inurl:dashboard site:gov
- inurl:wp-content/plugins/

✅ Locate admin panels and login pages.

✅ Find hidden dashboards on government websites.

✅ Search for WordPress plugin vulnerabilities.

☐ OSINT Use Case:

If you want to find government admin pages, try:

- inurl:admin site:gov

This may expose government agency login portals.

5. cache: – View a Cached Version of a Page

Google saves cached versions of web pages, even if they are deleted or changed.

🔍 Example Searches:

- cache:example.com

✅ Recover deleted information.

✅ View a site before it was modified.

✅ Find historical records of webpages.

☐ OSINT Use Case:

If a whistleblower's website suddenly disappears, try:

- cache:whistleblower-website.com

This may retrieve the last version indexed by Google.

6. - (Minus) – Exclude Words from Search Results

This operator removes unwanted words from search results.

🔍 Example Searches:

- "data breach" -news -blog
- filetype:pdf "confidential" -site:gov

✅ Filter out news articles to focus on primary sources.

✅ Exclude government websites when searching for leaked files.

☐ OSINT Use Case:

If you're looking for real leaked reports but don't want media coverage, try:

- "internal memo" -news -blog -press

This removes news articles and focuses on original documents.

7. OR – Search for Multiple Terms at Once

This operator broadens searches by allowing multiple keywords.

🔍 Example Searches:

- filetype:pdf OR filetype:xls "salary report"
- inurl:admin OR inurl:dashboard

✅ Search for multiple file types at once.

✅ Find various login panels on different sites.

☐ OSINT Use Case:

If you want to find both PDFs and Word documents about leaked government data, try:

- filetype:pdf OR filetype:docx site:gov "leaked"

This finds both formats without needing separate searches.

3. Combining Search Operators for Advanced OSINT

🔍 **Example 1:** Finding Leaked Spreadsheets on a Government Site

- site:gov filetype:xls "classified"

🔎 **Potential Results**: Government Excel sheets containing restricted data.

🔍 **Example 2:** Locating Exposed WordPress Admin Panels

- inurl:wp-admin site:edu

🔎 **Potential Results**: University WordPress admin portals.

🔍 **Example 3:** Discovering Open Webcams & Security Cameras

- intitle:"webcamXP 5" OR inurl:"/view.shtml"

🔎 **Potential Results**: Live, unsecured camera feeds.

4. Ethical & Legal Considerations

🔒 What You Should NOT Do:

✗ Use search operators to access private or password-protected data.

✗ Attempt to exploit vulnerabilities found through OSINT.

✗ Search for personal information in a way that violates privacy laws.

💡 What You CAN Do:

✓ Use search operators for open-source research.

✓ Perform security audits (with proper authorization).

✓ Locate leaked information that is already publicly available.

⚠️ **Reminder**: Some organizations monitor Google Dorking activity. Excessive use of certain queries may trigger security alerts.

5. Conclusion: Becoming a Google Search Master

Google search operators are a core skill for OSINT professionals. By combining multiple operators, analysts can extract hidden insights, track down leaks, and uncover intelligence that would otherwise remain buried.

2.3 Finding Hidden & Exposed Documents Online

The internet is full of sensitive documents that were never meant to be public, yet they remain exposed due to poor security practices, misconfigurations, or sheer oversight. OSINT (Open-Source Intelligence) analysts can uncover financial records, internal reports, contracts, legal documents, and even classified information simply by knowing where and how to look.

This chapter explores techniques to find hidden and exposed documents online, leveraging search engines, Google Dorking, metadata analysis, and alternative search tools.

1. Why Are Documents Exposed Online?

Organizations and individuals often unknowingly leak documents due to:

◆ **Misconfigured web servers** – Publicly accessible folders that should be private.
◆ **Cloud storage mistakes** – Misconfigured Google Drive, Dropbox, or Amazon S3 buckets.
◆ **Search engine indexing** – Websites failing to block sensitive files from Google crawlers.
◆ **Forgotten or abandoned websites** – Old subdomains and archives that were never secured.
◆ **Employee mistakes** – Internal documents accidentally uploaded to public websites.

Understanding these vulnerabilities allows OSINT analysts to track down hidden data using search engines and specialized tools.

2. Using Google Dorking to Find Exposed Documents

Google indexes millions of publicly accessible documents, many of which were not meant to be found. Using advanced search operators (Google Dorking), we can extract these files efficiently.

A. Searching for Specific File Types

Google allows you to search for documents by their format using the filetype: operator.

🔍 **Example Dorks:**

- filetype:pdf "confidential"
- filetype:xls "salary report"
- filetype:docx site:gov "internal memo"

☑ Finds PDFs, Excel spreadsheets, and Word documents containing sensitive information.

☐ **OSINT Use Case:**

If you're investigating a leaked military report, try:

- filetype:pdf site:mil "classified"

This searches for classified PDFs on .mil (military) domains.

B. Finding Open Directories

Some websites have unprotected directories where files are stored without security measures.

🔍 Example Dorks:

- intitle:"index of" "documents"
- intitle:"index of" "backup"

✓ Exposes open file directories containing reports, logs, and archives.

☐ OSINT Use Case:

To find leaked financial data, try:

intitle:"index of" "budget"

This may expose spreadsheets with financial projections.

C. Searching for Internal Reports & Leaked Data

Many organizations upload internal documents to their websites without realizing they are public.

🔍 Example Dorks:

- site:company.com filetype:pdf "internal use only"
- site:gov filetype:xls "not for public release"

✓ Finds reports labeled "internal use only" or "not for public release."

☐ OSINT Use Case:

To locate government procurement reports, try:

- site:gov filetype:pdf "contract award"

This can reveal contracts between governments and private companies.

D. Searching for Exposed Login Credentials

Some documents mistakenly contain usernames and passwords.

🔍 Example Dorks:

- filetype:txt site:pastebin.com "password"
- filetype:xls "username" "password"

✅ Finds text files or spreadsheets containing leaked credentials.

🗆 OSINT Use Case:

To check for leaked corporate login details, try:

- filetype:txt site:example.com "admin password"

⚠️🗆 **Warning**: Searching for leaked credentials is legally sensitive. Always follow ethical OSINT guidelines.

3. Searching for Documents on Alternative Search Engines

Google isn't the only search engine indexing exposed documents. Some alternative search engines specialize in uncovering overlooked or hidden data.

A. Bing Search Operators

Microsoft Bing indexes different results than Google, often capturing files that Google doesn't.

🔍 Example Bing Queries:

- filetype:pdf "internal report" site:edu
- intitle:"index of" "client list"

✅ Finds education reports, client databases, and internal memos.

B. Yandex: Russian Search Engine with Powerful Indexing

Yandex can reveal files, images, and archives that are harder to find on Google.

🔍 Example Yandex Queries:

- filetype:xls "financial report" site:example.com

✅ Useful for finding spreadsheets and databases in different languages.

C. Specialized OSINT Search Engines

Some search engines are designed for deep research and intelligence gathering:

◆ **Shodan.io** – Finds exposed databases, webcams, and IoT devices.
◆ **Censys.io** – Searches for unprotected servers and files.
◆ **Wayback Machine (Archive.org)** – Retrieves deleted documents from old versions of websites.

4. Finding Documents in Cloud Storage (Google Drive, Dropbox, Amazon S3)

Many organizations use cloud storage services but fail to secure their files. OSINT investigators can search for publicly accessible cloud files.

A. Google Drive Exposed Files

Google Drive often leaks PDFs, spreadsheets, and internal presentations.

🔍 Example Dork:

- site:drive.google.com "confidential"

✅ Finds confidential files stored in publicly shared Google Drive folders.

B. Amazon S3 Buckets (Unsecured Cloud Storage)

Many companies misconfigure AWS S3 storage, leaving files unprotected.

🔍 Example Dork:

- site:s3.amazonaws.com "passwords"

✅ Can reveal exposed databases, login credentials, and backups.

5. Analyzing Metadata in Exposed Documents

Even if a document doesn't contain sensitive data, its metadata might.

A. Extracting Metadata from Documents

Metadata can reveal:

- ◆ Author names (who created the document)
- ◆ Editing history (previous document versions)
- ◆ Software used (which tools were used to create it)

☐ How to Extract Metadata:

Using ExifTool (Command Line Tool)

- exiftool document.pdf

- Using Online Tools (e.g., Metadata2Go.com)
- Upload a document to analyze hidden metadata.

6. Ethical & Legal Considerations

🚨 What You Should NOT Do:

✗ Download or access restricted, private, or password-protected files.

✗ Use found documents for malicious or illegal purposes.

✘ Distribute sensitive personal data found through OSINT techniques.

♥ What You CAN Do:

✓ Use publicly available documents for legitimate research and analysis.

✓ Assess your own organization's security vulnerabilities.

✓ Report critical data leaks to responsible parties when necessary.

⚠ **Important**: Some search activities may trigger security alerts. Always follow ethical OSINT practices.

7. Conclusion: Becoming a Master of Document Discovery

Finding hidden and exposed documents online is one of the most valuable skills in OSINT investigations. By mastering Google Dorking, alternative search engines, cloud storage searches, and metadata analysis, analysts can extract sensitive intelligence from public sources.

2.4 Searching for Publicly Exposed Databases & Logins

The internet is filled with misconfigured databases, unsecured login portals, and exposed credentials, often due to weak security settings, mismanagement, or a failure to restrict access. OSINT (Open-Source Intelligence) analysts can leverage search engines, Google Dorking, IoT search engines, and alternative techniques to uncover publicly accessible databases and login pages, many of which contain sensitive or even critical data.

In this chapter, we explore techniques for identifying open databases, unsecured login pages, and exposed credentials, while emphasizing the ethical and legal considerations of OSINT research.

1. Why Are Databases & Logins Exposed Online?

Many organizations unknowingly leave databases and login pages exposed, often due to:

◆ **Misconfigured cloud storage** – Public Amazon S3, Google Cloud, or Azure databases.

◆ **Unprotected web services** – Elasticsearch, MongoDB, Firebase, and SQL databases left open.

◆ **Poor security settings** – Default admin passwords or unrestricted access.

◆ **Search engine indexing** – Google or Bing indexing database management interfaces.

◆ **Forgotten or abandoned websites** – Unsecured legacy portals and internal tools.

These security flaws expose personal data, corporate secrets, financial records, and government information—a goldmine for OSINT investigators and a serious risk for organizations.

2. Using Google Dorking to Find Exposed Databases & Logins

Google indexes more than just websites—it also captures database interfaces, login portals, and admin dashboards when they are not properly secured. By using advanced search operators, OSINT analysts can find:

✅ **Exposed login pages** (admin panels, employee portals).

✅ **Database dashboards** (MongoDB, MySQL, Elasticsearch, Firebase).

✅ Unprotected server directories containing backups or logs.

A. Finding Login Pages & Admin Panels

Many websites do not restrict access to admin pages, making them easy to find with Google Dorking.

🔍 **Example Dorks:**

- inurl:admin login
- intitle:"admin panel" "login"
- inurl:wp-admin site:edu

✅ Locates WordPress admin panels, login portals, and control dashboards.

☐ **OSINT Use Case:**

To find corporate login pages, try:

- inurl:login site:company.com

This may expose employee login pages for further analysis.

B. Finding Exposed SQL & NoSQL Databases

Many SQL and NoSQL databases are accessible without authentication, often due to misconfigured servers.

🔍 **Example Dorks:**

- inurl:phpmyadmin "Welcome to phpMyAdmin"
- inurl:admin intext:"MongoDB"
- intitle:"Index of /" "mysql" OR "database"

✅ Uncovers open database management systems (DBMS).

☐ **OSINT Use Case:**

To locate unprotected MySQL interfaces, try:

- inurl:phpmyadmin intext:"Welcome to phpMyAdmin"

This may reveal database control panels where credentials are stored.

C. Finding Unsecured Cloud Storage

Many organizations fail to properly secure Amazon S3 buckets, Google Drive links, and Dropbox folders.

🔍 **Example Dorks:**

- site:s3.amazonaws.com "confidential"
- site:drive.google.com "restricted"

✅ Locates exposed cloud storage containing internal files.

☐ **OSINT Use Case:**

To check for publicly available financial reports, try:

- site:s3.amazonaws.com filetype:xlsx "budget"

This could uncover financial spreadsheets stored in misconfigured S3 buckets.

D. Finding Exposed API Keys & Passwords in Public Repositories

Developers often accidentally upload API keys, passwords, and credentials to public repositories like GitHub and GitLab.

🔍 Example Dorks:

- site:github.com "AWS_ACCESS_KEY_ID"
- site:pastebin.com "database password"

✅ Finds leaked API keys, credentials, and sensitive code.

☐ OSINT Use Case:

To check for leaked API keys, try:

- site:github.com "PRIVATE_KEY"

⚠☐ **Warning**: Accessing or using exposed credentials is illegal. Always follow ethical guidelines.

3. Using IoT & Database Search Engines for Deeper OSINT

Some specialized search engines index exposed databases, login portals, and misconfigured servers, making them excellent tools for OSINT investigations.

A. Shodan: The Search Engine for Exposed Servers

Shodan.io indexes publicly exposed IoT devices, databases, and admin panels.

🔍 **Example Searches:**

- port:27017 MongoDB
- title:"phpMyAdmin"
- port:9200 Elasticsearch

✅ Finds unsecured MongoDB, MySQL, and Elasticsearch instances.

☐ **OSINT Use Case:**

To find unprotected Elasticsearch databases, try:

- port:9200 title:"Elasticsearch"

This may reveal databases containing sensitive user records.

B. Censys: Another Deep Web Search Engine

Censys.io scans open ports, SSL certificates, and publicly exposed services.

🔍 **Example Searches:**

- tags: "database" AND services.mongodb
- metadata.product: "MySQL"

✅ Identifies exposed databases and login portals.

☐ **OSINT Use Case:**

To locate open MySQL databases, try:

- metadata.product: "MySQL"

This may uncover databases that should be private.

4. Searching the Dark Web for Leaked Credentials

Many stolen credentials and breached databases end up being sold on dark web marketplaces or shared in hacker forums. OSINT analysts can search for leaks using:

◆ **Have I Been Pwned (https://haveibeenpwned.com/)** – Checks if an email has been part of a breach.

◆ **Dehashed (https://www.dehashed.com/)** – Searches leaked credentials, hashes, and database dumps.

◆ **Intelligence X (https://intelx.io/)** – Indexes dark web content, leaks, and exposed databases.

◻ **OSINT Use Case:**

To check if company credentials were leaked, enter the domain into Have I Been Pwned to see past breaches.

5. Ethical & Legal Considerations

🔐 **What You Should NOT Do:**

✘ Access password-protected databases or login pages.

✘ Exploit misconfigured servers or APIs.

✘ Download sensitive data from unsecured storage.

💡 **What You CAN Do:**

✓ Report vulnerabilities to organizations when appropriate.

✓ Use findings to improve cybersecurity awareness.

✓ Search for publicly accessible information only.

⚠️ **Important**: Some organizations monitor database access attempts. Avoid triggering security alerts by conducting responsible OSINT research.

6. Conclusion: The Power & Risk of Finding Exposed Data

Finding publicly exposed databases and login pages is one of the most powerful yet risky OSINT techniques. By using Google Dorking, IoT search engines like Shodan, and dark web databases, analysts can uncover valuable intelligence, but they must always stay within legal and ethical boundaries.

2.5 Extracting Metadata from Indexed Documents

Metadata is the hidden layer of information embedded within digital files such as PDFs, Word documents, images, and spreadsheets. For OSINT (Open-Source Intelligence) investigators, metadata can reveal author names, document creation dates, software versions, GPS coordinates, and even hidden notes. When documents are indexed by search engines and publicly accessible, analysts can extract this metadata to uncover crucial intelligence about the source, context, and authenticity of the document.

In this chapter, we explore how to locate indexed documents, extract metadata, and analyze it for OSINT investigations.

1. Understanding Metadata & Why It Matters

Every digital file contains metadata, which is background information stored within the document. Metadata can provide valuable OSINT insights, including:

- **Author & Organization** – Identifies who created or edited the document.
- **Creation & Modification Dates** – Tracks document history and timeline.
- **Software & Version** – Reveals the tools used to create the file.
- **Hidden Comments & Notes** – Often overlooked but can contain internal discussions.
- **GPS Coordinates (for Images & PDFs)** – Reveals the location where a document or photo was created.

☐ OSINT Use Case Example:

If a leaked government document is found online, its metadata might show:

- Who wrote it
- When it was last modified
- If it was ever altered before being uploaded

This information can help verify the document's authenticity and track down its source.

2. Finding Indexed Documents Using Google Dorking

Before extracting metadata, we need to locate relevant documents. Google indexes millions of publicly accessible files, including PDFs, Word documents, Excel spreadsheets, and PowerPoint slides.

A. Finding Specific File Types

Google's filetype: operator allows us to search for specific document formats.

🔍 Example Dorks:

- filetype:pdf "confidential"
- filetype:xls "salary report"
- filetype:docx site:gov "internal memo"

✅ Finds PDFs, Excel files, and Word documents related to sensitive topics.

☐ OSINT Use Case:

To locate military reports, try:

- filetype:pdf site:mil "classified"

This searches for classified PDFs on .mil (military) domains.

B. Finding Metadata-Rich Documents

Some documents contain hidden comments, author names, and history logs.

🔍 Example Dorks:

- filetype:docx "tracked changes"
- filetype:pptx "internal use only"
- filetype:xlsx "password"

✅ Extracts documents with hidden notes, tracked changes, or embedded passwords.

☐ OSINT Use Case:

If investigating corporate leaks, try:

- filetype:docx site:company.com "confidential"

This may reveal internal memos and reports with metadata.

C. Locating Government & Legal Documents

Many government agencies unknowingly expose metadata in public reports.

🔍 Example Dorks:

- site:gov filetype:pdf "draft report"
- site:edu filetype:docx "research study"

✅ Finds government draft reports and academic research papers.

□ OSINT Use Case:

To analyze publicly available court documents, try:

- site:courts.state.tx.us filetype:pdf "case number"

Metadata may reveal judge names, law firm authors, or case updates.

3. Extracting Metadata from Documents

Once a document is found, the next step is extracting its metadata. There are several tools that can retrieve hidden details from files.

A. Using ExifTool (Command-Line Metadata Extractor)

ExifTool is a powerful command-line tool for extracting metadata from almost any file type.

□ How to Install ExifTool:

Windows: Download from ExifTool Official Site.

Linux/Mac: Install via Terminal:

- sudo apt install exiftool   # Debian-based systems
- brew install exiftool   # macOS (using Homebrew)

□ How to Extract Metadata from a Document:

- exiftool document.pdf

✅ Displays author name, timestamps, software used, and hidden metadata.

◆ **Key Metadata Fields to Look For:**

- **Author** – Who created or last modified the document.
- **Title/Subject** – Often used for internal categorization.
- **Creation Date/Modification Date** – Identifies if the document was edited.
- **Software Used** – Can hint at the organization or tools used.

B. Using Online Metadata Extraction Tools

For users who prefer web-based tools, several online services allow quick metadata extraction:

- **Metadata2Go** – Upload a document to extract metadata.
- **FOCA** – Extracts metadata from bulk documents.
- **Get-Metadata** – Web-based tool for fast metadata retrieval.

☐ **OSINT Use Case:**

If a leaked PDF is found online, upload it to Metadata2Go to check:

- Who wrote it
- When it was created
- If any sensitive info is embedded

⚠️ **Warning**: Do not upload sensitive documents to third-party sites if confidentiality is required.

4. Extracting Metadata from Images & PDFs

Some documents contain embedded images, which also store metadata, including GPS coordinates.

A. Extracting GPS Data from Images

Photos taken on smartphones or digital cameras often include geolocation (GPS) metadata.

☐ **Extracting GPS Metadata with ExifTool:**

- exiftool image.jpg

✓ Displays latitude, longitude, and location details (if available).

☐ **OSINT Use Case:**

If an image is found in a leaked document, its metadata may reveal where it was taken.

B. Extracting Hidden Comments & Annotations from PDFs

PDFs often contain hidden comments, redactions, and embedded notes.

☐ **How to Extract Annotations from PDFs:**

- Open the PDF in Adobe Acrobat or PDF-XChange Viewer.
- Look for "Comments" or "Annotations".

Use exiftool to check for hidden text layers:

- exiftool -All document.pdf

✓ Extracts hidden author names, timestamps, and internal notes.

5. Ethical & Legal Considerations

🏛 **What You Should NOT Do:**

✗ Download confidential, password-protected, or illegally obtained documents.

✗ Use metadata analysis for malicious intent (e.g., blackmail, hacking).

✗ Share sensitive metadata without permission.

💡 **What You CAN Do:**

✅ Use metadata to verify sources and document authenticity.

✅ Report publicly exposed metadata risks to organizations.

✅ Check your own company's metadata security to prevent leaks.

⚠️ **Important**: Many organizations forget to strip metadata from public files. OSINT analysts should handle this data responsibly.

6. Conclusion: The Power of Metadata in OSINT Investigations

Extracting metadata from indexed documents is an essential skill for OSINT investigators. By using Google Dorking, metadata extraction tools like ExifTool, and online analysis platforms, analysts can uncover hidden intelligence in digital files.

2.6 Case Study: Real-World Google Dorking Investigations

Google Dorking, also known as Google Hacking, is a powerful OSINT (Open-Source Intelligence) technique used to uncover hidden and sensitive data through advanced search queries. Over the years, investigators, ethical hackers, and even malicious actors have used Google Dorking to find exposed databases, login portals, security vulnerabilities, and confidential documents.

In this chapter, we'll explore real-world case studies where Google Dorking played a critical role in OSINT investigations. These examples will demonstrate both the power and the risks of improperly secured data and how OSINT professionals can responsibly use this technique.

Case Study 1: Exposing a Government's Unsecured Documents

Background

A security researcher discovered that a government agency had accidentally exposed classified documents on a publicly accessible web server. The researcher used Google Dorking to find internal memos, confidential reports, and legal files that were not meant to be publicly accessible.

Google Dork Used

- site:gov filetype:pdf "confidential" OR "classified"

✅ This search query targeted government domains (.gov) and searched for PDF documents containing sensitive keywords like "confidential" or "classified".

Findings

The researcher uncovered:

- Internal military strategy reports stored on an unprotected web directory.
- Confidential legal opinions and draft legislation before public release.
- Email exchanges between government officials discussing security protocols.

Impact

🏛 The researcher responsibly reported the findings to the government agency, which then secured the files and improved its document storage practices. This case highlighted how poor cybersecurity hygiene can lead to major intelligence leaks.

Case Study 2: Uncovering Exposed Security Camera Feeds

Background

An OSINT analyst conducting research on IoT vulnerabilities used Google Dorking to identify publicly accessible security camera feeds. Many businesses and homeowners fail to secure their surveillance systems, allowing anyone to access live video streams.

Google Dork Used

- inurl:view/view.shtml

✅ This query finds IP camera web interfaces that are publicly exposed.

Findings

The analyst discovered:

- Live security camera feeds from businesses, parking lots, and even private residences.

- Cameras showing sensitive locations like government buildings and hospitals.
- Several cameras with default login credentials (e.g., admin/admin).

Impact

◎ The analyst reported the findings to affected businesses and cybersecurity teams, leading to improved security awareness. This case highlights the risks of misconfigured IoT devices and the need for strong passwords and firewall protections.

Case Study 3: Finding a Company's Exposed Employee Passwords

Background

A cybersecurity researcher was investigating corporate data leaks when they found that a company had accidentally exposed an internal employee database on a public-facing website.

Google Dork Used

- filetype:xlsx site:company.com "password"

✓ This query searched for Excel spreadsheets (.xlsx) on the company's domain that contained the word "password".

Findings

- An Excel file containing employee login credentials was accidentally uploaded to a public directory.
- The file included usernames, plaintext passwords, and email addresses.
- The company was completely unaware that this data was indexed by Google.

Impact

◎ The researcher immediately alerted the company, which removed the exposed document and reset employee credentials. This case highlights how improper file storage and poor password management can put organizations at risk.

Case Study 4: Discovering Unprotected Medical Records

Background

A journalist investigating data privacy in the healthcare sector used Google Dorking to see if medical records were being exposed online.

Google Dork Used

- site:clinic.com filetype:pdf "patient records"

✓ This search looked for PDF documents containing patient records on healthcare websites.

Findings

- Hundreds of patient records were available online due to misconfigured cloud storage.
- Some records included names, medical conditions, and insurance details.
- The clinic had no idea that these files were accessible via search engines.

Impact

⚖ The journalist reported the issue to the clinic and later published a story on healthcare data security risks. This case revealed how human error and lack of cybersecurity awareness can lead to serious data breaches.

Case Study 5: Identifying Exposed Law Enforcement Reports

Background

An OSINT investigator researching police transparency discovered that law enforcement agencies sometimes unknowingly publish sensitive reports without properly restricting access.

Google Dork Used

- site:police.gov filetype:docx "arrest report"

✅ This query searched for Word documents (.docx) containing "arrest report" on official police websites.

Findings

- Internal police reports containing suspect details were publicly available.
- Some reports included witness names and addresses, posing a privacy risk.
- Certain documents were indexed by Google but were never intended to be public.

Impact

🚨 The investigator reported the findings to the agencies involved, which immediately secured the data. This case demonstrated how government agencies must take cybersecurity seriously to protect sensitive information.

Key Takeaways from These Case Studies

◆ **Google Dorking is extremely powerful** – It can uncover sensitive and confidential data that organizations unintentionally expose.

◆ **Many data leaks are caused by human error** – Companies and government agencies fail to restrict access to sensitive files, leaving them indexed by search engines.

◆ **OSINT professionals must act ethically** – If you find exposed data, never exploit it. Instead, report it responsibly.

◆ **Organizations must improve cybersecurity** – The use of strong passwords, proper file permissions, and regular security audits can prevent data leaks.

Conclusion: The Responsible Use of Google Dorking

Google Dorking is one of the most powerful OSINT techniques, but it comes with great responsibility. As these case studies show, unsecured databases, login portals, and confidential documents are often indexed by search engines due to misconfigurations and poor security practices.

Ethical OSINT professionals, cybersecurity researchers, and journalists can use Google Dorking to uncover and report security flaws—helping to prevent potential data breaches and cyberattacks.

3. Search Engine Pivoting: Extracting Hidden Data

Search engine pivoting is the art of uncovering deeper layers of information by strategically altering search queries based on discovered data points. Instead of relying on a single query, OSINT analysts pivot by using email addresses, usernames, domain names, or document metadata to expand their search and connect the dots. For example, finding an email in one search result can lead to social media profiles, leaked databases, or forum posts through refined queries. Leveraging reverse image searches, cached pages, and alternative search engines further enhances this process. By continuously refining and redirecting searches based on new findings, analysts can extract hidden data that would otherwise remain buried in the vastness of the internet.

3.1 Understanding Search Pivoting in OSINT Investigations

Search pivoting is an advanced OSINT (Open-Source Intelligence) technique used to extract hidden or interconnected data by following digital clues found in search results. Instead of stopping at a single query, pivoting involves iterative searches that refine and expand the scope of an investigation. By identifying key data points—such as email addresses, usernames, domains, or document metadata—analysts can uncover deeper layers of intelligence that were not immediately visible in the first search.

Pivoting is essential in OSINT investigations because:

✓ It expands intelligence gathering beyond basic search queries.

✓ It connects fragmented pieces of information to form a complete picture.

✓ It helps identify hidden relationships between individuals, organizations, and assets.

✓ It allows analysts to find alternative sources when primary data is removed or restricted.

In this chapter, we will explore different types of search pivoting, how to leverage search engines effectively, and real-world examples of pivoting in OSINT investigations.

1. How Search Pivoting Works

Search pivoting follows a step-by-step process where each discovered data point leads to a new search query, allowing investigators to gradually uncover deeper intelligence.

☐ **The Pivoting Cycle:**

1☐ **Start with a Core Query** → Find an initial search result (e.g., a leaked email, a document, a username).

2☐ **Extract Key Data Points** → Identify names, emails, domains, metadata, or unique identifiers from the result.

3☐ **Construct a New Search Query** → Use the extracted data to refine or expand the search.

4☐ **Repeat the Process** → Continue searching and connecting the pieces until the full intelligence picture emerges.

☐ **Example**: Uncovering More Information About a Person

Let's say an OSINT investigator finds an email address john.doe@example.com in a data breach.

🔍 **Initial Google Dork:**

- "john.doe@example.com"

✅ **Finds**: A public forum post where the email was used.

📌 **Pivot #1:** Extract the username from the forum post (johndoe1990).

🔍 **New Search:**

- "Johndoe1990"

✅ **Finds**: More profiles using the same username on other platforms (LinkedIn, Twitter, GitHub).

📌 **Pivot #2**: Extract a workplace domain from LinkedIn (companyxyz.com).

🔍 **New Search:**

- site:companyxyz.com "John Doe"

✅ **Finds**: A work-related document containing internal email formats (firstname.lastname@companyxyz.com).

📌 **Pivot #3:** Use Google Dorking to find company leaks.

🔍 **New Search:**

- site:pastebin.com "companyxyz.com"

✅ **Finds**: A data breach leak containing employee passwords.

This pivoting process expands intelligence step by step, moving from an email address to usernames, social media profiles, work history, and even potential security risks.

2. Types of Search Pivoting in OSINT

There are several pivoting techniques that analysts use depending on the investigation type.

A. Domain & Subdomain Pivoting

Often, organizations use multiple domains and subdomains that can be connected through pivoting.

🔍 **Google Dork Example**: Find related domains of a company

- site:example.com OR site:*.example.com

✅ Expands the investigation to subdomains like secure.example.com or internal.example.com.

🔍 **Pivot Further**: Check for leaked credentials linked to a domain

- "@example.com" filetype:xlsx OR filetype:txt

✅ Finds lists of emails or credentials from data leaks.

B. Email & Username Pivoting

Emails and usernames are unique identifiers that can link multiple accounts together.

🔍 **Google Dork Example**: Find usernames connected to an email

- "john.doe@example.com"

✅ May reveal forum posts, social media accounts, and data breaches.

🔍 **New Pivot**: Search for other accounts using the same username

- "Johndoe1990"

✅ Can uncover more online identities on platforms like GitHub, Reddit, and old blog posts.

C. Document Metadata Pivoting

Documents often contain hidden metadata, including author names, timestamps, and software details.

🔍 **Find Documents with Metadata**

- site:gov filetype:pdf "internal use only"

✅ Finds government documents that may contain metadata.

☐ **Use ExifTool to extract metadata:**

- exiftool document.pdf

📌 **Pivot Further**: Use the author's name found in metadata to search for more documents:

- "Author: John Doe" filetype:pdf

✅ Uncovers additional files linked to the same author.

D. Image & EXIF Data Pivoting

Photos contain EXIF metadata, including GPS coordinates, timestamps, and camera details.

☐ Extract EXIF Data from an Image

- exiftool image.jpg

✅ May reveal location, time taken, and device used.

📌 **Pivot Further**: If GPS coordinates are found, search them in Google Maps:

- "40.7128, -74.0060"

✅ May show locations linked to the image's origin.

E. Dark Web & Breach Data Pivoting

Data breaches and dark web leaks can reveal passwords, emails, and internal documents.

🔍 Find Breached Data Using Google Dorks

- site:pastebin.com "example.com"

✅ Finds potential leaks containing employee emails or sensitive data.

📌 **Pivot Further**: Use HAVE I BEEN PWNED to check for breached emails:

🔗 https://haveibeenpwned.com/

✓ May reveal where an email has been compromised.

3. Real-World Example: Using Pivoting to Track a Cybercriminal

Background

An OSINT investigator was tasked with tracking a suspected cybercriminal using only a username from an online forum (DarkHunter99).

Step-by-Step Pivoting Process:

1️ Google Dork for the Username

🔍 Search: "DarkHunter99"
✓ Found multiple social media accounts using the same username.

2️ Extract Email from a Social Media Profile

🔍 Search: "DarkHunter99@gmail.com"
✓ Found forum posts discussing hacking tools.

3️ Search the Email in Data Breach Repositories

🔍 Have I Been Pwned Search: DarkHunter99@gmail.com
✓ Found a password leak from an old database breach.

4️ Check If the Username Appears in Cybercrime Forums

🔍 Search: site:darkwebmarket.com "DarkHunter99"
✓ Found active listings for stolen data.

Outcome:

By pivoting through usernames, emails, and breached data, investigators linked the suspect to multiple online identities and dark web activities, leading to their identification.

4. Conclusion: The Power of Search Pivoting in OSINT

Search pivoting is one of the most effective techniques in OSINT investigations, allowing analysts to:

✅ Expand intelligence gathering beyond surface-level searches.

✅ Connect data points across different platforms and leaks.

✅ Uncover hidden relationships between people, organizations, and online footprints.

By mastering search pivoting, OSINT professionals can track individuals, identify cyber threats, and uncover critical intelligence that would otherwise remain hidden.

3.2 Using One Data Point to Find More Related Information

In OSINT investigations, a single piece of information—an email address, username, phone number, IP address, domain name, or even a document—can serve as a pivot point to uncover a wealth of related intelligence. This process, often referred to as search pivoting, allows analysts to trace connections, identify patterns, and gather actionable insights.

By strategically leveraging search engines, social media platforms, data breach repositories, and specialized OSINT tools, an investigator can turn one small data point into a complete intelligence profile.

1. The OSINT Pivoting Mindset

Effective OSINT investigations rely on a structured approach to pivoting. Here's how analysts think about expanding a single data point into a full investigation:

🔍 The OSINT Pivoting Process

1️⃣ **Start with One Data Point** → Identify a username, email, phone number, IP, or document.

2⃞ **Extract Additional Identifiers** → Find linked emails, domains, social profiles, or metadata.

3⃞ **Search Using New Identifiers** → Run targeted queries on search engines, social media, and data leaks.

4⃞ **Cross-Reference & Validate** → Confirm links between different data sources to build a reliable profile.

By following this cycle, analysts can expand a small clue into a detailed intelligence report.

2. Case Study: Investigating a Username

Imagine an OSINT analyst receives the username "ShadowHunter99" and needs to uncover more information about the person behind it.

Step 1: Searching the Username on Google

🔍 **Google Search Query:**

- "ShadowHunter99"

✓ Found results from gaming forums, Reddit, and a Twitter account using the same username.

📌 **Pivot #1:** Extract any email addresses or links from these profiles.

Step 2: Searching the Username on Social Media

🔍 Checking Twitter, Instagram, and Reddit for the username.
✓ The username appears on Reddit and GitHub.

📌 **Pivot #2**: Extract bio details, past posts, linked accounts, and IP clues.

- Reddit profile mentions: "I work in cybersecurity."
- GitHub repository contains a personal website link.

Step 3: Searching for Email Addresses

🔍 Google Dork to find emails linked to the username:

- "ShadowHunter99@gmail.com"

✅ Found an old forum post where the user shared their email for contact.

📌 **Pivot #3:** Use this email to search data breach repositories and LinkedIn profiles.

Step 4: Searching Data Breaches for More Information

🔍 Using Have I Been Pwned (https://haveibeenpwned.com/)
✅ Email appears in a 2018 breach, revealing a real name and partially exposed password.

📌 **Pivot #4**: Use the real name to refine the search.

Step 5: Searching Public Records & Domain Ownership

🔍 Check WHOIS records for the domain found on GitHub.
✅ Domain is registered to John Doe, based in New York.

📌 **Final Pivot**: Cross-reference John Doe with the username to find more online activity.

Final Findings

From a single username, the investigator uncovered:

✅ **A real name** (John Doe).
✅ **A LinkedIn profile** (which mentions working in cybersecurity).
✅ **An email address** (found via old forum posts).
✅ **A domain registration** (traced via WHOIS records).
✅ **A data breach record** (containing a partially exposed password).

By using search pivoting, the analyst turned one anonymous username into a detailed intelligence profile.

3. Pivoting with Different Types of Data Points

A. Pivoting from an Email Address

🔍 Google Dork to find mentions of an email:

- "john.doe@example.com"

✅ Finds forum posts, social media accounts, and public records.

📌 **Next Pivot**: Use the email to check for breached passwords in Have I Been Pwned.

🔍 Check Breach Data:

- site:pastebin.com "john.doe@example.com"

✅ Finds a leaked password that may be reused elsewhere.

B. Pivoting from a Domain Name

🔍 Check WHOIS Records:

- whois example.com

✅ Finds registrant name, email, and phone number.

📌 **Next Pivot**: Search the registrant's email in Google to find more connections.

🔍 Find Other Sites Hosted on the Same Server:

- site:ipinfo.io [IP Address]

✅ Finds other domains owned by the same person or company.

C. Pivoting from a Phone Number

🔍 Google Search for a Phone Number:

- "555-123-4567"

✅ Finds classified ads, business listings, and social media profiles.

📌 **Next Pivot**: Use reverse phone lookup tools like Truecaller or OSINT databases to find more details.

D. Pivoting from an Image or Video

☐ **Use Reverse Image Search** (Google, Yandex, TinEye)
🔍 Upload an Image to Google Reverse Image Search
✅ Finds other places where the image appears (e.g., LinkedIn, Facebook).

📌 **Next Pivot**: Extract metadata (EXIF data) to find location, device, and timestamps.

4. Tools & Resources for Search Pivoting

Tool	Use Case	Website
Google Dorks	Advanced search queries	Google.com
WHOIS Lookup	Find domain ownership	who.is
Have I Been Pwned	Check for breached emails	haveibeenpwned.com
ExifTool	Extract image metadata	ExifTool
TinEye	Reverse image search	tineye.com
OSINT Framework	List of OSINT tools	osintframework.com

5. Conclusion: The Power of a Single Data Point

OSINT investigations often start with just one small clue, but through search pivoting, analysts can uncover a full intelligence profile. Whether it's a username, email, phone number, domain, or document, each data point serves as a stepping stone to more information.

By following structured search techniques and using OSINT tools, investigators can effectively track individuals, companies, and cyber threats—all from a single starting point.

3.3 Reverse Searching Usernames, Emails & Phone Numbers

Reverse searching is a crucial OSINT (Open-Source Intelligence) technique that allows investigators to trace usernames, emails, and phone numbers back to their sources. Unlike a regular search that starts with a broad keyword, reverse searching starts with a specific identifier (e.g., an email address or phone number) and uncovers all related information connected to it.

By using specialized search engines, social media platforms, and OSINT tools, investigators can:

✅ Link a username to multiple accounts across platforms

✅ Find social media profiles and breached data from an email address

✅ Identify the owner of a phone number and past usage history

This technique is widely used in cyber investigations, threat intelligence, fraud detection, and online profiling.

1. Reverse Searching Usernames

A username is one of the most valuable identifiers in OSINT investigations. Many people reuse usernames across different platforms, allowing analysts to connect multiple accounts and build a detailed profile.

🔍 Step 1: Google Dorking for Usernames

A simple Google search can often uncover multiple accounts associated with a username.

🔍 Google Search Query:

- "shadowhunter99"

✅ Finds gaming forums, social media profiles, and old blog comments.

🔍 Google Dork to Find Profiles:

- "shadowhunter99" site:twitter.com OR site:instagram.com OR site:reddit.com

✅ This search checks if the username is used on major platforms.

🔍 Step 2: Using OSINT Tools for Username Searches

Several tools can automate the process of searching usernames across hundreds of platforms.

☐ Top Tools for Reverse Username Searching:

Tool	Purpose	Link
WhatsMyName	Checks username across multiple sites	whatsmyname.app
Namechk	Finds username availability & accounts	namechk.com
Sherlock	OSINT tool for finding usernames across platforms	GitHub - Sherlock

📌 **Pivot Further**: If a username is found on GitHub, check for repositories that may contain emails, work projects, or sensitive data.

🔍 Google Dork for GitHub Repositories:

- "shadowhunter99" site:github.com

🔍 Step 3: Finding Username Variations

If an exact username doesn't return results, look for variations:

- shadowhunter1990 (adding a birth year)
- shadowhunter (using underscores)
- shadow.hunter99 (adding dots or numbers)

☐ Tool for Finding Similar Usernames:

LeakedSource Usernames – Checks variations in data breaches.

2. Reverse Searching Email Addresses

An email address is often the most valuable OSINT identifier since many platforms require it for account creation.

🔍 Step 1: Google Dorking for Email Addresses

🔍 Basic Search for Email Mentions:

- "john.doe@gmail.com"

✓ Finds old forum posts, social media profiles, and published documents.

🔍 Search for Email Mentions in Pastes and Leaks:

- site:pastebin.com "john.doe@gmail.com"

✓ Finds potential leaked credentials or hacked databases.

🔍 Step 2: Searching Data Breaches for Exposed Emails

☐ Best OSINT Tools for Checking Breached Emails:

Tool	Purpose	Link
TrueCaller	Identifies names & locations linked to a number	truecaller.com
SpyDialer	Searches public records for phone numbers	spydialer.com
NumLookup	Reverse search phone numbers for free	numlookup.com

📌 **Pivot Further**: If a breach reveals a password, search variations of that password in other databases to see if it's been reused elsewhere.

🔍 Step 3: Checking Social Media Accounts Linked to Emails

Many social media platforms allow you to find accounts using an email.

✅ **Facebook & Instagram**: Try entering an email into the "Forgot Password" feature to see if an account exists.

✅ **LinkedIn Email Lookup**:

- "john.doe@gmail.com" site:linkedin.com

✅ Finds LinkedIn profiles associated with the email.

📌 **Pivot Further**: Once you find a LinkedIn profile, extract company names, job titles, and locations for further searches.

3. Reverse Searching Phone Numbers

A phone number can provide direct links to social media accounts, business records, and past data breaches.

🔍 **Step 1: Google Dorking for Phone Numbers**

🔍 **Basic Search for a Phone Number:**

- "555-123-4567"

✅ Finds classified ads, business listings, or customer complaints.

🔍 **Google Dork for Business Listings:**

- site:yellowpages.com OR site:linkedin.com "555-123-4567"

✅ Finds company records or professionals linked to the number.

🔍 **Step 2: Using Reverse Phone Lookup Tools**

☐ **Top OSINT Tools for Reverse Phone Searches:**

Tool	Purpose	Link
TrueCaller	Identifies names & locations linked to a number	truecaller.com
SpyDialer	Searches public records for phone numbers	spydialer.com
NumLookup	Reverse search phone numbers for free	numlookup.com

★ **Pivot Further**: If the number belongs to a company, check the WHOIS records for their website to find emails or domain registration details.

🔍 Step 3: Finding Social Media Accounts with Phone Numbers

Many social media platforms allow users to register with a phone number.

✅ **Facebook & Instagram**: Use the "Forgot Password" feature to check if the number is linked to an account.

✅ **Telegram**: Add the number to Telegram and check profile pictures or usernames.

✅ **WhatsApp**: Save the number in contacts and check the WhatsApp profile.

★ **Pivot Further**: If a WhatsApp profile picture is visible, use reverse image search to find other instances of that image online.

4. Conclusion: Reverse Searching as an OSINT Power Tool

Reverse searching usernames, emails, and phone numbers opens doors to deeper intelligence. By systematically using search engines, breach data, social media, and OSINT tools, investigators can uncover hidden connections, track digital footprints, and expose online identities.

Key Takeaways:

✅ Usernames often link to multiple accounts across platforms.

✅ Emails are powerful for tracking social media profiles and breached data.

✅ Phone numbers can reveal business records, social accounts, and past associations.

✅ Combining Google Dorks, OSINT tools, and breach databases provides a complete intelligence profile.

3.4 Pivoting Through Social Media & Forum Mentions

In OSINT investigations, social media and forums are treasure troves of information. People discuss personal details, share opinions, and interact with others—often without realizing how much data they expose. By tracking mentions of usernames, email addresses, phone numbers, locations, or keywords, investigators can pivot from one clue to a network of related accounts, conversations, and connections.

This technique, known as social media and forum pivoting, is essential for:

✅ Identifying an individual's digital footprint

✅ Uncovering hidden accounts linked to the same person

✅ Tracking mentions of specific events, locations, or groups

✅ Monitoring discussions around specific topics or threats

In this section, we'll explore how to search across social media and forums, uncover hidden mentions, and pivot effectively for deeper intelligence gathering.

1. Searching for Mentions on Social Media

🔍 Step 1: Google Dorking for Social Media Mentions

Google indexes some public social media content. By using Google Dorks, we can find mentions of a specific username, email, or keyword.

☐ Google Dorks for Social Media Mentions

🔍 Find a username across social platforms:

- "shadowhunter99" site:twitter.com OR site:instagram.com OR site:facebook.com OR site:tiktok.com

✅ Finds profiles, mentions, and posts containing the username.

🔍 Find email addresses in social media posts:

- "john.doe@gmail.com" site:facebook.com OR site:linkedin.com

☑️ Identifies accounts and past discussions linked to the email.

🔍 Find discussions about a keyword or phrase:

- "insider leak" site:twitter.com OR site:reddit.com

☑️ Reveals posts where people discuss "insider leaks" on forums and social media.

📌 **Pivot Further**: If a username is found on Twitter, check if the same username exists on Instagram, Reddit, or Discord.

🔍 Step 2: Searching Social Media Platforms Directly

Many platforms don't allow Google to index posts, so you need to search within each platform manually.

☐ How to Search for Mentions on Different Social Media Platforms

Platform	How to Search for Mentions
Twitter (X)	Use Twitter Advanced Search here
Facebook	Use Facebook Graph Search or search "keyword" in the search bar
Instagram	Search with "@username" or hashtags related to the topic
LinkedIn	Use Boolean search: "John Doe" site:linkedin.com on Google
TikTok	Use the TikTok search bar and try variations of the username
Reddit	Use Reddit's advanced search at Reddit.com/search
Discord	Use Google Dorking: "keyword" site:discord.com

☑️ **Tip**: Some platforms require an account or specific access levels to search effectively.

📌 **Pivot Further**: If an account is private, look for mentions in replies, tagged posts, or interactions with other users.

🔍 Step 3: Using OSINT Tools for Social Media Pivoting

Several OSINT tools automate social media searches and help find related mentions.

☐ Top OSINT Tools for Social Media Investigations

Tool	Purpose	Link
SPOKEO	Reverse searches social media profiles	spokeo.com
SOCMINT	Social media intelligence gathering	socmint.osintcombine.com
Twint	Extracts Twitter data without an account	github.com/twintproject/twint
OSINT Combine Social Media Search	Finds accounts by name or email	osintcombine.com
Reddit Search Dorks	Finds discussions on Reddit	Pushshift.io

📌 **Pivot Further**: If a person's LinkedIn profile is found, check company websites, job boards, and professional events for more information.

2. Finding Mentions in Forums & Online Communities

Forums, discussion boards, and specialized online communities often contain valuable intelligence that isn't found on mainstream social media.

🔍 Step 1: Google Dorking for Forum Posts

Many forums are publicly indexed by Google, making them easy to search with Google Dorks.

☐ Google Dorks for Forum Searches

🔍 Find a username in forums:

- "shadowhunter99" site:forum.blueteamsec.com OR site:blackhatworld.com OR site:raidforums.com

✓ Finds mentions of the username in hacking, cybersecurity, and darknet forums.

🔍 Find discussions about a keyword:

- "hacking tools" site:forums.whirlpool.net.au OR site:malwaretips.com

✅ Reveals forum threads discussing hacking tools.

🔍 **Find posts containing an email address:**

- "john.doe@gmail.com" site:breachforums.is OR site:darknetmarkets.com

✅ Checks dark web forums for email mentions in data leaks or discussions.

📌 **Pivot Further**: If a forum post contains an IP address, domain, or business name, use WHOIS lookups to trace the owner.

🔍 **Step 2: Searching Forums Directly**

Some forums have internal search engines that are more effective than Google.

✅ **Top Forums for OSINT Investigations:**

- **Cybersecurity & Hacking Forums** → BlackHatWorld, Exploit.in, BreachForums
- **Tech & Software Forums** → Stack Overflow, Whirlpool, XDA Developers
- **Underground Marketplaces** → Darknet forums (requires TOR access)
- **Local Community Forums** → City-specific forums & classifieds

📌 **Pivot Further**: If a forum post contains an image, run a reverse image search to find where else it appears.

3. Case Study: Tracking a User Through Forum Mentions

Imagine an OSINT investigator is tracking a user with the email john.doe@gmail.com.

Step 1: Google Dorking

🔍 **Query:**

- "john.doe@gmail.com" site:reddit.com OR site:blackhatworld.com

✅ Finds Reddit comments where the user discussed cryptocurrency.

Step 2: Searching Forum Databases

🔍 **Using Dehashed & BreachForums**

✅ Finds a leaked password used in past breaches.

📌 **Pivot Further**: Try the username "JohnDoeCrypto" (from the Reddit profile) on Twitter & Telegram.

Step 3: Searching Social Media

🔍 **Check Twitter, LinkedIn, and Telegram**

✅ Finds a matching username on Telegram selling crypto services.

🔍 **Google Dork to check Telegram mentions:**

- "JohnDoeCrypto" site:t.me

✅ Finds a public Telegram group where the user is active.

📌 **Final Pivot**: Investigate other members of the Telegram group for further connections.

Conclusion: Social & Forum Pivoting for Deeper OSINT

- Social media and forums are rich sources of intelligence.
- Google Dorks, OSINT tools, and manual searches help uncover hidden connections.
- Pivoting from a single mention (email, username, or phone) can reveal a full identity.

3.5 Finding Hidden Connections Using Search Techniques

In OSINT investigations, individual data points—usernames, emails, phone numbers, locations, IP addresses, or company names—are just pieces of a puzzle. The real power comes from finding hidden connections between them. By using advanced search techniques, metadata extraction, and cross-referencing, we can link seemingly unrelated information to reveal a person's or entity's full digital footprint.

This chapter explores how to correlate different data points using:

✅ Advanced search operators to discover hidden connections

✅ Metadata extraction from files, images, and websites

✅ Social network analysis to map relationships

✅ Cross-referencing multiple sources to verify intelligence

1. Cross-Referencing Data Using Search Engines

The first step in uncovering hidden connections is using search engines strategically.

🔍 Step 1: Cross-Referencing Names, Emails & Usernames

Many people reuse the same username, email, or name across different platforms. By searching for variations, we can connect different accounts.

☐ Google Dorks for Cross-Referencing Identities

🔍 Find profiles linked to an email:

- "john.doe@gmail.com"   site:linkedin.com   OR   site:facebook.com   OR site:instagram.com

✅ Identifies social media accounts connected to the email.

🔍 Find usernames linked to a real name:

- "John Doe" AND "shadowhunter99" site:twitter.com

✅ Confirms if a real name and username belong to the same person.

🔍 Find multiple accounts with a phone number:

- "555-123-4567" site:facebook.com OR site:whatsapp.com OR site:telegram.org

✅ Locates social media accounts tied to a phone number.

📌 **Pivot Further**: If an email address appears in a data breach, check the associated passwords for clues about username patterns.

🔍 Step 2: Finding Related Domains & Websites

Sometimes, people own multiple domains or websites under the same email or business name.

☐ **Google Dorks for Finding Related Websites**

🔍 **Find all websites associated with an email:**

- "john.doe@gmail.com" site:whois.domaintools.com

✅ Shows domains registered under a specific email.

🔍 **Find websites hosted on the same server (IP address):**

- Ip:192.168.1.1

✅ Lists all domains linked to a server, revealing hidden sites.

📌 **Pivot Further**: Use WHOIS lookups on the domains to check company names, registration details, and historical ownership changes.

2. Extracting Metadata from Files & Images

Hidden data often exists inside files, images, and documents. Metadata extraction helps link files to their original creators.

🔍 Step 1: Extracting Metadata from Documents

Documents such as PDFs, Word files, and images often contain hidden metadata revealing usernames, creation dates, and locations.

☐ OSINT Tools for Metadata Extraction

Tool	Purpose	Link
ExifTool	Extracts metadata from images & documents	ExifTool
FOCA	Finds metadata in PDFs, Word docs, & Excel sheets	FOCA Metadata
Metagoofil	Extracts metadata from public documents	Metagoofil

📌 **Pivot Further**: If an author name appears in a document's metadata, search for it on social media and professional websites to find the document creator.

🔍 Step 2: Reverse Searching Images to Find Hidden Connections

A person's profile picture, company logo, or any uploaded image can be traced to its origins.

☐ Reverse Image Search Tools

Tool	Purpose	Link
Google Reverse Image Search	Finds where an image appears online	Google Images
Yandex Reverse Search	Better for finding social media profiles	Yandex
TinEye	Tracks modified or cropped images	TinEye

📌 **Pivot Further**: If an image is found on a social media profile, check comments and tagged locations for additional connections.

3. Mapping Hidden Social & Business Connections

Social and professional networks leave behind relationship traces that can reveal hidden associations between people.

🔍 Step 1: Finding Connections on Social Media

Even if someone's profile is private, their interactions (likes, comments, tagged posts) can link them to other accounts.

☐ OSINT Tools for Social Network Analysis

Tool	Purpose	Link
Maltego	Maps relationships between people, companies, & websites	Maltego
OSINT Combine	Finds related accounts using social graphs	OSINT Combine
Gephi	Visualizes social network links	Gephi

📌 **Pivot Further**: If a user likes or comments on specific brands or topics, investigate those topics further to build a profile of their interests.

🔍 Step 2: Identifying Business & Financial Links

Many OSINT investigations require connecting people to businesses or financial activity.

☐ OSINT Tools for Business & Financial Research

Tool	Purpose	Link
OpenCorporates	Finds business ownership records	OpenCorporates
Company House (UK)	Searches registered companies in the UK	Company House
SEC EDGAR (USA)	Finds U.S. corporate filings	SEC EDGAR

📌 **Pivot Further**: If an individual owns multiple companies, check their financial transactions, legal cases, or partnerships for additional leads.

4. Case Study: Connecting the Dots in an OSINT Investigation

Imagine an OSINT investigator is researching John Doe, a suspected cybercriminal.

Step 1: Start with a Google Dork Search

🔍 Query:

- "John Doe" site:linkedin.com OR site:twitter.com OR site:facebook.com

✅ Finds a LinkedIn profile for John Doe, showing he works in cybersecurity.

Step 2: Reverse Search the Profile Picture

🔍 Using Yandex Image Search

☑ Finds the same image on a forum discussing hacking tools under the username "ShadowHunter99".

Step 3: Extract Metadata from a Leaked PDF

🔍 Using ExifTool on a leaked document

☑ Finds a hidden author name, matching John Doe's LinkedIn username.

Step 4: Check Business Ownership Records

🔍 Using OpenCorporates

☑ Finds that John Doe owns a cybersecurity consulting company that shares an address with another suspicious firm.

📌 **Final Pivot**: Investigate the connections between the two companies and their transactions.

Conclusion: Turning Disconnected Data into Intelligence

⬥ **People leave digital traces everywhere**—connecting them requires smart search techniques.
⬥ Cross-referencing usernames, emails, and phone numbers reveals hidden links.
⬥ Metadata from files and images provides crucial insights into individuals and businesses.
⬥ Mapping social and business connections exposes hidden relationships.

3.6 Practical Search Pivoting Exercises

Now that we've covered the theory behind search engine pivoting, it's time to put these skills to the test. Practical exercises will help you refine your ability to uncover hidden connections, extract intelligence from data points, and think like an OSINT investigator.

In this section, you'll practice:

✅ Google Dorking for usernames, emails, and documents

✅ Cross-referencing data points to expand your search

✅ Using metadata extraction tools for deeper insights

✅ Social media investigations to track digital footprints

✅ Finding hidden websites, business records, and leaked data

Each exercise includes a scenario, step-by-step walkthrough, and a challenge for you to solve.

Exercise 1: Finding a User's Online Footprint

Scenario:

You receive an anonymous tip about a user with the username "ShadowHunter99" who is active on multiple platforms. Your goal is to find all related accounts, social media profiles, and any other digital traces.

Step-by-Step Guide:

Step 1: Google Dorking for Social Media Profiles

🔍 **Search Query:**

- "ShadowHunter99" site:twitter.com OR site:facebook.com OR site:instagram.com OR site:reddit.com

✅ Finds potential profiles under the same username.

Step 2: Reverse Search the Username on OSINT Tools

✅ **Use sites like:**

- **Namechk** – Checks username availability across platforms
- **WhatsMyName** – Finds accounts linked to a username
- **CheckUsernames** – Searches multiple platforms

📌 **Pivot Further**: If the username is found on Reddit, search for their posts to uncover interests, locations, or connections.

Challenge:

Can you find an email address or phone number linked to this username? Use Google Dorking, data leaks, or metadata analysis.

Exercise 2: Extracting Hidden Data from Documents

Scenario:

A leaked PDF document is circulating online, and you suspect it was created by a company insider. Your task is to extract metadata to identify the author and find more related documents.

Step-by-Step Guide:

Step 1: Use Metadata Extraction Tools

✅ Download the document and run it through ExifTool:

- exiftool leaked-document.pdf

✅ This will reveal author name, creation date, software used, and sometimes even a device ID.

Step 2: Google Dorking for Related Documents

🔍 **Search Query:**

- "CompanyName" filetype:pdf OR filetype:docx OR filetype:xlsx

✅ Finds more publicly exposed documents from the same company.

📌 **Pivot Further**: If an author name is found in the metadata, search for that name on LinkedIn to find their job role.

Challenge:

Can you find out where else the author's name appears online? Use Google search, social media, and company records.

Exercise 3: Investigating a Leaked Email Address

Scenario:

You come across the email johndoe@gmail.com in a forum post. Your goal is to find where else this email has been used and whether it appears in any data breaches, social media accounts, or website registrations.

Step-by-Step Guide:

Step 1: Google Dorking for Email Mentions

🔍 **Search Query:**

- "johndoe@gmail.com"   site:linkedin.com   OR   site:facebook.com   OR site:twitter.com

✅ Finds social media profiles associated with the email.

Step 2: Check Data Breaches for Exposed Passwords

✅ Use sites like:

- **Have I Been Pwned** – Checks data breaches
- **DeHashed** – Searches leaked databases
- **LeakCheck** – Finds exposed credentials

✦ **Pivot Further**: If the email appears in a breach, use the leaked password patterns to predict other usernames or accounts.

Challenge:

Can you link the email address to any business records or domain registrations? Use WHOIS lookups or company databases.

Exercise 4: Mapping Hidden Social Connections

Scenario:

You're investigating a Twitter user @CryptoWhale99 who is suspected of running a cryptocurrency scam. Your goal is to find out who they interact with, their linked accounts, and possible real-world identity.

Step-by-Step Guide:

Step 1: Use Twitter Advanced Search

🔍 **Search Query:**

- from:CryptoWhale99 OR to:CryptoWhale99 OR @CryptoWhale99

✅ Reveals who they interact with and what topics they discuss.

Step 2: Cross-Reference Username Across Other Platforms

✅ Use Namechk or WhatsMyName to see if CryptoWhale99 exists on Instagram, Reddit, or Telegram.

Step 3: Analyze Their Followers & Mentions

✅ Use Twint (OSINT Twitter Tool) to download all tweets and interactions for offline analysis.

📌 **Pivot Further**: If the Twitter account is linked to a Telegram group, investigate group members for additional connections.

Challenge:

Can you find a real name or email linked to this Twitter account? Check mentions, metadata, or past tweets for clues.

Exercise 5: Tracking a Business Owner's Online Activity

Scenario:

You are investigating XYZ Technologies, a cybersecurity company. Your goal is to find its owner, related businesses, and any hidden online activity.

Step-by-Step Guide:

Step 1: Find Business Registration Records

✅ Use OSINT business search tools:

- **OpenCorporates** – Global company records
- **SEC EDGAR** – US company filings
- **Company House UK** – UK business records

Step 2: Find Related Domains & Websites

🔍 **Google Dorking for Related Websites**

- "XYZ Technologies" site:whois.domaintools.com

✅ Identifies other domains registered to the same company or owner.

Step 3: Reverse Search the Owner's Name

✅ Once you find the company owner's name, search for their LinkedIn, Twitter, or business partnerships.

★ **Pivot Further**: If the business has multiple addresses, investigate them on Google Maps or Street View to verify legitimacy.

Challenge:

Can you find if the company is linked to any legal disputes or government contracts? Use government records and legal case searches.

Conclusion: Strengthening Your OSINT Skills Through Practice

- ◆ Search pivoting is a skill that improves with hands-on practice.
- ◆ Every data point—username, email, IP address, or document—can lead to deeper intelligence.
- ◆ Combining multiple OSINT tools and techniques helps uncover hidden connections.
- ◆ Real-world scenarios prepare you for professional OSINT investigations.

4. Alternative Search Engines for OSINT

While Google dominates the search landscape, relying solely on it limits the scope of OSINT investigations. Alternative search engines like Bing, Yandex, DuckDuckGo, and Baidu index different parts of the web, often revealing unique results that Google may filter out. Specialized search engines such as Shodan (for internet-connected devices), Censys (for network reconnaissance), and Wayback Machine (for archived web pages) provide even deeper intelligence. Dark web search engines like Ahmia and OnionLand allow analysts to explore hidden networks inaccessible via traditional searches. By diversifying search tools, OSINT practitioners can bypass algorithmic biases, access broader datasets, and uncover intelligence that remains invisible within mainstream search engines.

4.1 Why Google is Not Enough: Exploring Alternative Search Engines

Google is the most powerful and widely used search engine, but it is not always the best option for OSINT investigations. While it indexes a massive amount of web content, it also has significant limitations that can hinder intelligence gathering:

◆ **Filtered Search Results** – Google personalizes results based on your location, browsing history, and previous searches.
◆ **Censorship & De-indexing** – Many websites, including forums, government databases, and leaked content, are removed or hidden from Google's index.
◆ **Deep & Dark Web Exclusion** – Google only covers the surface web; anything behind a login or in non-indexed databases is invisible.
◆ **Anti-Scraping Measures** – Google limits automated searches (scraping), making large-scale OSINT investigations difficult.

To overcome these barriers, OSINT analysts must explore alternative search engines that provide different indexing methods, regional focus, or specialized datasets. This chapter covers the best Google alternatives for intelligence gathering.

1. Privacy-Focused Search Engines for Unbiased Results

Google tailors search results based on your activity. This means that two users searching for the same term might see different results due to Google's ranking algorithms. OSINT investigators need neutral, unfiltered search engines to get global and unbiased results.

🔍 Alternative Search Engines for Neutral Results

Search Engine	Why Use It for OSINT?	Link
DuckDuckGo	No tracking, different indexing from Google	DuckDuckGo
Startpage	Google results but without personalization	Startpage
Mojeek	Independent search index, no tracking	Mojeek
Searx	Aggregates multiple search engines anonymously	Searx

📌 **OSINT Tip**: If Google filters out certain results due to government regulations, use DuckDuckGo or Startpage to see uncensored content.

2. Search Engines for Finding Hidden & Technical Information

Google focuses on popular websites but often ignores technical, academic, and underground sources. For OSINT investigations, alternative search engines can help locate hidden technical data, software repositories, and forgotten web pages.

🔍 Alternative Search Engines for Technical Searches

Search Engine	Why Use It for OSINT?	Link
Yandex	Excellent reverse image search & deep web indexing	Yandex
Bing	Indexes some sites Google does not show	Bing
Qwant	Privacy-focused, good for EU searches	Qwant
Brave Search	Independent indexing, no tracking	Brave

📌 **OSINT Tip**: Yandex is better than Google at finding obscure social media profiles and reverse searching images.

3. Search Engines for Academic, Government & Legal Data

Many intelligence investigations require searching academic papers, government reports, patents, and legal cases. These databases often do not appear on Google or require specialized search engines to access.

🔍 Alternative Search Engines for Academic & Government Research

Search Engine	Why Use It for OSINT?	Link
Google Scholar	Best for academic papers, citations	Google Scholar
BASE	Open-access academic research	BASE
CORE	Millions of research papers	CORE
WorldWideScience	Global government & scientific research	WorldWideScience

📌 **OSINT Tip**: If an academic paper is behind a paywall, search for its title in BASE or CORE—there's often a free version available.

4. Search Engines for Social Media & Forum Intelligence

Google struggles to index social media due to platform restrictions. OSINT analysts must use specialized search tools to extract intelligence from Twitter, Facebook, Instagram, Reddit, Telegram, and dark web forums.

🔍 Alternative Search Engines for Social Media & Forums

Tool	Why Use It for OSINT?	Link
Social Searcher	Searches social media posts & mentions	Social Searcher
TweetDeck	Monitors Twitter in real-time	TweetDeck
AllMyTweets	Extracts complete Twitter timelines	AllMyTweets
RedditSearch.io	Advanced Reddit search	RedditSearch.io

📌 **OSINT Tip**: RedditSearch.io helps find deleted Reddit posts, useful for investigating past conversations.

5. Search Engines for the Deep & Dark Web

The deep web (content behind logins) and the dark web (hidden Tor sites) are not indexed by Google. To investigate hidden forums, leaked data, or underground marketplaces, OSINT analysts need specialized search engines.

🔍 Alternative Search Engines for the Deep & Dark Web

Search Engine	Why Use It for OSINT?	Link
Ahmia	Searches .onion (dark web) sites	Ahmia
OnionLand	Dark web search engine	OnionLand
Hunchly Dark Web Search	OSINT tool for deep web research	Hunchly

📌 **OSINT Tip**: Always use a VPN and Tor browser when accessing dark web search engines for anonymity.

6. Case Study: How Alternative Search Engines Reveal Hidden Data

Scenario:

A journalist is investigating a fake cybersecurity expert who has been spreading misinformation online.

Google Search:

🔍 Searching JohnDoeCybersecurity on Google returns only his personal website and social media.

Yandex Search:

🔍 Searching the same name on Yandex finds an old forum post where JohnDoeCybersecurity admitted to running a fake certification scam.

BASE & CORE Search:

🔍 Searching John Doe cybersecurity on BASE and CORE finds no published research under his name, proving his academic claims are false.

Ahmia (Dark Web Search):

🔍 Searching JohnDoeCybersecurity on Ahmia reveals a dark web post offering hacking services, linking him to underground cybercrime activities.

📌 **Key Takeaway**: Alternative search engines can uncover information Google completely misses.

Conclusion: Expanding Your OSINT Toolkit Beyond Google

◆ Google is powerful but has limitations—alternative search engines help fill the gaps.
◆ Privacy-focused search engines like DuckDuckGo & Startpage provide unbiased results.
◆ Technical & academic search engines reveal hidden information.
◆ Social media & dark web search engines expose underground data.
◆ A skilled OSINT analyst must use multiple search engines for the most complete intelligence.

4.2 Bing, Yandex, and Baidu: Their Strengths & Weaknesses

While Google dominates the search engine market, it has significant limitations for OSINT investigations. Alternative search engines like Bing, Yandex, and Baidu offer different indexing algorithms, regional advantages, and unique capabilities that can help uncover hidden intelligence.

In this chapter, we explore:

✅ **Bing** – A strong alternative to Google with different indexing priorities.
✅ **Yandex** – Superior reverse image search and deep web indexing.
✅ **Baidu** – The dominant Chinese search engine, useful for Asia-focused investigations.

Each of these search engines has strengths and weaknesses, making them valuable for specific OSINT tasks.

1. Bing: Microsoft's Alternative to Google

Bing, operated by Microsoft, is the second-largest search engine globally. It indexes content differently from Google, often surfacing pages that Google does not show due to ranking differences.

◆ Strengths of Bing for OSINT

✓ **Less Personalization** – Bing personalizes search results less aggressively than Google, providing more neutral results.

✓ **Better Indexing of Old & Niche Websites** – Bing indexes older pages and deep links that may be filtered out by Google's freshness algorithm.

✓ **More Filetype Search Support** – Bing allows searches for specific filetypes (PDF, DOCX, XLSX, etc.) similar to Google.

✓ **Video & Image Search is More Detailed** – Bing's video search is better at indexing smaller platforms and adult content.

▼ Weaknesses of Bing for OSINT

✗ **Smaller Search Index** – Bing indexes far fewer web pages than Google.

✗ **Weaker Social Media Indexing** – Google is better at finding Facebook, Twitter, and LinkedIn pages.

✗ **Geographic Bias** – Bing is heavily U.S.-centric and performs worse for searches outside North America and Europe.

📌 OSINT Use Case: Finding Older or Deindexed Content

If a webpage has been removed from Google's index, try searching for it on Bing:

🔍 Search Query:

- site:example.com "target phrase"

This often retrieves older, archived content that Google no longer displays.

2. Yandex: The OSINT Investigator's Secret Weapon

Yandex is Russia's largest search engine, but it has gained global popularity among OSINT professionals due to its powerful image search and deep indexing.

◆ Strengths of Yandex for OSINT

✓ **Best Reverse Image Search** – Yandex outperforms Google & Bing in facial recognition, object detection, and finding duplicate images.

✓ **Better Deep Web Indexing** – Yandex indexes Russian forums, dark web pages, and hidden content that Google ignores.

✓ **Finds Social Media Profiles Better** – Yandex is better than Google at finding VK, Telegram, and Instagram accounts.

▼ **Weaknesses of Yandex for OSINT**

✗ **Russian Language Bias** – Yandex prioritizes Russian content, making it less effective for searches in English, French, or Spanish.

✗ **Government Censorship** – Yandex complies with Russian laws, meaning some politically sensitive information may be censored.

✗ **Limited Filetype Searches** – Unlike Google and Bing, Yandex does not support advanced filetype operators.

📌 **OSINT Use Case: Reverse Image Searching for Identity Verification**

To find other places an image appears online, upload it to Yandex Image Search:

🔍 **URL**: https://yandex.com/images/

✅ This method is highly effective for identifying people, objects, and landmarks.

3. Baidu: The Gateway to Chinese Intelligence

Baidu is China's largest search engine, controlling over 70% of the Chinese search market. It is an essential OSINT tool for investigating Chinese businesses, people, and government activity.

◆ **Strengths of Baidu for OSINT**

✓ **Best Search Engine for Chinese Content** – Baidu indexes more Chinese websites than Google or Bing.

✓ **Access to Chinese Business & Government Records** – Many corporate, legal, and academic records are searchable only through Baidu.

✓ **Better for Researching Chinese Social Media** – Google and Bing struggle to index Weibo, WeChat, and QQ content, but Baidu provides better results.

▼ Weaknesses of Baidu for OSINT

✗ **Heavily Censored** – Baidu complies with Chinese government censorship laws, meaning politically sensitive topics are blocked.
✗ **Poor for English Content** – If you search in English, Baidu's results are far less useful than Google's.
✗ **Requires a Chinese IP for Best Results** – Many Baidu services work better when accessed from China or with a VPN set to China.

📌 OSINT Use Case: Investigating Chinese Businesses

To research a Chinese company or CEO, search for their name in Chinese characters:

🔍 Search Query:

- "公司名称" site:baidu.com

✔ This often reveals hidden corporate records, financial data, and legal disputes that Google does not index.

4. Comparison: Bing vs. Yandex vs. Baidu for OSINT

Feature	Bing	Yandex	Baidu
Best for Reverse Image Search	✗	✅ Best	✗
Best for English Results	✅	✗	✗
Best for Finding Social Media Accounts	✗	✅	✗
Best for Investigating Chinese Content	✗	✗	✅ Best
Best for Old or Deindexed Websites	✅	✗	✗
Best for Business & Legal Records	✗	✗	✅ Best
Best for Finding Leaked Documents	✅	✗	✗
Best for Censorship-Free Results	✅	✗	✗

📌 Key Takeaway:

- Use Yandex for images & social media investigations.

- Use Bing for old or hidden web content.
- Use Baidu for Chinese intelligence & corporate research.

Conclusion: Using the Right Search Engine for OSINT Success

◆ No single search engine is perfect—each has unique strengths and weaknesses.

◆ Bing is useful for uncovering old, deindexed, and technical content.

◆ Yandex is unmatched for reverse image searches and Russian deep web research.

◆ Baidu is essential for investigating China-based subjects, businesses, and government data.

◆ A skilled OSINT investigator must master multiple search engines to uncover the full picture.

4.3 Privacy-Focused Search Engines: DuckDuckGo & Startpage

When conducting OSINT investigations, privacy and anonymity are critical. Google, Bing, and other mainstream search engines track users through:

◆ **IP address logging** – Recording your location.

◆ **Search history tracking** – Personalizing results based on past activity.

◆ **Cookies and fingerprinting** – Identifying your device and browser.

For OSINT analysts, this compromises investigations by:

⚠️ Altering search results based on past activity.

⚠️ Exposing investigative queries to third parties.

⚠️ Risking detection when researching targets.

Privacy-focused search engines like DuckDuckGo and Startpage offer anonymity, neutrality, and unfiltered results, making them essential tools for intelligence gathering.

1. DuckDuckGo: The Leading Privacy Search Engine

DuckDuckGo (DDG) is the most popular privacy-focused search engine, with a strong commitment to user anonymity. It does not track searches, store history, or personalize results.

◆ Strengths of DuckDuckGo for OSINT

✓☐ **No Tracking, No Logging** – It does not store IP addresses, cookies, or search history.

✓☐ **Neutral & Unbiased Results** – Unlike Google, results are not influenced by past searches or location.

✓☐ **Instant Search Shortcuts (Bangs)** – Allows quick access to specific sites using shortcuts (e.g., !gh for GitHub, !yt for YouTube).

✓☐ **Deep Web & Alternative Content Indexing** – Often surfaces results ignored by Google, especially on dark web-related topics.

✓☐ **Tor-Friendly** – Works well with Tor Browser for anonymous searching.

▼ Weaknesses of DuckDuckGo for OSINT

✗ Smaller Index than Google – It pulls results primarily from Bing and its own crawler, missing some Google-only content.

✗ Weaker Local Search – Since it avoids tracking locations, results for local investigations may be less useful.

✗ Limited Advanced Search Operators – It lacks Google's complex search syntax (e.g., AROUND() proximity searches).

✦ OSINT Use Case: Anonymous Searching Without Google Tracking

To search without Google's tracking algorithms, use DuckDuckGo's search:

🔍 Example Query:

- intitle:"confidential" filetype:pdf

✅ This finds confidential PDFs without logging your search.

2. Startpage: Google Search Without the Tracking

Startpage is a privacy-focused search engine that provides Google results anonymously. It acts as a proxy, allowing users to access Google's powerful index without being tracked.

◆ Strengths of Startpage for OSINT

✓☐ **Google Results Without Tracking** – Retrieves Google's search index without logging IP addresses or search history.

✓☐ **Anonymous Proxy Browsing** – Each result has an option to view anonymously via a proxy, hiding the user's identity.

✓☐ **Neutral, Unbiased Searches** – Avoids Google's personalization algorithms, providing pure, raw search results.

✓☐ **Worsk Well with OSINT Search Operators** – Supports Google's advanced operators (e.g., site:, filetype:, intitle:).

▼ **Weaknesses of Startpage for OSINT**

✕ **Blocked in Some Regions** – Since it uses Google's results, some searches may be censored in certain countries.

✕ **No Alternative Index** – Unlike DuckDuckGo, Startpage only relies on Google and does not pull from Bing or independent sources.

✕ **Less Effective for Image & Video Search** – Since it proxies Google results, image and video searches lack depth.

📌 **OSINT Use Case: Viewing Websites Anonymously**

Startpage allows you to visit websites anonymously without revealing your IP.

🔍 **Example Search:**

- site:leakeddata.com "username database"

✅ Click "Anonymous View" next to a result to visit the site without exposing your identity.

3. DuckDuckGo vs. Startpage: Which One Should You Use?

◆ Strengths of DuckDuckGo for OSINT

✓ **No Tracking, No Logging** – It does not store IP addresses, cookies, or search history.

✓ **Neutral & Unbiased Results** – Unlike Google, results are not influenced by past searches or location.

✓ **Instant Search Shortcuts (Bangs)** – Allows quick access to specific sites using shortcuts (e.g., !gh for GitHub, !yt for YouTube).

✓ **Deep Web & Alternative Content Indexing** – Often surfaces results ignored by Google, especially on dark web-related topics.

✓ **Tor-Friendly** – Works well with Tor Browser for anonymous searching.

▼ Weaknesses of DuckDuckGo for OSINT

✗ **Smaller Index than Google** – It pulls results primarily from Bing and its own crawler, missing some Google-only content.

✗ **Weaker Local Search** – Since it avoids tracking locations, results for local investigations may be less useful.

✗ **Limited Advanced Search Operators** – It lacks Google's complex search syntax (e.g., AROUND() proximity searches).

✦ **OSINT Use Case**: Anonymous Searching Without Google Tracking

To search without Google's tracking algorithms, use DuckDuckGo's search:

🔍 Example Query:

- intitle:"confidential" filetype:pdf

✅ This finds confidential PDFs without logging your search.

2. Startpage: Google Search Without the Tracking

Startpage is a privacy-focused search engine that provides Google results anonymously. It acts as a proxy, allowing users to access Google's powerful index without being tracked.

◆ Strengths of Startpage for OSINT

✓☐ **Google Results Without Tracking** – Retrieves Google's search index without logging IP addresses or search history.

✓☐ **Anonymous Proxy Browsing** – Each result has an option to view anonymously via a proxy, hiding the user's identity.

✓☐ **Neutral, Unbiased Searches** – Avoids Google's personalization algorithms, providing pure, raw search results.

✓☐ **Worsk Well with OSINT Search Operators** – Supports Google's advanced operators (e.g., site:, filetype:, intitle:).

▼ Weaknesses of Startpage for OSINT

✗ **Blocked in Some Regions** – Since it uses Google's results, some searches may be censored in certain countries.

✗ **No Alternative Index** – Unlike DuckDuckGo, Startpage only relies on Google and does not pull from Bing or independent sources.

✗ **Less Effective for Image & Video Search** – Since it proxies Google results, image and video searches lack depth.

📌 OSINT Use Case: Viewing Websites Anonymously

Startpage allows you to visit websites anonymously without revealing your IP.

🔍 Example Search:

- site:leakeddata.com "username database"

✅ Click "Anonymous View" next to a result to visit the site without exposing your identity.

3. DuckDuckGo vs. Startpage: Which One Should You Use?

Feature	DuckDuckGo	Startpage
Privacy & No Tracking	Best (No logging at all)	Google results but private
Search Index	Bing-based + Independent	Google-based
Advanced Search Operators	✕ Limited	Full Google operators
Anonymous Website Viewing	✕ No	Yes (via proxy)
Reverse Image Search	✕ No	✕ No
Best for Local Searches	✕ Weaker	Uses Google's local data
Dark Web & Privacy Focus	Better for anonymity	✕ Google still filters some results

📌 Key Takeaway:

- Use DuckDuckGo for pure privacy and deep web-related searches.
- Use Startpage for Google-level results without tracking.

4. Combining Privacy-Focused Search Engines with OSINT Tools

For maximum effectiveness, combine DuckDuckGo and Startpage with other OSINT techniques:

◆ Use DuckDuckGo with a VPN or Tor for fully anonymous investigations.
◆ Use Startpage to leverage Google's power without revealing your search patterns.
◆ Use Searx.me – An open-source meta-search engine that queries multiple search engines anonymously.
◆ Use browser isolation – Conduct searches in a separate browser or virtual machine to reduce fingerprinting.

5. Case Study: Using Privacy Search Engines for Investigative Journalism

Scenario:

A journalist is investigating corporate corruption involving a CEO who is hiding financial transactions.

Google Search:

🔍 Searching the CEO's name on Google results in personalized, PR-controlled news articles.

DuckDuckGo Search:

🔍 Searching on DuckDuckGo surfaces an older, deleted article about financial fraud allegations.

Startpage Search:

🔍 Searching the CEO's name on Startpage retrieves Google results but without tracking, revealing a hidden lawsuit document in PDF format.

📌 **Key Takeaway**: Privacy-focused search engines help bypass tracking, uncover hidden data, and protect the investigator's identity.

Conclusion: The Power of Private Search Engines in OSINT

◆ Google tracks searches, filters results, and personalizes content, limiting OSINT investigations.
◆ DuckDuckGo is a strong choice for anonymous searches and deep web-related topics.
◆ Startpage provides full Google results without tracking and allows anonymous website viewing.
◆ Combining privacy-focused search engines with VPNs, Tor, and alternative OSINT tools maximizes investigative power.

4.4 Academic & Government Search Engines for OSINT

Most OSINT investigations rely on traditional search engines like Google and Bing, but these often fail to index specialized academic and government databases. Many valuable official records, research papers, and legal documents are hidden inside government portals, university repositories, and scientific archives.

For OSINT analysts, these databases offer:

✅ **Access to authoritative data** – Verified reports, regulations, and legal filings.

✓ **Corporate, legal, and financial records** – Government archives often store contracts, patents, and court rulings.

✓ **Scientific and technical intelligence** – Research papers contain deep insights into emerging technologies, security threats, and political analysis.

This chapter explores the best academic and government search engines for OSINT investigations and how to use them effectively.

1. Google Scholar: Finding Academic & Legal Intelligence

Google Scholar is a powerful yet underused tool for OSINT. It indexes:

♦ **Academic papers** – Research from universities, think tanks, and government agencies.

♦ **Legal cases** – U.S. court rulings, patents, and regulatory filings.

♦ **Technical reports** – Scientific studies related to cybersecurity, defense, and technology.

◆ Strengths of Google Scholar for OSINT

✓ **Finds credible, peer-reviewed information** – Useful for verifying claims.

✓ **Accesses government-funded research** – Many intelligence agencies, defense organizations, and policy institutes publish here.

✓ **Legal case search** – Helpful for investigating corporate and criminal cases.

▼ Weaknesses of Google Scholar for OSINT

✗ **Paywalls** – Some papers require a university login or paid access.

✗ **Limited news or public records** – Primarily academic and legal content.

📌 **OSINT Use Case**: Investigating a Technology Patent

🔍 **Example Query:**

- "cybersecurity threat detection" site:scholar.google.com

✅ This retrieves scientific papers, technical reports, and government studies on cybersecurity threats.

2. WorldWideScience.org: Multinational Scientific OSINT

WorldWideScience.org is a global search engine that indexes:

- Government-funded research from multiple countries.
- Scientific, medical, and technical studies.
- Defense and intelligence-related papers.

◆ Strengths of WorldWideScience for OSINT

✓☐ **Access to international research** – Sources include NASA, the Department of Energy (DOE), and European research centers.
✓☐ **Multilingual search** – Translates foreign studies into English.
✓☐ **Focus on science & security topics** – Ideal for tracking emerging cyber threats, biosecurity risks, and military technologies.

📌 **OSINT Use Case**: Tracking Global Cybersecurity Trends

🔍 **Example Query:**

- "AI-based cyber attacks" site:worldwidescience.org

✅ This finds government-funded research on AI-related cyber threats.

3. USA.gov & Federal Government Portals

USA.gov is the official search engine for U.S. government documents, offering:

- Legal records & court filings.
- Regulatory & policy reports.
- Business & contractor information.

◆ Strengths of USA.gov for OSINT

✓☐ Direct access to official records – Avoids misinformation.

✓☐ Includes public reports from agencies like the FBI, DHS, and SEC.

✓☐ Searches multiple federal databases at once.

★ **OSINT Use Case**: Investigating a Government Contractor

🔍 **Example Query:**

- "XYZ Corp" site:usa.gov

✅ This retrieves government contracts, SEC filings, and legal disputes involving the company.

4. CIA's World Factbook: Country & Geopolitical Intelligence

The CIA World Factbook provides open-source intelligence on:

◆ Political, economic, and security data for every country.

◆ Infrastructure, military, and intelligence agency profiles.

◆ Geopolitical risks and emerging threats.

◆ Strengths of the World Factbook for OSINT

✓☐ Authoritative geopolitical intelligence – Trusted source for country research.

✓☐ Useful for tracking political instability, economic trends, and defense policies.

★ **OSINT Use Case**: Investigating a Country's Cybersecurity Policies

🔍 **Example Query:**

- "China cybersecurity policy" site:cia.gov

✅ This retrieves official CIA assessments of China's cyber strategies.

5. European & International Government Search Engines

Beyond U.S. sources, international databases provide valuable intelligence:

Search Engine	Region	OSINT Use Cases
EU Open Data Portal	European Union	Government contracts, economic data, regulatory filings.
Gov.UK Search	United Kingdom	Public records, security policies, corporate data.
Australia Gov Data	Australia	Business registrations, environmental reports.
Canada Open Data	Canada	Corporate disclosures, legal documents.

6. ResearchGate & Academia.edu: Tracking Academic Intelligence

These platforms host millions of research papers, some of which are:

◆ Technical reports from defense contractors & intelligence analysts.
◆ Cybersecurity, AI, and disinformation studies.
◆ Government-funded research that's unavailable elsewhere.

🔍 Example Query on ResearchGate:

- "Deepfake detection methods" site:researchgate.net

✓ This retrieves scientific studies on deepfake identification—valuable for OSINT investigations.

7. Legal & Business OSINT: PACER & EDGAR

For corporate and legal investigations, use:

◆ **PACER** – U.S. court records (civil & criminal cases).
◆ **SEC EDGAR** – Public company financial filings.
◆ **OpenCorporates** – The world's largest database of company records.

8. Combining Government & Academic Search Engines for OSINT

◆ Use Google Scholar to find academic research on a topic.
◆ Use WorldWideScience.org to get global intelligence on cybersecurity, AI, and defense.
◆ Use USA.gov & Gov.UK to access legal, business, and regulatory data.

- Use CIA World Factbook to get country-level intelligence.
- Use ResearchGate to track scientific research trends.

📌 **Key Takeaway:**

Government and academic search engines provide data that Google and Bing cannot access.

Conclusion: The Power of Government & Academic OSINT

- Most official records and scientific intelligence are hidden from mainstream search engines.
- Google Scholar, WorldWideScience, and PACER offer powerful insights into legal, corporate, and geopolitical intelligence.
- OSINT professionals must leverage specialized government and academic search engines for deeper investigations.

4.5 Specialized Search Engines for Cyber Investigations

Google, Bing, and DuckDuckGo are great for general OSINT searches, but they miss a significant portion of cyber-related intelligence. Threat actors, hackers, and cybercriminals often communicate on forums, host malicious files, or leave digital traces that aren't indexed by traditional search engines.

For cybersecurity investigations, specialized search engines help uncover:

✅ **Compromised credentials & leaked databases** – Credentials exposed in breaches.
✅ **Malware & suspicious domains** – Finding malicious IPs, phishing sites, and attack indicators.
✅ **Exposed IoT & server vulnerabilities** – Identifying misconfigured systems.
✅ **Dark web discussions & threat intelligence** – Cybercriminal activities in underground markets.

This chapter explores the best specialized search engines for cybersecurity investigations and how OSINT analysts can use them effectively.

1. Shodan: The Search Engine for Internet-Connected Devices

Shodan is known as "Google for hackers" because it indexes:

- Exposed webcams, routers, and IoT devices.
- Misconfigured servers & databases.
- Industrial control systems (ICS) & critical infrastructure.

◆ Strengths of Shodan for Cyber OSINT

✓☐ **Detects open ports & vulnerable services** – Helps identify at-risk systems.
✓☐ **Finds exposed databases** – Useful for checking if MongoDB, Elasticsearch, or MySQL databases are public.
✓☐ **Searches by IP, domain, or organization** – Great for tracking attack surfaces.

▼ Weaknesses of Shodan

✗ Requires a paid plan for full data access.

✗ Does not cover the dark web or credential leaks.

✦ OSINT Use Case: Finding Exposed Security Cameras

🔍 Example Query:

- "webcam" port:554 country:US

✓ This lists publicly accessible security cameras in the U.S.

2. Censys: The Alternative to Shodan for Network Scanning

Censys is another internet scanning engine that provides:

- Real-time search of exposed services & SSL certificates.
- Identification of vulnerable servers & expired certificates.
- Historical data on IPs & domains.

◆ Strengths of Censys for Cyber OSINT

✓☐ More detailed SSL/TLS certificate information than Shodan.

✓☐ Free-tier access is more generous than Shodan's.

✓☐ Great for investigating phishing domains & malware servers.

📌 **OSINT Use Case**: Finding Servers with Expired SSL Certificates

🔍 **Example Query:**

- tags:expired_ssl country:RU

✅ This finds Russian websites with expired SSL certificates, a common sign of abandoned or compromised domains.

3. GreyNoise: Filtering Out Background Internet Noise

GreyNoise is an intelligence tool for distinguishing real cyber threats from background noise. It tracks:

◆ Mass internet scanning activity (e.g., botnets, reconnaissance tools).

◆ Malicious IP addresses launching attacks.

◆ Traffic trends for cybersecurity incidents.

◆ **Strengths of GreyNoise for Cyber OSINT**

✓☐ Identifies whether an IP is scanning the internet or launching attacks.

✓☐ Filters out false positives from mass scanning bots.

✓☐ Useful for incident response teams tracking active threats.

📌 **OSINT Use Case**: Checking if an IP is a Known Threat

🔍 **Example Query:**

- IP: 45.227.255.10

✅ This checks if the IP is linked to malicious activity.

4. VirusTotal: Investigating Malware, URLs, and IPs

VirusTotal is a multi-engine malware scanner used to analyze:

- **Suspicious files & URLs** – Checks for malware or phishing.
- **Malicious IPs & domains** – Cross-referenced with security vendors.
- Threat intelligence on cyber attacks.

◆ Strengths of VirusTotal for Cyber OSINT

✓☐ Aggregates results from over 70 security vendors.
✓☐ Scans uploaded files, hashes, and URLs.
✓☐ Tracks malware trends over time.

📌 **OSINT Use Case**: Checking if a Website is Malicious

🔍 **Example Query:**

- https://suspiciouswebsite.com

✓ This scans the site against multiple antivirus databases.

5. IntelligenceX: Searching Leaked Data & Dark Web Content

IntelligenceX specializes in searching:

- Leaked databases & credential dumps.
- Dark web marketplaces & forums.
- Archived content from Tor and I2P networks.

◆ Strengths of IntelligenceX for Cyber OSINT

✓☐ Searches leaked credentials, private documents, and sensitive data.
✓☐ Indexes content from the deep web & dark web.
✓☐ Provides historical snapshots of deleted content.

📌 **OSINT Use Case**: Checking if an Email Has Been Leaked

- email:john.doe@example.com

✅ This checks if the email has appeared in data breaches or dark web leaks.

6. Have I Been Pwned: Checking for Compromised Credentials

Have I Been Pwned (HIBP) is a free tool that allows users to:

- ◈ Check if an email address has been part of a data breach.
- ◈ Find leaked passwords from cyber attacks.
- ◈ Monitor for new credential leaks.

📌 **OSINT Use Case**: Investigating Breached Emails

🔍 **Example Query:**

- Email: victim@example.com

✅ This identifies if the email has been exposed in past breaches.

7. Hybrid Analysis: Deep Malware Investigation

Hybrid Analysis is a sandbox analysis platform that:

- ◈ Executes suspicious files in a controlled environment.
- ◈ Extracts behavioral patterns & network connections.
- ◈ Identifies malware used in cyberattacks.

📌 **OSINT Use Case**: Checking a Suspicious File Hash

🔍 **Example Query:**

- File hash: d41d8cd98f00b204e9800998ecf8427e

✅ This reveals if the file is linked to malware campaigns.

8. Combining Cyber Search Engines for OSINT Investigations

◆ Use Shodan or Censys to find exposed servers, webcams, or databases.

◆ Use VirusTotal & Hybrid Analysis to analyze suspicious files & domains.

◆ Use Have I Been Pwned & IntelligenceX to check for data breaches.

◆ Use GreyNoise to separate real cyber threats from background noise.

📌 Key Takeaway:

No single search engine provides complete cyber intelligence—combining multiple tools is essential.

Conclusion: Mastering Cyber OSINT with Specialized Search Engines

◆ Traditional search engines miss critical cybersecurity intelligence.

◆ Specialized tools like Shodan, VirusTotal, and IntelligenceX help track exposed data, malware, and cyber threats.

◆ By using a combination of cyber search engines, OSINT analysts can uncover hidden risks, detect leaks, and prevent cyberattacks.

4.6 Testing Search Engine Effectiveness in Real-World Scenarios

The effectiveness of a search engine varies depending on data type, indexing methods, and search algorithms. No single engine uncovers everything—Google is great for general queries, but it fails to index deep web databases, leaked credentials, and real-time cyber threats.

For OSINT analysts, testing multiple search engines is crucial for:

✅ Validating the accuracy of search results.

✅ Comparing data coverage between engines.

✅ Finding the best tool for specific intelligence needs.

This chapter explores real-world test cases comparing search engines and their effectiveness in OSINT investigations.

1. Testing Google vs. Alternative Search Engines

🔍 Test Case: Searching for a Missing Person

Imagine you're tracking John Doe, who was last active on social media in 2023. You start by searching his name.

◆ Google Search Results

✓☐ Retrieves LinkedIn, Twitter, and Facebook profiles.
✓☐ Shows news articles mentioning the person.
✗ Struggles to find forum discussions or old social media mentions.

🔍 Google Query:

- "John Doe" AND "New York" site:facebook.com OR site:twitter.com

◆ Yandex Search Results

✓☐ Finds cached versions of deleted social media profiles.
✓☐ More likely to show Russian and Eastern European sources.
✗ Results may contain more outdated or irrelevant data.

🔍 Yandex Query:

- "John Doe" AND "New York" site:vk.com OR site:ok.ru

📌 Takeaway:

Google is better for real-time and official sources, but Yandex may find older, hidden, or international data.

2. Testing People Search Engines for Background Investigations

🔍 Test Case: Finding Information on a Business Owner

You're investigating a small business owner, James Smith, in Florida.

◆ Google Search

✓ Finds LinkedIn, company website, and basic business listings.
✗ Fails to retrieve public records or legal cases.

🔍 Google Query:

- "James Smith" AND "Florida" site:linkedin.com OR site:companywebsite.com

◆ Pipl Search (People Search Engine)

✓ Retrieves phone numbers, addresses, and social media links.
✓ Shows past addresses and possible relatives.
✗ Requires a paid subscription for full details.

🔍 Pipl Query:

- James Smith, Florida

◆ TruthFinder / Spokeo

✓ Finds court records, criminal history, and email addresses.
✗ Some data is outdated or duplicated from other sources.

📌 Takeaway:

Google provides general information, while people search engines reveal deeper records—Pipl is excellent for OSINT investigations.

3. Testing Dark Web Search Engines for Leaked Data

🔍 **Test Case**: Checking If an Email Appears in Data Breaches

You're investigating if john.doe@example.com has appeared in leaked databases.

◆ Google Search

✗ Google does not index dark web leaks.

✗ No results from hacker forums or breach databases.

◆ IntelligenceX Search

✓☐ Finds email mentions in past data breaches.
✓☐ Retrieves dark web dumps, archived documents.

🔍 IntelligenceX Query:

- john.doe@example.com

◆ Have I Been Pwned (HIBP)

✓☐ Shows whether the email was part of a breach.

✗ Does not reveal full breach data—only confirms exposure.

📌 Takeaway:

For breach investigations, IntelligenceX and HIBP outperform Google by accessing underground data sources.

4. Testing Cyber Threat Search Engines for Malware Analysis

🔍 **Test Case**: Investigating a Suspicious Domain

A phishing email contains the link: suspiciousdomain.com.

◆ Google Search

✓☐ Finds basic WHOIS data and company website.

✗ Does not detect if the domain is malicious.

🔍 Google Query:

- whois suspiciousdomain.com

◆ VirusTotal Search

✓☐ Scans the domain for malware, phishing, and bad reputation.
✓☐ Shows historical records of malicious activity.

🔍 VirusTotal Query:

- suspiciousdomain.com

◆ Hybrid Analysis Search

✓☐ Provides behavioral analysis of files downloaded from the domain.
✓☐ Identifies malware connections and suspicious activity.

📌 Takeaway:

VirusTotal and Hybrid Analysis are more effective for cyber threat investigations than Google.

5. Testing Image Reverse Search Engines

🔍 **Test Case**: Identifying a Person from a Photo

You find a mysterious photo on social media and want to trace its origin.

◆ Google Reverse Image Search

✓☐ Finds matching images from indexed websites.
✗ Does not search social media profiles effectively.

◆ Yandex Reverse Image Search

✓☐ More effective at finding faces and social media profiles.
✓☐ Can retrieve profile pictures from VK, Facebook, and Instagram.

◆ PimEyes (Facial Recognition Search Engine)

✓ Advanced facial recognition for finding the same person across different photos.
✗ Paid service with limited free searches.

📌 Takeaway:

For general image matching, Google works, but Yandex and PimEyes are better for facial recognition.

6. Testing Search Engines for OSINT Automation

🔍 **Test Case**: Automating Search Queries

You need to automate Google Dorking and advanced searches for large-scale investigations.

◆ Google with Custom Scripts (SerpApi or Google CSE)

✓ Allows automated Google searches using Python scripts.
✓ Great for scaling OSINT workflows.

◆ Recon-ng & SpiderFoot

✓ Automates multi-source OSINT investigations.
✓ Extracts data from Google, Shodan, VirusTotal, and more.

📌 Takeaway:

Automating OSINT requires specialized tools like Recon-ng and APIs for search engines.

Conclusion: No Single Search Engine is Perfect

◆ Google is great for basic OSINT but fails in deep web, breach, and cyber investigations.
◆ Yandex excels in reverse image searches and cached social media data.
◆ Specialized tools like VirusTotal, IntelligenceX, and Have I Been Pwned provide deeper insights.
◆ Automating OSINT searches with APIs and tools like Recon-ng improves efficiency.

5. Metadata & Filetype Searches

Metadata and filetype searches are powerful techniques for extracting hidden intelligence from publicly available documents. Search engines index a vast range of file types, including PDFs, Word documents, Excel spreadsheets, and PowerPoint presentations, often containing valuable insights such as names, emails, IP addresses, and geolocation data. Using operators like filetype: in combination with site: or intitle: allows OSINT analysts to target specific file formats on particular domains. Additionally, examining document metadata through tools like ExifTool or FOCA can reveal authorship details, software versions, and even document revision history. By leveraging these methods, analysts can uncover sensitive data that organizations unknowingly expose, making metadata analysis a crucial skill in OSINT investigations.

5.1 What is Metadata & How It Affects OSINT

When you download a photo, document, or video, you're not just getting the visible content—you're also getting metadata, which is hidden information embedded in the file. This metadata can include:

✅ Who created the file (author name, username, or device info)

✅ When it was created & modified (timestamps)

✅ Where it was created (GPS coordinates in photos)

✅ How it was created (software used, camera model, file version history)

For OSINT analysts, metadata is a goldmine of intelligence. It helps track the origin of leaked documents, verify images, and uncover information that the creator didn't intend to share.

In this chapter, we'll break down:

◆ Types of metadata found in different files
◆ How metadata exposes sensitive information
◆ Real-world OSINT examples of metadata analysis

1. Types of Metadata in Different Files

◆ Image Metadata (EXIF Data)

EXIF (Exchangeable Image File Format) metadata is embedded in images and includes:

✓□ Camera model & settings (shutter speed, ISO, lens type)
✓□ GPS coordinates (where the photo was taken)
✓□ Date & time (when the photo was captured)

📌 Example:

A journalist uploads a photo of a confidential meeting. The EXIF data reveals the exact GPS coordinates, exposing the location.

🔍 Tool to Extract EXIF Data:

- exiftool photo.jpg

◆ Document Metadata (Word, PDF, Excel, etc.)

Office documents contain metadata that can expose:

✓□ **Author name & organization** (who created the document)
✓□ **Last edited timestamp** (when the document was last changed)
✓□ **Tracked revisions & comments** (previous versions of the file)

📌 Example:

A company publishes a redacted PDF report, but the hidden metadata still contains the names of employees who worked on it.

🔍 Tool to Extract Document Metadata:

- pdfinfo document.pdf

◆ Video & Audio Metadata

Multimedia files contain metadata such as:

✓☐ Device used (smartphone brand, editing software)
✓☐ Encoding information (codec, bit rate, frame rate)
✓☐ Timestamps (when the file was created or modified)

📌 Example:

A whistleblower uploads an anonymous audio recording, but metadata reveals the exact device and time of recording, making it traceable.

🔍 Tool to Extract Video/Audio Metadata:

- ffmpeg -i video.mp4

2. How Metadata Can Expose Identities & Locations

◆ Case Study: Tracking a Hacker Through Document Metadata

A hacker leaks classified documents online, believing they are anonymous. However, OSINT analysts extract the document metadata and find:

✓☐ The hacker's username from Microsoft Word's author field
✓☐ The organization name from the document's metadata
✓☐ A hidden file path revealing the hacker's operating system

🎯 **Result**: The hacker is traced and arrested due to a single overlooked metadata field.

◆ Case Study: Finding the Location of a Photo

A political activist posts a photo claiming to be in one country, but the EXIF metadata shows GPS coordinates from another location.

🔍 Tool to Extract GPS from an Image:

- exiftool -gpslatitude -gpslongitude photo.jpg

📌 OSINT Takeaway:

Metadata can prove deception by verifying timestamps, locations, and device details.

3. Removing & Manipulating Metadata

Because metadata can expose sensitive details, professionals often remove or modify it before sharing files.

◆ How to Remove Metadata

◈ **For images**: Strip EXIF data before uploading:

- exiftool -all= photo.jpg

◈ **For PDFs & Word Docs**: Use metadata removal tools like MAT2 (Metadata Anonymisation Toolkit):

- mat2 -r document.pdf

✦ **OSINT Tip:** If someone has removed metadata, it may indicate they are trying to hide something—which is valuable intelligence on its own.

4. OSINT Tools for Metadata Analysis

Here are the best tools for extracting metadata in investigations:

Tool Name	Use Case	Website/Command
ExifTool	Extracts image, video, and document metadata	exiftool file.jpg
pdfinfo	Extracts metadata from PDFs	pdfinfo document.pdf
ExifPilot	Windows tool for viewing EXIF metadata	ExifPilot
FOCA	Extracts metadata from bulk documents	FOCA
OSINT Framework	Collection of metadata tools	OSINT Framework

5. Conclusion: Why Metadata Matters in OSINT

◈ Metadata is often overlooked, but it's a powerful OSINT tool for tracking individuals, verifying media, and exposing hidden data.

◈ EXIF data in images can reveal GPS coordinates and timestamps, while document metadata can expose authors and file history.

◈ OSINT analysts can use specialized tools like ExifTool, FOCA, and MAT2 to extract, analyze, and remove metadata for investigations.

5.2 Extracting Metadata from PDF, Word & Image Files

Metadata embedded in PDF, Word documents, and image files can reveal critical intelligence during OSINT investigations. These hidden details can expose:

✓ Author names & organizations (who created the file)

✓ Timestamps (when the file was created, edited, or printed)

✓ Software used (which tool or device generated the file)

✓ GPS coordinates (where an image was taken)

✓ Version history & previous edits (what changes were made)

For OSINT professionals, metadata analysis can confirm authenticity, uncover identities, and track digital footprints. This chapter explores how to extract metadata from PDFs, Word documents, and images using powerful tools.

1. Extracting Metadata from PDF Files

◆ **What Metadata is Stored in PDFs?**

PDF metadata can contain:

✓ Author & creator details (username, organization)
✓ Creation & modification timestamps
✓ Software used to generate the PDF
✓ Document title, subject, and keywords
✓ Hidden annotations or comments

📌 **Example:**

A whistleblower leaks a classified PDF, thinking it's anonymous. However, metadata reveals:

✓☐ The author's real name
✓☐ The timestamp of document creation
✓☐ The company's internal software used to generate the file

◆ **Tools to Extract PDF Metadata**

📌 **Method 1: Using pdfinfo (Linux & Windows)**

pdfinfo is a simple command-line tool to extract metadata from PDFs.

🔍 **Run the following command:**

- pdfinfo secret_document.pdf

Example Output:

- **Title**: Confidential Report
- **Author**: JohnDoe
- **Producer**: Microsoft Word 2016
- **CreationDate**: 2024-02-10 12:30:00
- **ModDate**: 2024-02-12 15:45:00

✅ **Takeaway**: This document was created by JohnDoe using Microsoft Word 2016 and last modified two days later.

📌 **Method 2: Using ExifTool (Cross-platform)**

ExifTool extracts deep metadata beyond what pdfinfo finds.

🔍 **Run the command:**

- exiftool secret_document.pdf

✅ **Benefit**: Can extract hidden metadata, timestamps, and encryption details.

📌 **Method 3: Using FOCA (Windows)**

FOCA (Fingerprinting Organizations with Collected Archives) is a GUI tool for bulk metadata extraction from PDFs, DOCs, and images.

🔍 Steps to use FOCA:

1☐ Download and install FOCA (link)

2☐ Upload PDF files

3☐ Extract metadata & analyze hidden details

2. Extracting Metadata from Word & Office Documents

◆ What Metadata is Stored in Word, Excel, & PowerPoint?

Office files contain:

✓☐ Author & organization name

✓☐ Creation & last modification timestamps

✓☐ Editor history (who worked on the document)

✓☐ Hidden comments & tracked changes

📌 Example:

A company publishes an internal report. The metadata shows:

✓☐ Employee names who contributed

✓☐ The internal document ID

✓☐ Who last edited the file and when

◆ Tools to Extract Word Document Metadata

📌 Method 1: Using ExifTool

ExifTool works for Word, Excel, and PowerPoint files.

🔍 Run the command:

- exiftool confidential_report.docx

Example Output:

- Author: JaneSmith
- Company: XYZ Corp
- Last Modified By: AdminUser
- Created: 2024-02-10 09:15:00
- Modified: 2024-02-12 18:20:00
- Software Used: Microsoft Word 2019

✅ **Takeaway**: This document was originally created by JaneSmith from XYZ Corp but later modified by AdminUser.

📌 **Method 2: Using LibreOffice (GUI Tool for Windows/Linux)**

1️⃣ Open the .docx file in LibreOffice Writer

2️⃣ Click File → Properties → Custom Properties

3️⃣ View hidden metadata fields

📌 **Method 3: Using FOCA for Bulk Extraction**

FOCA can analyze multiple Office documents at once, revealing network paths, usernames, and hidden metadata.

3. Extracting Metadata from Image Files (EXIF Data)

◆ **What Metadata is Stored in Images?**

✓ Camera model & lens details
✓ Timestamps (when the photo was taken)
✓ GPS coordinates (where the image was taken)
✓ Software used to edit the photo

📌 **Example:**

A journalist uploads a photo claiming to be in Paris, but the EXIF data shows GPS coordinates from New York—proving deception.

◆ Tools to Extract Image Metadata

📌 Method 1: Using ExifTool

ExifTool works for JPEG, PNG, and RAW images.

🔍 Run the command:

- exiftool suspect_photo.jpg

Example Output:

- Camera Model: iPhone 14 Pro
- Date Taken: 2024-02-12 14:45:30
- GPS Latitude: 40.7128° N
- GPS Longitude: 74.0060° W (New York)
- Software: Adobe Photoshop

☑ **Takeaway**: The image was edited using Photoshop, and the GPS coordinates reveal the true location.

📌 Method 2: Using Jeffrey's EXIF Viewer (Online Tool)

1️⃣ Upload an image to Jeffrey's EXIF Viewer
2️⃣ View camera details, timestamps, and GPS

📌 Method 3: Using OSINT Tools like OSINTCombine's EXIF Scraper

☑ Works for bulk image analysis
☑ Identifies manipulated metadata

4. Removing Metadata to Maintain Anonymity

Since metadata can expose identities, professionals often remove it before sharing files.

◆ How to Remove Metadata from PDFs & Word Documents

📌 Method 1: Using mat2 (Metadata Anonymization Toolkit)

🔍 To remove metadata from PDFs, DOCX, or images:

- mat2 -r document.pdf

✅ **Benefit**: Works for multiple file formats, ensuring complete metadata removal.

📌 Method 2: Using Windows "Remove Properties" Tool

1️⃣ Right-click on the file → Click Properties
2️⃣ Go to Details Tab → Click Remove Properties and Personal Information
3️⃣ Choose "Remove all properties"

5. Conclusion: Why Metadata Matters in OSINT

◆ PDFs, Word docs, and images contain hidden metadata that can reveal authors, timestamps, and locations.
◆ Tools like ExifTool, pdfinfo, and FOCA extract metadata for intelligence gathering.
◆ Metadata can verify authenticity, expose deception, and track digital footprints.
◆ Removing metadata is crucial for privacy and anonymity in sensitive investigations.

5.3 Finding Publicly Exposed Metadata in Search Engines

Metadata isn't just stored inside files—it's also indexed by search engines, often unknowingly exposed to the public. Many websites, companies, and even government agencies accidentally leave sensitive documents available online, complete with their hidden metadata.

For OSINT analysts, these exposed documents can reveal:

✅ Internal author names & usernames

✅ Organization names & document history

✅ File locations on company servers

✅ Confidential reports, spreadsheets, and legal documents

This chapter will cover:

- How search engines index metadata-rich files
- Google Dorking techniques to find publicly available metadata
- Tools & methods for extracting metadata from online documents

1. How Metadata Ends Up on Search Engines

Many organizations upload PDFs, Word documents, and images online without stripping metadata. These files can be indexed by search engines, making them searchable using advanced search operators.

🔍 **Common mistakes that expose metadata:**

✓☐ Uploading internal documents to public-facing websites (without restricting access)
✓☐ Leaving backups or old reports on unprotected directories
✓☐ Forgetting to clean EXIF data from images before posting them online

📌 **Example:**

A company uploads a PDF report about an upcoming product launch. The metadata contains:

✓☐ **Author name**: John.Doe@company.com
✓☐ **Organization**: TechCorp R&D
✓☐ **Last modified date**: Two months before the official launch

✅ **OSINT Takeaway**: Analysts can use this information to identify employees, confirm leaks, and track internal activities.

2. Using Google Dorking to Find Exposed Metadata

Google indexes many file types that often contain metadata. We can use Google Dorking to search for specific documents, spreadsheets, and presentations uploaded online.

◆ **Search for Publicly Available PDFs**

- filetype:pdf site:example.com

✅ Finds all PDFs uploaded on a specific website.

🔍 **Example**: Searching for leaked government reports:

- filetype:pdf site:.gov confidential

✅ Finds government PDFs containing the word "confidential".

◆ **Search for Word & Excel Documents**

- filetype:docx OR filetype:xlsx site:example.com

✅ Finds Word and Excel documents on a specific website.

🔍 **Example**: Finding financial reports:

- filetype:xlsx site:example.com budget report

✅ Finds budget spreadsheets, which often contain hidden metadata.

◆ **Find Exposed Server Directories (Open File Listings)**

Some websites accidentally expose entire directories where files are stored.

- intitle:"index of" "parent directory" filetype:pdf OR filetype:docx

✅ Finds open directories containing PDFs and Word documents.

◆ **Find Images with EXIF Metadata**

- filetype:jpg OR filetype:png site:example.com

✅ Finds images that may still contain GPS and camera metadata.

🔍 **Example**: Searching for satellite images from research institutions:

- filetype:jpg site:nasa.gov satellite

✅ Finds NASA images that may contain metadata with location details.

3. Extracting Metadata from Online Documents

Once you've found a publicly available document, the next step is to extract its metadata.

◆ Extract Metadata from an Online PDF

1️⃣ Download the file
2️⃣ Use pdfinfo to analyze metadata:

- pdfinfo downloaded_document.pdf

✅ Reveals author, creation date, and software used.

◆ Extract Metadata from Online Word & Excel Files

1️⃣ Download the file
2️⃣ Use ExifTool:

- exiftool confidential_report.docx

✅ Extracts author name, organization, timestamps, and revision history.

◆ Extract Metadata from Online Images

1️⃣ Download the image
2️⃣ Use ExifTool to check GPS, camera details, and timestamps:

- exiftool leaked_photo.jpg

✅ If GPS data is present, it may reveal the exact location where the photo was taken.

4. Tools for Finding & Extracting Metadata Online

Tool Name	Use Case	Website/Command
Google Dorking	Finds exposed documents in search engines	`filetype:pdf site:example.com`
ExifTool	Extracts metadata from documents & images	`exiftool file.pdf`
FOCA	Bulk metadata extraction from online files	FOCA
Metagoofil	Searches & extracts metadata from public files	`metagoofil -d example.com -t pdf,docx -o output`
Jeffrey's EXIF Viewer	Extracts metadata from online images	EXIF Viewer

✅ **OSINT Tip**: Metagoofil is great for finding metadata from files already indexed online.

5. Case Study: Exposing a Fake Leaked Document

📌 **Scenario:**

A leaked government document appears online, making bold claims about classified projects. OSINT analysts analyze its metadata to verify authenticity.

🔍 **Investigation:**

✓☐ Google Dorking finds the document hosted on a random website.
✓☐ Downloading the PDF & running pdfinfo shows the author is "Anonymous".
✓☐ Examining metadata with ExifTool reveals it was created with "Microsoft Word 2023"
✓☐ Timestamp shows the document was edited AFTER it was supposedly leaked.

✅ **Conclusion**: The document is likely fake, as official government documents would not use such vague metadata fields.

6. Conclusion: Why Metadata Search is Crucial for OSINT

◈ Many documents online still contain hidden metadata, revealing authorship, timestamps, and software details.

◈ Google Dorking can help locate exposed PDFs, Word files, spreadsheets, and images with metadata.

◈ Metadata can confirm authenticity, expose deception, and track leaked documents back to their source.

◈ OSINT analysts can use tools like ExifTool, FOCA, and Metagoofil to extract metadata for intelligence gathering.

5.4 Using Search Operators to Locate Specific Filetypes

Many valuable intelligence sources—leaked documents, financial reports, government data, corporate records, and even login credentials—are stored in specific file formats like PDFs, Excel spreadsheets, Word documents, and PowerPoint presentations.

Search engines, particularly Google, Bing, and Yandex, allow users to search for specific filetypes using advanced search operators. This chapter will cover:

✅ How to use filetype search operators effectively

✅ Common file formats for OSINT investigations

✅ Real-world examples of extracting intelligence from specific filetypes

✅ Tools and techniques for automating file searches

1. Understanding the filetype: Search Operator

The filetype: operator allows OSINT professionals to target specific document formats that may contain sensitive or useful information.

◆ **Basic Syntax:**

- filetype:pdf "confidential report"

✅ Finds PDF documents containing the phrase "confidential report"

◆ Combine filetype: with site: for Targeted Searches

- site:gov filetype:xlsx "budget report"

✅ Finds Excel files related to budget reports on government websites

◆ Combine filetype: with Other Search Operators

- intitle:"passwords" filetype:txt

✅ Finds text files that contain the word "passwords" in the title

2. Common Filetypes for OSINT Investigations

Different file formats contain different types of intelligence. Here's a breakdown of useful filetypes and what they typically contain:

Filetype	Use in OSINT	Example Search
PDF	Leaked reports, government documents, corporate memos	`filetype:pdf site:example.com confidential`
DOCX	Internal memos, contracts, reports, employee lists	`filetype:docx site:gov classified`
XLSX	Financial records, employee salary data, budget plans	`filetype:xlsx "salary report"`
PPTX	Corporate or military presentations, classified briefings	`filetype:pptx "internal use only"`
TXT	Password lists, logs, plaintext databases	`filetype:txt "usernames and passwords"`
LOG	Server logs, error messages, debugging files	`filetype:log site:example.com`
CSV	Data leaks, account lists, transaction records	`filetype:csv "email,password"`
JSON	API responses, open data, leaked user credentials	`filetype:json "api key"`
XML	Configuration files, web service data, sensitive exports	`filetype:xml "database credentials"`

3. Advanced Filetype Search Techniques

◆ Finding Government & Corporate Leaks

- filetype:pdf site:.gov "confidential"

✅ Finds government PDFs labeled as confidential

- filetype:xlsx site:company.com "budget"

✅ Finds financial spreadsheets on a company's website

◆ Finding Password & Credential Leaks

- filetype:txt "password list"

✅ Finds plaintext password files accidentally exposed online

- filetype:log "login successful"

✅ Finds authentication logs that may contain leaked credentials

◆ Discovering Open Databases & API Keys

- filetype:json "api key"

✅ Finds exposed API keys in JSON files

- filetype:xml "database password"

✅ Finds database credentials accidentally stored in XML files

4. Real-World OSINT Case Studies

📌 Case Study 1: Discovering a Corporate Data Leak

An OSINT analyst was investigating a tech company suspected of mishandling user data. By using Google Dorking with the filetype: operator, they found:

✔️ A public Excel spreadsheet (filetype:xlsx) containing thousands of customer emails

✓☐ A leaked PDF document with internal security policies and vulnerabilities

✅ **Impact**: The company was forced to take down the files and address the security breach.

📌 **Case Study 2: Finding an Exposed Government Report**

An investigative journalist was researching military expenditures. By using:

- filetype:pptx site:.mil "budget proposal"

They found a PowerPoint presentation detailing upcoming military contracts before they were officially announced.

✅ **Impact**: The journalist was able to report on potential government overspending.

5. Automating Filetype Searches for OSINT

Searching for specific filetypes manually can be time-consuming. OSINT professionals can automate file searches using tools like:

◆ FOCA (Fingerprinting Organizations with Collected Archives)

✅ Finds metadata-rich files (PDF, DOCX, PPTX)

✅ Extracts metadata from discovered documents

◆ Metagoofil

✅ Scrapes filetype results from search engines

✅ Extracts metadata (author names, software details, etc.)

🔍 **Example usage:**

- metagoofil -d example.com -t pdf,docx,xlsx -o output_folder

🔗 **Tool: Metagoofil GitHub**

◆ GitHub Dorks for File Searches

Many leaked documents are stored on GitHub repositories.

- filetype:json site:github.com "password"

✓ Finds exposed API keys, passwords, and credentials

6. Ethical Considerations & Legal Boundaries

- ◆ Only use these techniques for ethical OSINT investigations
- ◆ Do not attempt to bypass authentication or hack into private systems
- ◆ Respect privacy laws and corporate policies

📌 **Reminder**: Just because a document is publicly accessible does not mean it is legal to use or share. Always verify responsible disclosure guidelines.

7. Conclusion: Mastering Filetype Search for OSINT

- ◆ The filetype: operator is one of the most powerful tools for uncovering exposed documents.
- ◆ PDFs, Word docs, spreadsheets, and JSON files can contain leaked intelligence, credentials, and sensitive data.
- ◆ Google Dorking, automation tools like FOCA, and GitHub searches help streamline OSINT file discovery.
- ◆ Always follow ethical guidelines when analyzing publicly available documents.

5.5 Reverse Searching Metadata for Clues & Connections

Metadata—often referred to as data about data—can reveal hidden connections between documents, images, and other files. OSINT professionals can extract metadata from publicly available files and use it to track authorship, uncover relationships between people and organizations, and verify the authenticity of leaked documents.

In this chapter, we'll explore:

✅ How to extract metadata from different file formats

✅ Techniques for reverse searching metadata to find related documents or sources

✅ Real-world case studies where metadata led to critical intelligence

1. Extracting Metadata: Tools & Techniques

Before we can analyze metadata for connections, we need to extract it from target files. Different file formats store different types of metadata.

◆ Metadata Extraction for Documents (PDF, DOCX, XLSX, PPTX)

Many office documents store information about the author, organization, and software used.

☐ Tools to Extract Metadata from Documents:

- **ExifTool** (Command-line metadata extractor)
- **FOCA** (Windows tool for bulk metadata extraction)
- **Metagoofil** (OSINT tool to find and analyze metadata from indexed files)

🔍 **Example**: Extracting Metadata from a PDF using ExifTool

- exiftool leaked_document.pdf

✅ **Reveals**: Author name, creation date, software used, document version history

◆ Metadata Extraction for Images (JPG, PNG, TIFF, GIF, WebP)

Image metadata (EXIF data) can reveal:

✓☐ Camera model & settings
✓☐ GPS coordinates (if location data is embedded)
✓☐ Timestamps & software used to edit the image

🔍 **Example**: Extracting Metadata from an Image using ExifTool

- exiftool photo.jpg

✓ If GPS data is present, it may reveal the exact location where the photo was taken.

✦ **OSINT Tip**: Some websites (like Facebook & Twitter) strip metadata from uploaded images, but many others (like personal blogs or lesser-known forums) do not.

◆ **Metadata Extraction for Audio & Video Files (MP3, MP4, WAV, AVI)**

Audio and video files can contain:

✓☐ Encoding details (software used, timestamps)
✓☐ Embedded copyright metadata
✓☐ GPS location (in some smartphone-recorded videos)

🔍 **Example**: Extracting Metadata from a Video File

- exiftool video.mp4

✓ This can help verify if a video was truly recorded at a claimed location and time.

2. Reverse Searching Metadata to Find Related Documents

Once metadata is extracted, the next step is to use it to uncover related files, authors, or organizations.

◆ **Reverse Searching Author Names & Usernames**

Many documents contain author names or usernames in their metadata. We can search for other documents created by the same author.

🔍 **Example**: Searching for More Documents by an Author

If metadata reveals Author: JSmith_1987, we can use Google Dorking to find other documents by the same person:

- "JSmith_1987" filetype:pdf OR filetype:docx

✓ Finds all PDFs and Word documents where this username appears

◆ Tracking Software & Device Fingerprints

Some metadata reveals which software or devices were used to create a document.

🔍 **Example**: Searching for Other Files Created by the Same Software

If metadata shows a document was created using "Microsoft Word 2016 on Mac", we can look for other leaked documents that used the same software:

- "Microsoft Word 2016 on Mac" filetype:pdf OR filetype:docx

✓ This can help link multiple documents to the same source or organization.

◆ Reverse Searching GPS Coordinates from Images

If an image contains GPS metadata, we can check if other images were taken at the same location.

🔲 **Tools to Reverse Search GPS Metadata:**

- **Google Earth** (Manually input GPS coordinates)
- **ExifTool + Google Maps** (Extract GPS & plot location)
- **Yandex & Bing Reverse** Image Search (Find visually similar images from the same place)

🔍 **Example**: Finding More Photos from the Same Location

1️⃣ Extract GPS data from an image:

- exiftool photo.jpg | grep GPS

2️⃣ Use the coordinates to search in Google Maps or Yandex for related images.

✓ This method is useful in geolocation investigations to confirm authenticity.

3. Cross-Referencing Metadata with Public Data

Sometimes, metadata includes email addresses, company names, or domain names that can be cross-referenced with public data sources.

◆ Searching for Leaked Emails & Accounts

If an email is found in metadata (john.doe@company.com), we can check:

✓☐ Have there been any data breaches involving this email?
✓☐ Has this email been used to register accounts on forums, social media, or GitHub?

☐ Tools to Cross-Reference Emails:

- Have I Been Pwned (https://haveibeenpwned.com/)
- DeHashed (https://dehashed.com/)

⚲ Example: Finding Related Leaked Data

- "john.doe@company.com" site:pastebin.com OR site:github.com

✅ Finds any references to this email in pastes, leaks, or code repositories

4. Case Study: Identifying a Leaker Through Metadata

📌 Scenario:

A journalist received an anonymous leaked government document exposing corruption. The sender removed identifying information, but the journalist examined the metadata.

⚲ Investigation:

✓☐ Used ExifTool to extract metadata from the PDF
✓☐ Discovered the "Author" field contained a unique username
✓☐ Reverse searched the username on Google and found a LinkedIn profile
✓☐ The person worked in the exact department handling the leaked document

✅ **Outcome**: The journalist confirmed the authenticity of the document and identified the potential source.

5. Ethical Considerations & Legal Boundaries

While metadata can be a powerful tool for OSINT, investigators must be aware of legal and ethical boundaries:

⚠️ Do not use metadata searches to invade privacy or access protected data

⚠️ Ensure that findings are responsibly disclosed and handled ethically

⚠️ Metadata analysis should be used for investigative and security purposes—not for harassment or doxxing

📌 **Remember**: Even if metadata is publicly available, it doesn't always mean it's legal to use or distribute.

6. Conclusion: Mastering Metadata in OSINT

◆ Metadata holds valuable intelligence—author names, timestamps, GPS coordinates, and more.

◆ Reverse searching metadata can uncover hidden relationships between files, authors, and organizations.

◆ Techniques like Google Dorking, GPS tracking, and public data cross-referencing enhance OSINT investigations.

◆ Ethical considerations must always guide metadata analysis to avoid legal and privacy violations.

5.6 Case Study: Tracking a Target Through Metadata

Metadata—often overlooked by the average user—can be a goldmine for OSINT professionals. In this case study, we will walk through a real-world-style OSINT investigation where a target was tracked using document metadata, image EXIF data, and public records.

By the end of this chapter, you will understand how metadata can:

✅ Reveal hidden details about a person's identity or location

✅ Connect multiple pieces of seemingly unrelated information

✅ Help verify authenticity and track digital footprints

1. The Scenario: Investigating an Anonymous Leak

A journalist receives a leaked government document from an anonymous source. The document alleges corruption within a government agency but provides no indication of who leaked it. The journalist needs to:

✓ Verify the document's authenticity
✓ Determine who created or edited the document
✓ Find possible connections between the source and the agency

💡 OSINT Tools & Techniques Used:

♦ **Document Metadata Extraction** (ExifTool, FOCA, Metagoofil)
♦ **Reverse Searching Names & Usernames** (Google Dorking, LinkedIn)
♦ **Cross-referencing email domains** (Hunter.io, HaveIBeenPwned)
♦ **Tracking images and GPS data** (Google Reverse Image Search, EXIF GPS Extraction)

2. Step 1: Extracting Metadata from the Leaked Document

The leaked document is a PDF report. The first step is to analyze its metadata.

🔍 Using ExifTool to Extract Metadata

- exiftool leaked_report.pdf

✅ Results:

- Author: J.Doe
- Creator Tool: Microsoft Word 2019
- Last Modified By: J.Doe_87
- Timestamp: January 15, 2024

📌 Key Takeaways:

✓ The document was last modified by "J.Doe_87"
✓ It was created in Microsoft Word 2019 (suggesting a corporate or government-issued laptop)

✓☐ The timestamp shows the last edit date

3. Step 2: Reverse Searching the Author Name

The name J.Doe_87 is unusual—it might be a username rather than a real name. We use Google Dorking to check if it appears elsewhere.

🔍 **Google Search for J.Doe_87**

- "J.Doe_87" site:linkedin.com OR site:github.com OR site:twitter.com

✅ **Results:**

- A GitHub profile with the username J.Doe_87
- A LinkedIn profile for a "John Doe" working at the same government agency that the leak is about

📌 **Key Takeaways:**

✓☐ "J.Doe_87" matches a real person working at the agency
✓☐ The username is consistent across multiple platforms

4. Step 3: Investigating Publicly Available Emails

Now that we have a name, we check if the user's email has been leaked in data breaches or exposed in public databases.

🔍 **Using Hunter.io to Find Work Email**

- Company: [Government Agency Name]
- Employee: John Doe

✅ **Results:**

- Email format: jdoe@agency.gov

🔍 **Checking for Leaked Emails with HavelBeenPwned**

- https://haveibeenpwned.com/

✅ Results:

The email jdoe@agency.gov was found in an old data breach from a government supplier.

📌 Key Takeaways:

✓☐ This confirms the person works at the agency
✓☐ The email was compromised, meaning someone could have accessed his credentials

5. Step 4: Searching for Related Documents

Since J.Doe_87 was found in metadata, we check if he has authored any other publicly available documents.

🔍 Google Dorking for More Documents

- "J.Doe_87" filetype:pdf OR filetype:docx site:gov

✅ Results:

- A PowerPoint presentation authored by J.Doe on the agency's internal processes
- A Word document from a government conference, listing J.Doe as a speaker

📌 Key Takeaways:

✓☐ J.Doe has created multiple official documents
✓☐ This confirms he has access to internal agency files

6. Step 5: Analyzing Images for GPS Data

A few days later, the anonymous source sends a follow-up image via email. The image is claimed to be a photo of classified documents inside the agency's office.

🔍 Using ExifTool to Extract Image Metadata

- exiftool leaked_photo.jpg

✅ Results:

- Device: iPhone 13 Pro
- Timestamp: January 18, 2024, 14:23 UTC
- GPS Coordinates: 40.748817, -73.985428

🔍 Reverse Searching the GPS Coordinates

- Pasting 40.748817, -73.985428 into Google Maps reveals…

✅ The image was taken inside the government agency's headquarters!

📌 Key Takeaways:

✓☐ The image was taken inside a restricted office
✓☐ Confirms the leaker had physical access to these documents
✓☐ The device (iPhone 13 Pro) could match J.Doe's known work phone

7. Step 6: Confirming the Connection

🔎 By cross-referencing all the discovered data, the investigation now has a strong lead on the anonymous source:

Metadata Clue	What It Revealed
PDF Metadata	Author: J.Doe_87
Google Dorking	Found J.Doe_87's LinkedIn & GitHub
Email Search	Found leaked gov email
Document Search	Found other reports by J.Doe
Image Metadata	Photo taken inside agency HQ
GPS Data	Location matches J.Doe's workplace

📌 Final Conclusion:

✓☐ John Doe is likely the anonymous leaker

✓ The metadata strongly links him to the leaked document and photo

✓ Reverse searching metadata successfully connected digital traces to a real person

8. Ethical & Legal Considerations

📌 Key Ethical Rules for Metadata Investigations:

⚠ Do not manipulate or fabricate metadata to frame someone

⚠ Respect privacy laws—only use publicly available information

⚠ Always verify metadata findings with other sources

💡 Metadata should be used responsibly to verify truth, not to violate privacy or manipulate evidence.

9. Conclusion: Mastering Metadata Tracking in OSINT

✓ Metadata can expose critical clues about a document's origin, authorship, and location

✓ Reverse searching names, emails, and GPS data can connect digital breadcrumbs

✓ Using a combination of OSINT tools, an investigator can build a strong case

✓ Ethical considerations must always be a priority in metadata investigations

6. People Search Engines & Public Records

People search engines and public records databases are invaluable resources for OSINT investigations, providing access to personal details, social connections, and historical data. Platforms like Pipl, Spokeo, and BeenVerified aggregate information from social media, government databases, and public archives, offering insights into an individual's online footprint. Additionally, government and legal repositories host open records such as court filings, business registrations, and property records, which can be queried for investigative purposes. By cross-referencing names, emails, phone numbers, and addresses across multiple sources, OSINT analysts can construct detailed profiles, track digital movements, and verify identities—often uncovering connections that would otherwise remain hidden. However, ethical considerations and legal compliance must always guide the use of such information.

6.1 How People Search Engines Work

People search engines are specialized tools designed to help find information about individuals by aggregating public records, social media profiles, leaked databases, and other online sources. Unlike standard search engines like Google, these platforms focus specifically on people-related data, making them invaluable for OSINT (Open-Source Intelligence) investigations.

By the end of this chapter, you will understand:

✅ How people search engines collect and display data

✅ The key differences between free and paid people search tools

✅ The limitations and ethical considerations of using these platforms

1. What Are People Search Engines?

People search engines are platforms that index and aggregate publicly available personal information from multiple sources, such as:

✓☐ **Public records** (birth, marriage, divorce, criminal, and court records)
✓☐ **Social media profiles** (Facebook, Twitter, LinkedIn, etc.)
✓☐ **Online directories** (business listings, professional databases)

✓□ The metadata strongly links him to the leaked document and photo

✓□ Reverse searching metadata successfully connected digital traces to a real person

8. Ethical & Legal Considerations

📌 Key Ethical Rules for Metadata Investigations:

⚠️□ Do not manipulate or fabricate metadata to frame someone

⚠️□ Respect privacy laws—only use publicly available information

⚠️□ Always verify metadata findings with other sources

💡 Metadata should be used responsibly to verify truth, not to violate privacy or manipulate evidence.

9. Conclusion: Mastering Metadata Tracking in OSINT

✅ Metadata can expose critical clues about a document's origin, authorship, and location

✅ Reverse searching names, emails, and GPS data can connect digital breadcrumbs

✅ Using a combination of OSINT tools, an investigator can build a strong case

✅ Ethical considerations must always be a priority in metadata investigations

6. People Search Engines & Public Records

People search engines and public records databases are invaluable resources for OSINT investigations, providing access to personal details, social connections, and historical data. Platforms like Pipl, Spokeo, and BeenVerified aggregate information from social media, government databases, and public archives, offering insights into an individual's online footprint. Additionally, government and legal repositories host open records such as court filings, business registrations, and property records, which can be queried for investigative purposes. By cross-referencing names, emails, phone numbers, and addresses across multiple sources, OSINT analysts can construct detailed profiles, track digital movements, and verify identities—often uncovering connections that would otherwise remain hidden. However, ethical considerations and legal compliance must always guide the use of such information.

6.1 How People Search Engines Work

People search engines are specialized tools designed to help find information about individuals by aggregating public records, social media profiles, leaked databases, and other online sources. Unlike standard search engines like Google, these platforms focus specifically on people-related data, making them invaluable for OSINT (Open-Source Intelligence) investigations.

By the end of this chapter, you will understand:

✓ How people search engines collect and display data

✓ The key differences between free and paid people search tools

✓ The limitations and ethical considerations of using these platforms

1. What Are People Search Engines?

People search engines are platforms that index and aggregate publicly available personal information from multiple sources, such as:

✓□ **Public records** (birth, marriage, divorce, criminal, and court records)
✓□ **Social media profiles** (Facebook, Twitter, LinkedIn, etc.)
✓□ **Online directories** (business listings, professional databases)

✓ Data breaches and leaked records

✓ News articles and obituaries

Unlike Google, which searches the entire web, people search engines focus on structured data related to individuals, making them useful for:

✓ Investigative journalism

✓ Cybersecurity & fraud detection

✓ Missing person investigations

✓ Background checks

2. How Do People Search Engines Collect Data?

People search engines work by crawling, aggregating, and cross-referencing publicly available data from multiple sources. Let's break down the process:

◆ Step 1: Data Crawling & Collection

✓ Search engines crawl public databases (government, corporate, social media)

✓ They scrape social media profiles, business listings, and court records

✓ Some platforms purchase data from third-party data brokers

📌 **Example**: A search engine might extract an individual's phone number from a business directory and cross-reference it with their social media profile to create a more complete profile.

◆ Step 2: Data Aggregation & Indexing

Once collected, the data is structured and indexed, allowing users to quickly search by:

✓ Name & Location (e.g., "John Doe, New York")

✓ Phone Number (reverse phone lookup)

✓ Email Address (reverse email search)

✓ Username (searching social media and forum profiles)

📌 **Example**: A search for "Jane Smith, California" may return:

- Past and current addresses

- Relatives and known associates
- Social media profiles
- Property ownership records

◆ Step 3: Cross-Referencing & Data Enrichment

Some people search engines enhance their data by:

✓ Matching public records with social media activity
✓ Using AI to predict possible connections between people
✓ Combining multiple sources to verify accuracy

📌 **Example**: A people search engine may notice that two individuals:

- Have shared addresses in the past
- Are tagged together in social media photos
- Appear in the same company's employee directory

This can suggest a relationship between them (family, business, or otherwise).

3. Types of People Search Engines

There are three main categories of people search engines:

◆ 1. Free Public Search Engines

These tools provide basic information for free but may require payment for detailed records.

Popular Free People Search Tools:

🔍 **Google & Bing** – Can be used with advanced operators (e.g., "John Doe" site:linkedin.com")
☐ **Facebook & LinkedIn** – Social media searches
💼 **Whitepages (Basic Version)** – Phone & address lookups
🏛 **CourtListener & PACER** – Public legal records

📌 **Pros**: Free, easy to use
📌 **Cons**: Limited data, missing deeper records

◆ 2. Paid People Search Services

Paid services offer detailed reports including criminal records, financial history, and address history.

Popular Paid People Search Tools:

👤 **BeenVerified** – Contact info, employment history
🔍 **Spokeo** – Aggregates public records and social profiles
💼 **Intelius** – Background checks, property records
☐☐ **TruthFinder** – Deep background reports

📌 **Pros**: More detailed and accurate information
📌 **Cons**: Expensive, data may be outdated

◆ 3. OSINT-Specific People Search Engines

Designed for investigative use, these tools search for hidden connections, breached data, and underground forums.

Popular OSINT People Search Tools:

☐☐♂☐ **SpiderFoot** – Finds data across public & dark web sources
☐☐♀☐ **Intelligence X** – Searches leaked government and corporate records
💼 **Pipl** – Advanced deep web people search
🔍 **Skopenow** – Investigates social media, public records, and business databases

📌 **Pros**: Useful for advanced OSINT investigations
📌 **Cons**: May require professional access or subscriptions

4. Limitations & Accuracy Issues

While people search engines can be powerful, they are not always 100% accurate. Here's why:

🏛 1. **Outdated Data** – Records may not update frequently, leading to incorrect addresses or phone numbers.

🔍 2. **False Positives** – Common names can result in misidentifications (e.g., multiple "John Smiths").

🔍 3. **Incomplete Information** – Not all data is indexed, especially if the person uses strict privacy settings.

🔍 4. **Legal & Ethical Restrictions** – Some regions (e.g., EU under GDPR) restrict access to personal data.

📌 **OSINT Tip**: Always verify findings with multiple sources before acting on them.

5. Ethical & Legal Considerations

Using people search engines comes with serious ethical and legal responsibilities.

🔭 Legal Boundaries:

✓ Some countries restrict public access to personal data

✓ Using people search engines for stalking, harassment, or fraud is illegal

✓ Websites like Spokeo & BeenVerified prohibit employment decisions based on their data

⚠ Ethical Guidelines for OSINT Investigators:

✅ Only use legally accessible data

✅ Verify information before making conclusions

✅ Respect individuals' privacy rights

💡 **Remember**: Just because information is available doesn't mean it's ethical to use.

6. Conclusion: Mastering People Search Engines for OSINT

✅ People search engines aggregate public data from social media, business directories, and records

✅ Free search engines provide basic info, while paid services offer deeper insights

✅ OSINT tools like SpiderFoot and Intelligence X go beyond surface-level searches

✅ Always verify information from multiple sources and respect legal boundaries

6.2 Free vs. Paid People Search Services

People search services are essential tools in OSINT investigations, helping uncover contact details, addresses, social media profiles, and public records. However, not all services are created equal—some are free and accessible, while others require payment for deeper insights.

This chapter will help you understand:

✓ The key differences between free and paid people search tools

✓ What kind of data you can expect from each

✓ Which tools are best suited for OSINT investigations

1. Free People Search Services

Free people search tools offer basic information and are often the first step in an OSINT investigation. They collect publicly available data from websites, social media, and government records.

◆ Features of Free People Search Tools:

✓☐ Basic name, phone number, and address lookups
✓☐ Reverse searches for usernames, emails, and social profiles
✓☐ Public records like court filings, property records, and voter registration
✓☐ Limited access to deeper data (criminal records, employment history, financials, etc.)

🔍 Examples of Free People Search Tools

Tool	Features	Limitations
Google & Bing	Advanced search operators for finding people	Requires OSINT skills, not people-focused
Facebook, LinkedIn, Twitter	Social media profiles, workplace info	Privacy settings may limit access
Whitepages (Free Version)	Basic phone number and address lookup	No criminal or financial data
CourtListener & PACER	Public court records	Requires manual searching, may need registration
Hunter.io	Finds emails linked to domains	Limited free searches per month
HaveIBeenPwned	Checks if an email or password has been in a breach	No personal details beyond breach exposure

📌 **Pros**: Free, easy to use, no registration required

📌 **Cons**: Limited details, requires manual verification, may contain outdated data

2. Paid People Search Services

Paid services aggregate public records, social media data, and background checks into detailed reports. These tools are useful when free sources don't provide enough information.

◆ Features of Paid People Search Tools:

✓ Full address history & phone number tracking
✓ Background checks (criminal, financial, legal history)
✓ Deep social media searches (including deleted profiles & hidden data)
✓ Relationship mapping (family members, associates, business partners)

💰 Examples of Paid People Search Tools

Tool	Features	Pricing
BeenVerified	Contact details, criminal records, employment history	Starts at $26.89/month
Spokeo	Aggregates public records, social media profiles	Starts at $13.95/month
Intelius	Background checks, property ownership	Starts at $24.86/month
TruthFinder	Deep background reports, known associates	Starts at $28/month
Pipl	Advanced **deep web** search, connects hidden profiles	Business-only pricing

📌 **Pros**: Provides comprehensive and verified reports

📌 **Cons**: Expensive, some data may be inaccurate or outdated, legal restrictions apply

3. Comparing Free vs. Paid People Search Services

Factor	Free Services	Paid Services
Accuracy	Basic & unverified	More reliable, cross-referenced
Depth of Information	Names, addresses, phone numbers	Background checks, financial history, relationships
Social Media Access	Public profiles only	Can reveal hidden/deleted profiles
Criminal & Legal Records	Limited access	Detailed reports
Reverse Searches	Basic searches for emails & usernames	Advanced AI-powered connections
Cost	Free	Monthly subscription fees

📌 **Best for OSINT Beginners**: Free tools

📌 **Best for Deep Investigations**: Paid services

4. When to Use Free vs. Paid People Search Tools

◆ **Use Free Tools When:**

✓☐ You only need basic contact info

✓☐ You are looking for social media profiles

✓☐ You are conducting an initial OSINT scan

◆ Use Paid Tools When:

✓☐ You need detailed background checks
✓☐ You are investigating criminal or financial history
✓☐ You need to verify relationships & connections

📌 **OSINT Tip**: Start with free tools, verify data, then use paid services if necessary.

5. Legal & Ethical Considerations

Using people search tools comes with legal and ethical responsibilities.

⚖️☐ Legal Restrictions:

✓☐ Some paid services restrict use for employment, credit, or tenant screening
✓☐ EU's GDPR & California's CCPA limit how personal data can be used
✓☐ Using people search engines for harassment, stalking, or fraud is illegal

⚠️☐ Ethical OSINT Guidelines:

✅ Only use legally accessible data

✅ Verify accuracy before acting on information

✅ Respect privacy laws and ethical boundaries

📌 **Remember**: Just because you can find personal data doesn't mean you should use it irresponsibly.

6. Conclusion: Mastering People Search Services for OSINT

✅ Free people search tools provide basic info, while paid services offer deep background data

✅ OSINT professionals should start with free searches before considering paid tools

✅ Verify all findings, as both free and paid services can have outdated or inaccurate data

✅ Follow legal and ethical guidelines when conducting investigations

6.3 Finding Social Media, Phone Numbers & Addresses Online

In OSINT investigations, discovering social media profiles, phone numbers, and addresses can be crucial for verifying identities, tracking online activity, and mapping out a subject's digital footprint. However, this information is often scattered across multiple platforms, requiring strategic search techniques to locate it.

This chapter will cover:

✅ How to find social media profiles using usernames, emails, and phone numbers

✅ Methods for uncovering phone numbers and addresses through public records

✅ Ethical and legal considerations when searching for personal information

1. Finding Social Media Profiles

◆ Why Social Media is Key in OSINT

Social media accounts contain a wealth of personal data, including:

✓☐ Usernames & profile pictures
✓☐ Location check-ins & tagged photos
✓☐ Friend lists & business associations
✓☐ Workplaces & past employment history

Even when users attempt to hide their profiles, OSINT techniques can help uncover hidden or deleted accounts.

◆ Finding Social Media Profiles by Username

Most people use the same or similar usernames across different platforms. By conducting a reverse username search, you can often find linked accounts.

📌 Tools & Techniques:

✓☐ **Google Search Operators**: "john_doe" site:instagram.com

✓□ **Sherlock** – Checks for usernames across 300+ social media sites

✓□ **WhatsMyName** – OSINT tool for finding usernames

✓□ **Namechk & KnowEm** – Username availability checker (useful for tracking common handles)

💡 **Example**: Searching for "johndoe123" site:twitter.com may reveal a Twitter profile, which can lead to a LinkedIn or Instagram account using the same handle.

◆ Finding Social Media by Email Address

Some platforms allow reverse email lookups, revealing linked accounts.

📌 Where to Search:

✓□ **Facebook**: Try logging in and entering an email in the search bar

✓□ **LinkedIn**: Use email lookup tools like Hunter.io

✓□ **Pipl & Spokeo**: Paid services that link emails to social profiles

✓□ **HaveIBeenPwned**: Checks if an email has appeared in data breaches (which may include old social media accounts)

💡 **Example**: If an email appears in a LinkedIn breach, you can often guess the person's LinkedIn profile and cross-check details.

◆ Finding Social Media by Phone Number

Many platforms link accounts to phone numbers, which can be searched directly.

📌 Where to Search:

✓□ **Facebook & Instagram**: Try entering a phone number in the search bar

✓□ **WhatsApp & Telegram**: Add a number to your contacts and see if an account exists

✓□ **Truecaller**: Reverse lookup for phone numbers

✓□ **OSINT Tools**: Spokeo, Pipl, and Intelligence X

💡 **Example**: If a number is linked to a WhatsApp account, the profile picture and name may provide clues to the owner's identity.

2. Finding Phone Numbers & Addresses

◆ Finding Phone Numbers Online

Phone numbers can often be found in business directories, leaked data, and public records.

📌 Where to Look:

✔️ Google Dorking:

- "123-456-7890" site:linkedin.com (Searches LinkedIn for a phone number)
- "contact us" + "123-456-7890" (Searches business pages for contact numbers)

✔️ **Whitepages & Truecaller**: Reverse phone lookups

✔️ **Spokeo & Intelius**: Paid background checks

✔️ **Data Breach Databases**: HavelBeenPwned & DeHashed

💡 **Example**: A Google Dork search like "John Doe" + "phone number" might reveal contact details in a leaked document.

◆ Finding Addresses Online

Addresses can be found in property records, voter registrations, business filings, and social media check-ins.

📌 Where to Search:

✔️ Google Dorking:

- "John Doe" + "address"
- "1234 Main St" site:zillow.com (Finds property listings)

✔️ Public Records Databases:

- **Zillow, Redfin, and Realtor** – Property ownership details
- **County tax records** – Check government databases for registered addresses

✔️ People Search Engines: BeenVerified, Spokeo, Intelius

💡 **Example**: If a subject's address appears in property tax records, it may list co-owners, mortgage details, or past sales history.

3. Case Study: Tracking a Target's Digital Footprint

Scenario: You are conducting an OSINT investigation on John Doe and need to find his social media, phone number, and address.

◆ Step 1: Find Social Media Profiles

1️⃣ **Google search**: "John Doe" site:linkedin.com → Finds LinkedIn profile

2️⃣ **Use Sherlock**: Searches 300+ platforms → Finds matching username on Twitter

3️⃣ **Use email lookup on Hunter.io** → Reveals a Gmail linked to a Facebook profile

◆ Step 2: Find Phone Number

1️⃣ **Search "John Doe" + "contact" on Google** → Finds a phone number in a business listing

2️⃣ **Input number into Truecaller & WhatsApp** → Confirms identity with a profile picture

◆ Step 3: Find Address

1️⃣ Google Dorking: "John Doe" + "address" site:realtor.com → Finds property listing

2️⃣ Search county tax records → Confirms homeownership history

Result: You now have John Doe's LinkedIn, Twitter, phone number, and home address—all using OSINT techniques.

4. Ethical & Legal Considerations

⚖️ OSINT investigators must follow legal and ethical guidelines when gathering personal data.

🔍 Legal Restrictions:

✔️ **GDPR & CCPA**: Restrict personal data collection in the EU and California

✓☐ **Data Broker Laws**: Some states prohibit selling personal info without consent

✓☐ **Illegal Activities**: Using OSINT for harassment, stalking, or identity theft is illegal

⚠☐ **Ethical Guidelines:**

✓ Only use publicly available data

✓ Verify all findings before making conclusions

✓ Never use OSINT for malicious purposes

📌 **Reminder**: Just because information is available does not mean it should be misused.

5. Conclusion: Mastering OSINT Search Techniques for Personal Data

✓ Social media profiles can be found using usernames, emails, and phone numbers

✓ Phone numbers are often hidden in business directories, data breaches, and Google searches

✓ Addresses can be uncovered through property records, real estate listings, and voter registration

✓ Always respect privacy laws and ethical guidelines in OSINT investigations

6.4 Verifying Identities with Public Records & Data Leaks

In OSINT investigations, verifying an individual's identity is critical to ensure accuracy and credibility. Public records and data leaks offer valuable insights that can confirm or refute identities, track movements, and reveal hidden connections.

This chapter will cover:

✓ How to use public records to verify personal details

✓ Finding and analyzing data leaks for OSINT investigations

✓ Cross-referencing multiple sources to establish identity

✅ Legal and ethical considerations when using leaked data

1. Using Public Records for Identity Verification

◆ What Are Public Records?

Public records are government-maintained databases that include:

✓☐ Birth & death certificates
✓☐ Property & tax records
✓☐ Court & criminal records
✓☐ Business registrations
✓☐ Marriage & divorce records
✓☐ Professional licenses

Public records vary by country—some are freely accessible, while others require subscriptions or special permissions.

◆ Finding Public Records Online

📌 Where to Look for Public Records:

Record Type	Where to Search	Details Available
Property & Tax Records	County assessor websites, Zillow, Redfin	Homeownership, property value, co-owners
Business Registrations	SEC.gov, OpenCorporates, state databases	Business ownership, financial disclosures
Court & Criminal Records	PACER (U.S.), CourtListener, state databases	Lawsuits, criminal charges, bankruptcy filings
Professional Licenses	State licensing boards, FINRA (finance), NPI (medical)	Verified credentials, workplace history
Marriage & Divorce Records	State vital records, Ancestry.com	Relationship status, past name changes

💡 **Example**: If investigating "John Doe," a search on county property records may confirm his home address, co-owners, and past transactions.

📌 **Google Dorking for Public Records:**

- **"John Doe" site:opencorporates.com** → Finds business registrations

- **"John Doe" + "court case" site:pacer.gov** → Searches for legal filings

- **"John Doe" + "property tax" site:county.gov** → Finds tax and ownership records

2. Using Data Leaks to Confirm Identities

◆ What Are Data Leaks?

Data leaks occur when sensitive information (emails, passwords, addresses) is exposed due to hacks, misconfigurations, or accidental leaks. These leaks can reveal:

✓☐ Emails & passwords linked to an identity
✓☐ Past addresses & phone numbers
✓☐ Hidden social media profiles
✓☐ Employment history

💡 Why This Matters:

If a person's email appears in a data breach, it can confirm their digital footprint.
A password reuse across platforms might expose linked accounts.

◆ Finding & Analyzing Data Leaks

📌 Best Tools for Searching Data Leaks:

Tool	Function
HaveIBeenPwned	Checks if an email or phone number is in a breach
DeHashed	Advanced database search for emails, usernames, passwords
IntelX	Dark web & data breach search engine
Snusbase	Paid database for leaked credentials
BreachForums	(Caution) Often used by hackers to trade leaks

📌 **How to Use Data Leaks in OSINT:**

1☐ **Search the target's email in HavelBeenPwned** → Check for breaches

2☐ Use DeHashed to find linked usernames, IP addresses, and passwords

3☐ Google Dork leaked databases:

- "email: johndoe@gmail.com" site:pastebin.com
- "password list" + "JohnDoe123"

💡 **Example**: If John Doe's email was leaked with a LinkedIn password, that password might work on other sites, leading to more account discoveries.

📷 **Warning**: Accessing stolen or unauthorized data can be illegal—only use legal, publicly available sources.

3. Cross-Referencing Data for Identity Confirmation

Finding a person's records or leaked data isn't enough—you must verify accuracy by cross-referencing multiple sources.

◆ **Steps to Confirm an Identity:**

✓☐ **Step 1**: Locate the full name, email, and known aliases

✓☐ **Step 2**: Cross-check social media, business records, and property records

✓☐ **Step 3**: Search for their email or phone in data leaks

✓☐ **Step 4:** Use reverse image searches (Google Lens, PimEyes) to confirm photos

✓☐ **Step 5**: Verify employment history through LinkedIn, company filings, and leaks

💡 **Example:**

🔍 **John Doe's LinkedIn** → Mentions working at ABC Corp

🔍 **SEC Filings** → Lists John Doe as a shareholder at ABC Corp

🔍 **Data Breach (LinkedIn)** → His corporate email & password were leaked

✅ **Confirmed Identity**: John Doe really works at ABC Corp

4. Ethical & Legal Considerations in OSINT Identity Verification

⚖ Before searching for personal data, consider these legal & ethical factors:

⚖ Legal Restrictions:

✓ GDPR (EU) & CCPA (California) limit data collection and personal searches
✓ Accessing leaked/stolen data can be illegal
✓ Background checks on individuals may require consent

⚠ Ethical Guidelines for OSINT Investigators:

✓ Only use publicly available and legally obtained data

✓ Verify sources—incorrect data can lead to false accusations

✓ Respect privacy—just because you can find data doesn't mean you should use it

💡 **Good Practice**: If in doubt, consult legal professionals before using certain OSINT tools.

5. Case Study: Tracking a Fraud Suspect Using Public Records & Data Leaks

Scenario:

A cybersecurity investigator is tracking John Doe, suspected of financial fraud. They need to confirm his identity before further investigation.

◆ **Step 1: Check Public Records**

- **Business filings** → Finds a company registered under John Doe's name

- **Court records** → Shows lawsuits involving financial disputes

- **Property tax records** → Confirms his residential address

◆ **Step 2: Search Data Leaks**

- **HavelBeenPwned** → Finds his corporate email in a LinkedIn breach

- **DeHashed search** → Leaked credentials reveal reused passwords

◆ **Step 3: Cross-Check Details**

- **Company website** → His LinkedIn photo matches the official CEO photo
- **Reverse image search** → Finds other social profiles with similar details

✅ **Confirmed Identity**: John Doe's business records, email leaks, and public filings match—he is likely connected to the fraud case.

6. Conclusion: Mastering Identity Verification in OSINT

✅ Public records provide official identity confirmation

✅ Data leaks expose hidden connections & credentials

✅ Cross-referencing multiple sources increases accuracy

✅ Always follow ethical and legal guidelines when using OSINT

6.5 How to Cross-Reference Information for Accuracy

In OSINT investigations, finding information is only half the battle—ensuring its accuracy is what makes intelligence truly valuable. False or misleading data can lead to incorrect conclusions, wasted efforts, or even legal consequences. Cross-referencing multiple sources is the key to confirming identities, tracking movements, and verifying claims.

This chapter will cover:

✅ Why cross-referencing is critical in OSINT investigations

✅ Techniques to verify names, emails, phone numbers, and locations

✅ How to spot inconsistencies and false data

✅ Using automation & tools to speed up verification

1. Why Cross-Referencing is Essential in OSINT

◆ **The Risks of Relying on a Single Source**

Relying on one data source increases the chances of encountering:

✓☐ Outdated information (e.g., an old address no longer in use)
✓☐ Deliberate disinformation (fake social media accounts, manipulated leaks)
✓☐ Data entry errors (typos, mismatches in databases)
✓☐ Coincidences (two different people with the same name)

By cross-referencing multiple independent sources, you can:

✓☐ Confirm accuracy by checking for matching details across different platforms
✓☐ Detect inconsistencies that may indicate false information
✓☐ Strengthen intelligence reports by ensuring credibility

💡 **Example:**

A business listing shows "John Doe" as the CEO of ABC Corp, but court records list him as unemployed. Cross-referencing tax filings might confirm which claim is true.

2. Cross-Referencing Different Data Types

◆ **Verifying Names & Identities**

✅ Search across multiple platforms:

- **Google Dorking**: "John Doe" site:linkedin.com OR site:opencorporates.com
- **People Search Engines**: Pipl, Spokeo, BeenVerified
- **Government Databases**: Business registrations, professional licenses

✅ Check for inconsistencies:

- Does their LinkedIn job title match their business registration?
- Is the profile picture used elsewhere under a different name?

✅ Use reverse image searches:

- **Google Reverse Image, PimEyes** → Find other online appearances

- **Yandex Image Search** → Better for non-Western sources

💡 **Example**: A LinkedIn profile claims John Doe is a lawyer, but a state bar license check shows no active registration. The profile might be fake.

◆ **Verifying Emails & Phone Numbers**

✅ Check if an email appears in leaks:

- HaveIBeenPwned, DeHashed, IntelX
- If the email was leaked in a corporate breach, it's likely legitimate.

✅ Search for phone numbers in different sources:

- **TrueCaller, SpyDialer, Whitepages** → Phone number lookup

- **Facebook, WhatsApp, Telegram** → Try adding the number to contacts

✅ Use Google Dorking for hidden contact info:

- "contact me at" + "johndoe@gmail.com"
- "phone number" + "John Doe" site:linkedin.com

💡 **Example**: A phone number listed on a website contact page might match a company registration, confirming its authenticity.

◆ **Verifying Locations & Addresses**

✅ Cross-check location history:

- **Google Earth & Street View** → Confirm if an address exists

- **Zillow, Redfin, Realtor.com** → Check property ownership records

✅ Check social media for location tags:

- **Instagram, Twitter, Facebook** → Past check-ins at the location
- **Google Dorking**: "John Doe" + "visited" + "Los Angeles"

✓ Use map tools for verification:

- **Google Timeline (if accessible)** → Tracks a subject's past movements
- **What3Words, OpenStreetMap** → Pinpoint exact locations

💡 **Example**: If someone claims to live at 123 Main St, NYC, but property records show it's a commercial building, they may be lying about their residence.

◆ **Verifying Social Media Accounts**

✓ Cross-check usernames across platforms:

- **Sherlock, WhatsMyName** → Check if a username is used on multiple sites
- **Google Dorking**: "johndoe123" site:twitter.com OR site:instagram.com

✓ Look for behavioral consistency:

- Do they post about the same topics across different platforms?
- Are their friends/followers overlapping across social media sites?

✓ Use metadata & timestamps:

- **FotoForensics** → Analyze timestamps in images
- **EXIF Metadata Extractor** → Find location & device data in uploaded images

💡 **Example**: A Twitter user claims to be a journalist, but their LinkedIn and Facebook have no references to journalism—this could be a fake identity.

3. How to Detect False or Manipulated Data

◆ **Signs of False Information**

⚠️ **Mismatched details** → A LinkedIn job title doesn't match government filings

⚠️ **Recently created accounts** → Social media or websites created very recently

⚠️ **Stock images as profile pictures** → Use reverse image search to check

⚠️ **Too much vague or generic information** → Fake profiles often lack specifics

📌 **Tools to Identify Fake Data:**

- **Fake Name Generator** → Helps compare with real profiles
- **Social Blade** → Analyzes social media growth for bots
- **Scamwatcher.com** → Checks for fraudulent websites

💡 **Example**: A job applicant lists a degree from Harvard University, but Harvard's alumni database has no record of them—this is likely a fabricated credential.

4. Automating Cross-Referencing with OSINT Tools

Manually verifying information is time-consuming, so automation can help speed up the process.

📌 **Recommended OSINT Tools for Cross-Referencing:**

Tool	Purpose
SpiderFoot	Automates email, IP, and domain lookups
Maltego	Maps connections between people, companies, and social media
IntelX	Searches breached data, paste sites, and government records
OSINT Framework	Categorized list of OSINT tools for verification
DataSploit	Extracts and correlates data from multiple sources

💡 **Example**: Maltego can take a single email and map all linked social media profiles, domains, and related leaks.

5. Case Study: Verifying a Suspicious Online Profile

Scenario:

An OSINT investigator is verifying John Doe, who claims to be a financial advisor.

Step 1: Cross-Check Social Media Profiles

- **LinkedIn Profile** → Says he works at "Wealth Advisors Inc."
- **Google Search** → No business registration for this company.

Step 2: Verify Contact Information

- **Email (johndoe@wealthadvisors.com)** → No website or LinkedIn matches
- **Phone number lookup** → Found on a scam warning site

Step 3: Check for Leaked Data

- **DeHashed** → His email was in a previous scam-related data breach

Conclusion:

🚨 **John Doe is likely a fraudster**—his company does not exist, his contact details were flagged in scams, and his email was leaked in fraud databases.

6. Conclusion: Mastering Cross-Referencing for OSINT Accuracy

✅ Always verify names, emails, phone numbers, and addresses across multiple sources

✅ Use reverse image searches and metadata to detect fake profiles

✅ Automate verification using OSINT tools like Maltego & SpiderFoot

✅ Watch for inconsistencies and signs of manipulation in data

6.6 Ethical & Legal Considerations in People Searches

People searches are one of the most powerful yet sensitive aspects of OSINT investigations. Whether tracking a missing person, verifying an identity, or investigating fraud, OSINT professionals must navigate legal boundaries and ethical considerations.

Misuse of personal data can lead to privacy violations, legal consequences, and reputational damage.

This chapter will cover:

✅ Legal frameworks governing OSINT and people searches

✅ Ethical considerations in handling personal information

✅ Responsible use of public records, data leaks, and social media

✅ Best practices to stay compliant with laws and industry standards

1. Understanding Legal Frameworks in OSINT People Searches

Different countries have varying laws regulating the collection and use of personal data. OSINT investigators must ensure their methods are legally compliant.

◆ Key Global Privacy Laws Affecting OSINT

Law/Regulation	Region	Impact on OSINT
GDPR (General Data Protection Regulation)	European Union	Restricts personal data collection, requires consent for processing
CCPA (California Consumer Privacy Act)	USA (California)	Gives individuals the right to request data deletion
FCRA (Fair Credit Reporting Act)	USA	Regulates background checks and employment screening
ECPA (Electronic Communications Privacy Act)	USA	Protects against unauthorized access to emails and online accounts
PIPEDA (Personal Information Protection & Electronic Documents Act)	Canada	Limits how personal data can be collected and stored
Right to Be Forgotten	EU, some countries	Allows individuals to request removal of personal data from search engines

💡 **Example**: Under GDPR, scraping personal information from EU citizens without consent could lead to legal action.

◆ What Data is Legal to Collect?

✅ Generally Allowed:

✓☐ Public records (business filings, court records, property data)
✓☐ Social media profiles (if publicly accessible)
✓☐ News articles, blogs, and press releases
✓☐ Government-published documents

✖ Legally Restricted:

⚠☐ Hacked or leaked data (unauthorized breaches, stolen credentials)
⚠☐ Private conversations (emails, direct messages, call logs)
⚠☐ Financial data (bank records, credit card info)
⚠☐ Medical records (HIPAA-protected in the US)

💡 **Tip**: Always verify that the data source is publicly available and legally accessible before using it in an investigation.

2. Ethical Considerations in People Searches

Even when something is legal, it may not be ethical. OSINT professionals must follow ethical guidelines to ensure responsible investigations.

◆ Core OSINT Ethical Principles

✅ **Respect Privacy**: Don't expose private details unnecessarily.
✅ **Minimize Harm**: Only collect and share data that is necessary.
✅ **Verify Before Acting**: False information can harm innocent people.
✅ **Avoid Unethical Tactics**: No social engineering, impersonation, or hacking.

💡 **Example**: If searching for a missing person, sharing their last known location in a public forum might put them in danger.

3. Responsible Use of Public Records & Data Leaks

Public records are valuable for verifying identities, but they should be used ethically and responsibly.

◆ How to Use Public Records Ethically

✅ Use them for legitimate investigations (fraud detection, identity verification).

✅ Cross-check with multiple sources to avoid false assumptions.

✅ Be cautious when sharing sensitive findings.

◆ Ethical Concerns with Using Data Leaks

🏛 Data breaches contain stolen information, and using them may violate laws.

🏛 Leaked passwords and financial data can harm victims if misused.

🏛 Accessing unauthorized databases may be criminal hacking (CFAA in the US).

💡 **Rule of Thumb**: If you need to ask whether it's legal to use a data source, it's probably unethical.

4. Social Media & OSINT: Balancing Privacy & Investigation

Social media is a goldmine for OSINT, but investigators must avoid crossing ethical lines.

◆ Ethical Social Media OSINT

✅ Only collect publicly available posts and profiles.

✅ Don't engage with or manipulate targets (no fake friend requests).

✅ Respect platform policies (scraping may violate terms of service).

◆ Gray Areas: Is It Ethical?

Scenario	Legal?	Ethical?
Using Google Dorking to find social media posts	✅ Legal	✅ Ethical
Creating a fake profile to access someone's private account	✕ Often illegal	✕ Unethical
Downloading and analyzing an entire social media platform's data	✕ Violates TOS	✕ Unethical
Looking up a user's location based on Instagram check-ins	✅ Legal	⚠ Questionable

💡 **Example**: If a journalist wants to confirm a politician's past statements, they can search old tweets, but they shouldn't impersonate someone to gain access to private messages.

5. Best Practices for Ethical & Legal OSINT Investigations

To ensure compliance with laws and ethical standards, follow these best practices:

◆ 1. Stick to Public & Open-Source Data

✅ Use government records, company filings, and public social media posts.

✖ Avoid hacking, phishing, or accessing restricted databases.

◆ 2. Always Verify Information Before Acting

✅ Cross-check multiple sources to avoid false accusations.

✖ Don't assume one data point is conclusive.

◆ 3. Understand the Law in Your Region

✅ Research privacy laws before conducting an investigation.

✅ Use VPNs and anonymization tools if your research is sensitive.

◆ 4. Keep Investigation Logs & Documentation

✅ Record data sources to prove your research was legal and ethical.

✅ This protects against accusations of misconduct.

◆ 5. Avoid Harassment & Unnecessary Exposure

✅ If investigating fraud, report findings to relevant authorities—not Twitter.

✅ Be mindful that exposing private individuals can have real-world consequences.

💡 **Example**: A researcher uncovering an anonymous whistleblower's identity should not publicly expose them, even if the information is legally accessible.

6. Case Study: Ethical OSINT vs. Unethical Practices

Scenario:

An investigator is tracking an online scammer, "John Doe," who has defrauded multiple victims.

Ethical Approach:

✅ Uses Google Dorking to find his business registrations & LinkedIn.

✅ Cross-checks records in public databases.

✅ Reports findings to law enforcement or a relevant authority.

Unethical Approach:

✖ Hacks into John Doe's private email to gather evidence.

✖ Uses a fake identity to befriend him on social media.

✖ Publicly exposes his home address, putting him at risk.

💡 **Outcome**: The ethical approach leads to a lawful, effective investigation, while the unethical approach could result in criminal charges against the investigator.

7. Conclusion: Responsible OSINT in People Searches

✅ Know the law before conducting any OSINT investigation.

✅ Respect privacy and avoid exposing unnecessary personal details.

✅ Use ethical tools and techniques—no hacking, impersonation, or harassment.

✅ Cross-check data to avoid spreading false information.

7. Academic & Government Database Searches

Academic and government databases are treasure troves of verified, high-quality information often overlooked in standard OSINT investigations. Platforms like Google Scholar, Semantic Scholar, and CORE provide access to research papers, theses, and technical reports that can offer deep insights into specialized subjects. Government databases, such as SEC filings, patent registries, court records, and FOIA archives, contain valuable public records that reveal corporate dealings, legal proceedings, and regulatory actions. By utilizing targeted search techniques, including Boolean operators and site-specific queries, OSINT analysts can extract critical intelligence from these authoritative sources. Navigating these databases effectively enables deeper research into individuals, organizations, and global events while ensuring credibility and accuracy in intelligence gathering.

7.1 What Information is Available in Public Databases?

Public databases are a goldmine for OSINT investigations. Governments, universities, and organizations maintain vast collections of public records, research archives, and official filings. These sources can provide accurate, legally accessible intelligence without relying on questionable data leaks or social engineering.

This chapter will cover:

✅ Types of public databases and what they contain

✅ How government, academic, and corporate databases support OSINT

✅ Best practices for searching public databases effectively

✅ Ethical and legal considerations in using public records

1. Understanding Public Databases

A public database is any openly accessible collection of structured information maintained by a government, institution, or private organization.

◆ **Why Use Public Databases for OSINT?**

✓☐ **Legally accessible** – No need to worry about hacking or privacy violations.
✓☐ **Highly reliable** – Maintained by official sources (government, universities, etc.).
✓☐ **Diverse information** – Covers identities, businesses, laws, court cases, patents, research, and more.

💡 **Example**: A journalist investigating a politician's finances might use SEC filings, court records, and real estate ownership databases instead of unreliable rumors.

2. Types of Public Databases & What They Contain

◆ A. Government Databases

Governments maintain vast amounts of publicly accessible data that can be used for OSINT investigations.

Database Type	Examples	What You Can Find
Company & Business Registrations	SEC (USA), Companies House (UK), OpenCorporates	Business ownership, directors, financial filings
Court & Legal Records	PACER (USA), ECLI (EU), UK Courts	Lawsuits, criminal records, judgments
Real Estate & Property Records	Zillow (USA), Land Registry (UK)	Ownership, mortgages, property value
Patent & Trademark Databases	USPTO (USA), WIPO (Global)	Inventions, intellectual property, ownership history
Government Expenditures & Contracts	USAspending.gov, EU Tenders	Who gets government money and contracts
Legislation & Laws	Congress.gov (USA), EUR-Lex (EU)	Laws, bills, amendments

💡 **Example**: Investigating a company's legitimacy? Search business registrations, tax records, and court filings to check for lawsuits or financial troubles.

◆ B. Academic & Research Databases

Universities, think tanks, and research institutions publish scientific studies, papers, and statistics that can be useful for OSINT.

Database	What It Contains	Best Used For
Google Scholar	Research papers, legal opinions	Academic research
PubMed	Medical and health research	Medical OSINT
SSRN	Social science research	Economics, policy research
arXiv	Preprint scientific papers	AI, cybersecurity research
World Bank Open Data	Global economic & social statistics	Financial, geopolitical intelligence

💡 **Example**: Need background on cybersecurity trends? Search arXiv and SSRN for the latest hacking research papers.

◆ C. Corporate & Financial Databases

Businesses and financial institutions publish market reports, corporate filings, and trade data that can reveal hidden connections.

Database	What It Contains	Best Used For
SEC EDGAR	US corporate financial reports	Investigating company finances
OpenCorporates	Global business registry	Mapping business ownership
Orbis / Bureau van Dijk	Private company data	Corporate due diligence
Trade Map (ITC)	Global trade statistics	Identifying supply chains

💡 **Example**: Want to track a shady company's financial history? Use SEC EDGAR to check their financial statements and investor reports.

◆ D. Intelligence & Open-Source Crime Databases

Law enforcement and security organizations maintain crime databases, sanctions lists, and investigative records.

Database	What It Contains	Best Used For
Interpol Red Notices	Wanted criminals list	International crime investigations
OFAC Sanctions List	US sanctions list	Checking if an entity is blacklisted
UN Sanctions List	Global sanctioned individuals & entities	Geopolitical investigations
Europol's Most Wanted	EU criminal watchlist	Criminal intelligence

💡 **Example**: A journalist investigating money laundering might use the OFAC Sanctions List to check if a business is linked to sanctioned individuals.

3. How to Search Public Databases Effectively

◆ A. Using Advanced Search Techniques

✅ Google Dorking for Public Databases

Use Google search operators to find hidden records in databases.

Search inside a database:

- site:pacer.gov "John Doe" (Finds court records for John Doe)
- site:opencorporates.com "XYZ Ltd" (Finds business records for XYZ Ltd)

Find PDFs, XLSX, or DOCX documents:

- site:gov filetype:pdf "financial report"

Search for related terms:

- "John Doe" AND "Company X" AND "lawsuit"

◆ B. Cross-Referencing for Accuracy

Since public databases are not always 100% accurate, cross-checking multiple sources is critical.

✅ Compare business registrations with court records to detect fraud.

✅ Cross-check real estate records with Google Street View for property confirmation.

✅ Verify research papers with multiple sources before citing them.

💡 **Example**: A company claiming to be worth $10M but has no financial filings in corporate databases might be a fraudulent operation.

4. Ethical & Legal Considerations in Public Database Searches

Even though public databases are legally accessible, OSINT professionals must follow ethical guidelines.

◆ A. Privacy & Legal Boundaries

✅ Follow GDPR, CCPA, and other privacy laws.

✅ Avoid scraping or automating searches on databases that prohibit it.

✅ Do not publish sensitive personal details unnecessarily.

◆ B. Responsible Use of Data

✅ Use OSINT findings for legitimate investigations (fraud detection, journalism, research).

✅ Be mindful of misinterpretation—data can be outdated or incomplete.

✅ If uncertain, consult legal experts before publishing findings.

💡 **Example**: Finding someone's address in a public property database doesn't mean you should expose it online—that could be doxxing.

5. Case Study: Investigating a Shell Company Using Public Databases

Scenario:

A suspicious company, XYZ Holdings, claims to be a multimillion-dollar investment firm, but no one knows who owns it.

Investigation Steps:

✅ **Business Registration Search** → Found on OpenCorporates, lists a fake address.

✅ **SEC Filings Check** → No financial reports filed → Likely not a real investment firm.

✅ **Court Record Search** → Lawsuits found in PACER, indicating fraud cases.

✅ **Property Ownership Search** → No assets linked to XYZ Holdings, confirming suspicions.

⚖ XYZ Holdings is a fraudulent shell company—its fake registrations, lawsuits, and lack of financial records exposed it.

6. Conclusion: Maximizing OSINT from Public Databases

✅ Government, academic, corporate, and crime databases contain valuable intelligence.

✅ Google Dorking and cross-referencing sources improve accuracy.

✅ Always follow legal and ethical guidelines when using public records.

7.2 Using Google Scholar & Research Papers for OSINT

While OSINT investigations often focus on social media, government records, and financial databases, one of the most underutilized yet powerful resources is academic research. Google Scholar, university archives, and open-access journals contain peer-reviewed studies, technical reports, and legal opinions that can provide credible intelligence on almost any topic.

This chapter will cover:

✅ How to use Google Scholar for OSINT

✅ Finding hidden intelligence in research papers

✅ Extracting useful data from citations and references

✅ Using academic sources for cybersecurity, geopolitics, and corporate research

1. Understanding Google Scholar for OSINT

◆ What is Google Scholar?

Google Scholar (scholar.google.com) is a specialized search engine that indexes:

✓☐ Research papers
✓☐ Legal opinions
✓☐ Patents
✓☐ Technical reports
✓☐ University theses

Unlike regular Google searches, Google Scholar focuses on high-quality, reliable sources.

💡 **Example**: Investigating cybersecurity threats? Searching for "zero-day vulnerabilities site:arxiv.org" on Google Scholar can lead you to cutting-edge cybersecurity research.

2. How to Search Google Scholar for OSINT

◆ Advanced Search Operators for Google Scholar

Google Scholar supports powerful search operators that help refine searches.

Search Operator	Function	Example
"exact phrase"	Finds exact matches	"deepfake detection methods"
author:	Searches by author name	author:"Edward Snowden"
intitle:	Finds words in the paper title	intitle:"OSINT techniques"
site:	Limits to a specific domain	site:researchgate.net "threat intelligence"
filetype:	Finds specific document formats	filetype:pdf "financial fraud investigation"
before: & after:	Filters by publication date	"cyber warfare" after:2020

💡 **Example**: Want classified intelligence leaks? Try:

- "leaked government documents" site:ssrn.com filetype:pdf

This searches SSRN (a research database) for PDFs discussing leaked documents.

3. Finding Hidden Intelligence in Research Papers

◆ Research Papers as OSINT Goldmines

Academic papers analyze, expose, and document real-world events, providing data that traditional OSINT sources miss.

OSINT Focus	How Research Papers Help
Cybersecurity	Explains hacking techniques, malware behaviors, and zero-day vulnerabilities
Geopolitics & Intelligence	Analyzes conflicts, military strategies, and intelligence operations
Corporate OSINT	Provides case studies on fraud, financial crimes, and corruption
Social Media Analysis	Tracks disinformation campaigns and bot networks

💡 **Example**: Investigating Russian disinformation campaigns? Searching "Russia disinformation site:ssrn.com" might uncover studies on bot networks and influence operations.

4. Extracting Useful Data from Citations & References

One of the most overlooked OSINT tactics is following citations in research papers to uncover more data sources.

◆ Why Citations Matter

✓☐ They link to official government reports
✓☐ They reference news articles, leaked documents, and interviews
✓☐ They provide alternative data sources

💡 **Example**: A research paper on illegal arms trafficking might cite:

1☐ UN reports with real smuggling routes
2☐ Financial records linking arms dealers to shell companies
3☐ Declassified government intelligence

How to find citations?

🔍 **Scroll to the bottom of a research paper** → Find the References section → Search for linked sources on Google.

5. Using Research Papers for Cybersecurity & Threat Intelligence

⬥ **Case Study**: Investigating a Cyber Threat Using Google Scholar

Scenario:

A cybersecurity researcher wants to investigate North Korean hacking groups for OSINT intelligence.

Step 1: Search on Google Scholar

📌 **Query**: "North Korea APT hacking site:arxiv.org OR site:ssrn.com"

🔍 **Findings:**

✓☐ Academic papers analyzing Lazarus Group's malware
✓☐ Research on phishing campaigns linked to North Korean hackers
✓☐ Technical breakdowns of North Korean cyber-attacks

Step 2: Cross-Check Citations

📌 **Action**: Follow citations in research papers to find:

✓☐ Leaked intelligence reports from government agencies
✓☐ Industry reports from cybersecurity firms (FireEye, Kaspersky, etc.)
✓☐ Historical data on past cyberattacks

6. Google Scholar for Corporate & Financial OSINT

◆ **How Research Papers Reveal Business Intelligence**

Corporate research papers analyze:
✓☐ Financial fraud & money laundering

✓☐ Supply chain vulnerabilities

✓☐ Offshore tax havens

💡 **Example**: Investigating a suspicious company?

Search:

- "XYZ Corp fraud investigation" site:ssrn.com OR site:researchgate.net

This may uncover:

✓☐ Financial misconduct studies involving the company

✓☐ Lawsuits & bankruptcy filings

✓☐ Links to offshore accounts

7. Academic Sources for Government & Military OSINT

◆ Research Papers on Military Operations & Intelligence

Academic papers often analyze military strategy, foreign intelligence operations, and classified events.

OSINT Focus	Example Search
Military Strategy	"US drone warfare tactics" site:jstor.org
Foreign Intelligence	"China espionage case study" site:arxiv.org
Covert Operations	"CIA black ops history" site:ssrn.com

💡 **Example**: Searching "Wagner Group military strategy site:ssrn.com" can uncover studies on Russia's private military contractors.

8. Ethical & Legal Considerations in Using Research Papers

Although research papers are publicly accessible, OSINT professionals should:

✅ Check copyright restrictions before publishing excerpts.

✅ Verify findings—peer-reviewed ≠ always accurate.

✅ Avoid relying on outdated research (look for papers published after:2020).

9. Case Study: Tracking an International Money Laundering Network Using Google Scholar

Scenario:

A journalist is investigating a global money laundering network.

Step 1: Search for Relevant Papers

📌 **Query**: "money laundering networks site:ssrn.com OR site:researchgate.net"

🔍 **Findings:**

✓☐ Research on how criminals use shell companies
✓☐ Case studies on past money laundering schemes
✓☐ Breakdowns of offshore tax havens

Step 2: Follow Citations & References

🔍 Found UN financial crime reports citing real-world case studies.
🔍 Found SEC filings linking shady companies to offshore accounts.

Step 3: Cross-Verify with Other OSINT Sources

✅ Checked OpenCorporates for company ownership.

✅ Checked Panama Papers leaks for hidden assets.

🚀 **Outcome**: The journalist uncovered a fraudulent company laundering millions through offshore banks.

10. Conclusion: Maximizing OSINT with Google Scholar

✅ Google Scholar reveals intelligence hidden from regular search engines.

✅ Follow citations to uncover classified reports, government data, and financial records.

✅ Use research papers for cybersecurity, geopolitics, and corporate investigations.

7.3 Searching Government & Legal Databases for Intelligence

Legal and government databases are some of the most powerful yet underutilized OSINT sources. They contain court filings, business records, financial disclosures, sanctions lists, and more—all of which can help expose fraud, track criminal activity, and verify identities.

This chapter will cover:

✅ Where to find legal and government databases

✅ How to search for court records, lawsuits, and legal disputes

✅ Using business registries to uncover hidden corporate networks

✅ Tracking individuals through official filings and sanctions lists

✅ Advanced search techniques for legal intelligence

1. Understanding Legal & Government Databases

◆ What Types of Information Can You Find?

Legal and government records document real-world events, making them valuable OSINT assets. These databases include:

Type of Database	What You Can Find
Court Records	Lawsuits, criminal cases, judgments, bankruptcy filings
Business Registries	Company ownership, financial statements, directorships
Sanctions Lists	Individuals and companies blacklisted by governments
Real Estate & Property Records	Property ownership, mortgages, rental histories
Government Filings & Contracts	Government spending, contractor details, procurement data
Legislation & Regulatory Databases	Laws, policies, government decisions

💡 **Example**: A journalist investigating a corrupt politician could use court records to find lawsuits and business registries to track shell companies in their name.

2. Searching Court Records & Lawsuits for OSINT

Court records are highly valuable in OSINT investigations because they reveal legal disputes, criminal histories, and financial troubles.

◆ Where to Find Court Records?

Country	Court Database	Access
USA	PACER (pacer.uscourts.gov)	Paid
UK	The National Archives (caselaw.nationalarchives.gov.uk)	Free
EU	ECLI (e-justice.europa.eu)	Free
Australia	AustLII (austlii.edu.au)	Free
Canada	CanLII (canlii.org)	Free
India	eCourts (services.ecourts.gov.in)	Free

💡 **Example**: Want to know if a company is being sued? Search PACER for lawsuits against them or check CanLII for Canadian corporate disputes.

◆ Google Dorking for Court Records

If a legal database doesn't have a built-in search, you can use Google Dorking to find court documents.

📌 Search for lawsuits against a company or person:

- "John Doe" lawsuit site:pacer.uscourts.gov
- "XYZ Corporation" court case site:canlii.org

📌 Find bankruptcy or fraud cases:

- "bankruptcy filing" site:pacer.uscourts.gov
- "fraud charges" site:austlii.edu.au

💡 **Example**: Searching "fraud charges site:e-justice.europa.eu" could reveal European court cases involving financial crimes.

3. Business Registries & Corporate OSINT

Business registries help OSINT investigators:

✓☐ Uncover company ownership
✓☐ Track financial filings
✓☐ Find hidden connections between businesses and individuals

◆ **Where to Find Business Registrations?**

Database	Country	What It Provides
SEC EDGAR	USA	Corporate financial reports
Companies House	UK	Business owners, directors, filings
OpenCorporates	Global	Business networks, offshore entities
Orbis / Bureau van Dijk	Global	Private company data (paid)
Business.gov.nl	Netherlands	Dutch company registrations

💡 **Example**: If a company denies connections to another firm, checking OpenCorporates might show the same directors in both businesses.

◆ **How to Search Business Registries for OSINT**

📌 **Find a company's financial health:**

- site:sec.gov "XYZ Corporation" annual report

📌 **Track company ownership:**

- site:opencorporates.com "XYZ Holdings"

📌 **Uncover offshore shell companies:**

- site:icij.org "XYZ Corporation" Panama Papers

💡 **Example**: Searching for a company's financial statements in SEC EDGAR can reveal suspicious money movements.

4. Tracking Individuals in Sanctions & Watchlists

Sanctions lists reveal criminals, terrorists, corrupt officials, and companies banned from doing business.

◆ **Where to Find Sanctions Lists?**

Sanctions List	Organization	What It Includes
OFAC SDN List	US Treasury	Individuals & companies under US sanctions
EU Sanctions List	European Union	EU-restricted persons & entities
UN Sanctions List	United Nations	Global sanctions targets
Interpol Red Notices	Interpol	Wanted criminals worldwide
World Bank Debarred Firms	World Bank	Banned businesses from financial projects

💡 **Example**: A fraudster trying to start a new company may appear on OFAC, EU sanctions lists, or the World Bank's banned businesses list.

◆ **Searching for Sanctioned Individuals or Companies**

📌 **Check if someone is on a sanctions list:**

- "John Doe" site:home.treasury.gov
- "XYZ Corporation" site:sanctionsmap.eu

📌 **Find links between people and sanctioned companies:**

- "John Doe" AND "XYZ Corporation" site:icij.org

💡 **Example**: Searching "XYZ Corporation site:sanctionsmap.eu" may reveal if the company is blacklisted for illegal dealings.

5. Investigating Government Contracts & Spending

Government contracts expose financial relationships between businesses and officials.

◆ Where to Find Government Contracts?

Database	Country	What It Includes
USAspending.gov	USA	Federal contracts & grants
EU Tenders Electronic Daily	EU	European government contracts
UK Contracts Finder	UK	Public procurement data
Australia AusTender	Australia	Government tenders & spending

💡 **Example**: A company winning millions in government contracts despite no prior experience may indicate corruption or favoritism.

6. Case Study: Exposing a Corrupt Business Network Using Legal Databases

Scenario:

A journalist is investigating a politician accused of corruption.

Step 1: Search Business Registries

📌 **Findings**: The politician secretly owns shares in XYZ Holdings, a company receiving government contracts.

Step 2: Check Sanctions & Court Records

📌 **Findings:**

✓☐ The company is flagged in EU sanctions lists.
✓☐ The politician is named in lawsuits involving bribery.

Step 3: Verify Government Contracts

📌 **Findings**: USAspending.gov reveals XYZ Holdings has received millions in public funds.

🚀 **Outcome**: The investigation confirms corruption and fraud, leading to a government inquiry.

7. Conclusion: Using Legal & Government Databases for OSINT

✅ Court records, business filings, and sanctions lists reveal hidden financial and criminal connections.

✅ Google Dorking & advanced search operators help find hidden legal documents.

✅ Cross-referencing government spending databases exposes corrupt business deals.

7.4 Extracting Information from Business & Corporate Filings

Corporate filings are one of the most powerful OSINT sources for uncovering hidden financial networks, money laundering, fraud, and corporate espionage. Governments and regulatory agencies require companies to submit financial statements, ownership details, and operational disclosures—making these documents a goldmine for investigators.

This chapter will cover:

✅ Where to find business and corporate filings

✅ How to extract ownership details, financial statements, and hidden connections

✅ Using SEC filings, shareholder reports, and offshore leaks for OSINT

✅ Advanced search techniques for corporate intelligence

1. Understanding Business & Corporate Filings

◆ What Are Corporate Filings?

Corporate filings are official documents submitted by businesses to regulatory bodies. These documents provide:

✓☐ **Ownership & directorship details** (Who controls the company?)
✓☐ **Financial reports & revenue data** (Is the company profitable?)
✓☐ **Legal disclosures & lawsuits** (Is the company in legal trouble?)
✓☐ **Mergers, acquisitions & investments** (Who is funding the business?)
✓☐ **Offshore registrations & shell companies** (Is the company hiding assets?)

💡 **Example**: Investigating a suspicious company? Corporate filings can reveal its real owners, financial backers, and offshore connections.

2. Where to Find Corporate Filings?

◆ Major Corporate Filings Databases

Database	Country	What It Provides	Access
SEC EDGAR	USA	Financial reports, IPOs, executive compensation	Free
Companies House	UK	Company directors, shareholders, annual reports	Free
OpenCorporates	Global	Business ownership & connections	Free
Orbis / Bureau van Dijk	Global	Private company financials & corporate networks	Paid
ICIJ Offshore Leaks	Global	Shell companies, offshore accounts	Free
Australian Business Register	Australia	Business owners & financial records	Free
Hong Kong Companies Registry	Hong Kong	Business ownership & filings	Paid
European Business Registry	EU	Company registrations across Europe	Paid

💡 **Example**: Searching SEC EDGAR for "XYZ Corporation annual report" can reveal revenue, shareholders, and corporate risks.

3. Extracting Ownership & Shareholder Information

◆ Why Ownership Details Matter

✓☐ Exposes hidden business relationships
✓☐ Reveals conflicts of interest
✓☐ Identifies politically exposed persons (PEPs) or sanctioned individuals

◆ How to Find Company Owners & Directors?

📌 Search the official corporate registry (e.g., Companies House, OpenCorporates).
📌 Use Google Dorking for leaked filings:

- "XYZ Corporation" shareholders site:sec.gov
- "XYZ Holdings" directors site:opencorporates.com

- "John Doe" business partner site:offshoreleaks.icij.org

📌 Cross-check multiple databases to detect ownership structures hidden behind shell companies.

💡 **Example**: A UK-based firm winning suspicious government contracts might be linked to a politician via Companies House records.

4. Analyzing Financial Statements & Revenue Reports

◆ Why Financial Data is Critical for OSINT

✓☐ Reveals financial stability (or bankruptcy risks)
✓☐ Identifies money laundering patterns
✓☐ Tracks suspicious investments & fund transfers

◆ Where to Find Financial Reports?

📌 **SEC EDGAR** (USA): Public company filings, including Form 10-K (annual reports).
📌 **Companies House** (UK): Balance sheets, profit/loss statements.
📌 **Stock Exchange Filings** (Global): Search Bloomberg, Reuters, or company investor pages.

💡 **Example**: Investigating corporate fraud? A company that reports massive revenue in one country but zero tax filings elsewhere may be hiding profits offshore.

5. Identifying Shell Companies & Offshore Registrations

◆ What Are Shell Companies?

✓☐ Companies with little to no real operations
✓☐ Used for money laundering, tax evasion, and fraud
✓☐ Often registered in offshore tax havens

◆ How to Find Offshore & Shell Companies?

📌 **Use the ICIJ Offshore Leaks Database**

🔗 https://offshoreleaks.icij.org/

📌 **Search OpenCorporates for international business links**

🔗 https://opencorporates.com/

📌 **Google Dorking for leaked documents:**

- "XYZ Holdings" offshore company site:icij.org
- "XYZ Corporation" tax haven site:opencorporates.com
- "XYZ Ltd" Cayman Islands registration

💡 **Example**: A company winning a government contract but hiding its real owners in the British Virgin Islands (BVI) could indicate corruption or fraud.

6. Tracking Mergers, Acquisitions & Investments

◆ **Why Track Mergers & Acquisitions?**

✓☐ Identifies corporate takeovers & foreign influence
✓☐ Reveals hidden financial backers
✓☐ Exposes monopolistic behavior

◆ **Where to Find M&A Data?**

📌 **SEC EDGAR (USA):** Search Form 8-K filings for mergers.
📌 **Reuters & Bloomberg**: Track corporate acquisitions.
📌 **European Business Registry**: Search for cross-border takeovers.

📌 **Google Dorking for M&A Filings:**

- "XYZ Corporation" merger site:sec.gov
- "ABC Holdings" acquisition site:bloomberg.com
- "Company takeover announcement" site:reuters.com

💡 **Example**: Investigating a Chinese company acquiring European tech firms? Searching "China tech investment Europe site:bloomberg.com" can reveal geopolitical business strategies.

7. Advanced Search Techniques for Corporate Filings

◆ Google Dorking for Leaked Business Records

📌 Find confidential financial reports:

- "Confidential financial report" site:sec.gov
- "internal company report" site:leakbase.pw

📌 Track leaked emails & business communications:

- "internal memo" "XYZ Corporation" filetype:pdf
- "executive email leak" site:pastebin.com

💡 **Example**: Searching leaked business reports can expose fraud, financial manipulation, or unethical business practices.

8. Case Study: Uncovering a Corrupt Business Network

Scenario:

A journalist is investigating a politician suspected of corruption.

Step 1: Search Business Registries

📌 **Findings**: The politician secretly owns shares in XYZ Holdings, a company winning government contracts.

Step 2: Check SEC & Companies House Filings

📌 **Findings:**

✓☐ XYZ Holdings is linked to offshore accounts in Panama.
✓☐ The politician's family members are listed as directors in another shell company.

Step 3: Cross-Check Sanctions & Financial Reports

📌 **Findings:**

✓ EU Sanctions List flags the company for money laundering risks.

✓ SEC filings show a $10 million unexplained transaction.

🏴 Outcome: The journalist uncovers a fraudulent business empire, leading to legal action and financial penalties.

9. Conclusion: Mastering Corporate OSINT Investigations

✅ Corporate filings reveal hidden business structures, financial crimes, and corruption.

✅ SEC EDGAR, Companies House, OpenCorporates, and ICIJ Offshore Leaks are critical OSINT tools.

✅ Google Dorking can uncover leaked business reports and confidential filings.

7.5 Historical Records & Archives: Finding the Past Online

Historical records and archives are critical sources of intelligence for uncovering past business dealings, property ownership, legal disputes, and personal histories. Whether investigating a political figure, corporate entity, or criminal network, understanding their historical footprint can expose hidden connections, undisclosed assets, or patterns of misconduct.

In this chapter, we will cover:

✅ Where to find online archives and historical records

✅ Using newspaper archives for OSINT investigations

✅ Tracking changes in websites and online content over time

✅ Exploring historical corporate, property, and government records

✅ Advanced search techniques for finding past information

1. Understanding the Value of Historical OSINT

◆ **Why Are Historical Records Important?**

✓☐ Uncover hidden connections between people, businesses, and events
✓☐ Verify claims and detect inconsistencies in personal or corporate histories
✓☐ Identify long-term patterns of fraud, corruption, or organized crime
✓☐ Retrieve deleted or altered information

💡 **Example**: A journalist investigating a politician's wealth might find previous property records, old lawsuits, or past financial disclosures that contradict their public statements.

2. Where to Find Historical Records & Archives?

◆ Major Online Archives for OSINT

Archive Type	Database/Website	What It Provides	Access
Newspaper Archives	Newspapers.com, Google News Archive, Chronicling America	Old news articles, obituaries, legal notices	Free/Paid
Wayback Machine	archive.org/web/	Website history, deleted pages	Free
Corporate & Business Archives	SEC EDGAR, Companies House, OpenCorporates	Past company filings, director history	Free
Government & Legal Records	National Archives (UK, USA, EU), Courtlistener	Laws, court cases, historical rulings	Free
Property & Land Records	Land Registry (UK), Zillow (USA), Historic Aerials	Ownership history, real estate changes	Free/Paid
Genealogy & People Archives	Ancestry.com, MyHeritage, FamilySearch	Birth/death records, census data	Paid
Digital Libraries	HathiTrust, Project Gutenberg, Google Books	Old books, reports, and scanned documents	Free
Social Media Archives	Politwoops, Social Searcher	Deleted tweets, historical social media posts	Free

💡 **Example**: Searching an old business name in OpenCorporates can reveal previous owners, defunct companies, or renamed corporations used for fraud.

3. Investigating Old News Articles & Newspaper Archives

Newspapers are a rich source of intelligence, containing:

✓☐ Legal notices (bankruptcies, lawsuits, business formations)

✓☐ Corporate & government announcements

✓☐ Obituaries (useful for genealogy or inheritance tracking)

✓☐ Political & financial scandals

◆ How to Search Newspaper Archives?

📌 **Google News Archive** (news.google.com/newspapers) – Free scanned newspapers

📌 **Chronicling America** (chroniclingamerica.loc.gov) – US historical newspapers

📌 **Newspapers.com** – Paid access to global archives

📌 Google Dorking for Old News Articles:

- "John Doe fraud" site:news.google.com
- "XYZ Corporation lawsuit" site:chroniclingamerica.loc.gov
- "Real estate scandal" site:newspapers.com

💡 **Example**: Searching a company's name in old newspapers might uncover past fraud cases or regulatory fines.

4. Recovering Deleted Websites & Online Content

◆ Using the Wayback Machine (Archive.org)

✓☐ View deleted or altered webpages

✓☐ Track how a company or individual's website has changed over time

✓☐ Recover evidence for investigations

📌 How to Search the Wayback Machine?

- Go to https://archive.org/web/
- Enter the URL of the website
- Browse past snapshots of the page

📌 Google Dorking for Archived Pages:

- site:archive.org "XYZ Corporation website"

- site:archive.org/web/ "John Doe bio page"

💡 **Example**: If a company removes a controversial statement from their website, you can retrieve it using the Wayback Machine.

5. Extracting Historical Corporate & Business Information

Corporate filings change over time, so tracking a company's history can reveal:

✓ Previous owners, directors, and investors
✓ Changes in business structure or rebranding
✓ Past financial statements and regulatory issues

◆ Where to Find Old Business Filings?

📌 **SEC EDGAR (USA)** – Old annual reports, financial statements
📌 **Companies House (UK)** – Historical company ownership records
📌 **OpenCorporates** – Past registrations & corporate changes

📌 Google Dorking for Historical Business Data:

- "XYZ Corporation" past filings site:sec.gov
- "Old financial report" site:companieshouse.gov.uk
- "Company renamed" site:opencorporates.com

💡 **Example**: A company involved in a scandal may have changed its name—searching old business filings can connect it to its past.

6. Finding Historical Property & Land Ownership Records

Property records don't just show real estate ownership—they help uncover hidden assets, money laundering, and financial fraud.

◆ Where to Find Historical Property Records?

📌 **UK Land Registry** (gov.uk/search-property-information) – Past ownership details
📌 **Zillow (USA)** – Property history & valuation changes
📌 **Historic Aerials (historicaerials.com)** – Compare past and present land use

📌 **Google Dorking for Real Estate History:**

- "John Doe property records" site:gov.uk
- "XYZ Corporation real estate purchase" site:zillow.com

💡 **Example**: A politician claiming no assets might be linked to properties owned under a family member's name in historical records.

7. Social Media Archives: Recovering Deleted Posts

Many high-profile individuals delete tweets, posts, or statements, but OSINT tools can retrieve them.

◆ **Tools for Social Media Archiving**

📌 **Politwoops** – Archives deleted tweets from politicians
📌 **Social Searcher** – Tracks old social media posts
📌 **Wayback Machine** – Stores historical versions of profiles

📌 **Google Dorking for Deleted Social Media Posts:**

- "Deleted tweet by John Doe" site:politwoops.com
- "XYZ CEO racist tweet" site:socialsearcher.com

💡 **Example**: Investigating a CEO's past statements? Searching Politwoops might reveal deleted controversial tweets.

8. Advanced Search Techniques for Historical OSINT

📌 **Google Dorking for Old Versions of Documents:**

- "XYZ Corporation 2010 report" filetype:pdf
- "Historical SEC filing" site:sec.gov

📌 **Searching Digital Libraries & Book Archives:**

- "Old financial fraud cases" site:hathitrust.org
- "Historical court rulings" site:books.google.com

📌 **Cross-Referencing Multiple Archives:**

✓☐ Use newspapers for past events

✓☐ Check business filings for financial history

✓☐ Review real estate records for hidden assets

💡 **Example**: Searching "John Doe lawsuit 1995" in newspaper archives might reveal past crimes or bankruptcies.

9. Conclusion: Leveraging the Past for OSINT Investigations

✅ Newspaper archives, corporate filings, and real estate records expose hidden histories.

✅ The Wayback Machine can retrieve deleted or altered webpages.

✅ Social media archives help track deleted tweets and controversial statements.

✅ Cross-referencing historical data can uncover financial fraud and corruption.

7.6 Case Study: Using Government Data for OSINT Investigations

Government databases contain a wealth of publicly accessible information that can be invaluable for OSINT investigations. Whether you're tracking a corporation's financial history, verifying an individual's identity, or uncovering hidden assets, government records can provide hard evidence that supports your findings.

In this case study, we'll walk through a real-world OSINT investigation using publicly available government data. We'll demonstrate how to:

✅ Access government records, business filings, and legal databases

✅ Cross-reference multiple data points for verification

✅ Use advanced search techniques to extract actionable intelligence

The Case: Investigating a Suspicious Business Network

A journalist is investigating a mysterious shell company that recently won a multi-million-dollar government contract. The company, XYZ Solutions Ltd., was relatively unknown before securing the contract, raising suspicions of corruption and cronyism.

The investigation aims to answer:

✓☐ Who owns XYZ Solutions Ltd.?
✓☐ What is the company's financial and legal history?
✓☐ Are there any connections to government officials?

Step 1: Searching for Business Registration Records

Tools & Databases Used:

📌 **Companies House (UK)** – Business ownership and registration details
📌 **SEC EDGAR (USA)** – Public company filings
📌 **OpenCorporates** – Global corporate database

Using OpenCorporates, the journalist searches for XYZ Solutions Ltd. and finds:

◆ The company was registered only six months before winning the contract
◆ It has one listed director: John Doe
◆ The registered address is a virtual office space, not a real office

💡 **Red Flag**: The company's recent formation and lack of operational history raise concerns about its legitimacy.

Step 2: Investigating the Company Director

Tools & Databases Used:

📌 **UK Land Registry** – Property ownership records
📌 **US Treasury Sanctions List** – Identifying blacklisted individuals
📌 **Courtlistener** – Searching for past legal disputes

A search for "John Doe" in court databases reveals:

✓☐ He was involved in a previous fraud case linked to another company
✓☐ That company was shut down for financial irregularities
✓☐ He has multiple business aliases, using slight name variations

💡 **Red Flag**: The company's director has a history of financial misconduct.

Step 3: Cross-Referencing Government Contracts Database

Tools & Databases Used:

📌 **USA Spending (US Federal Contracts)** – Identifying recipients of government funds
📌 **UK Contracts Finder** – Tracking public procurement contracts

A search in UK Contracts Finder reveals:

◆ XYZ Solutions Ltd. received a £5 million contract from the government
◆ The contract was awarded without competitive bidding
◆ The official who approved the contract is a former business associate of John Doe

💡 **Major Red Flag**: A potential conflict of interest between John Doe and the government official approving the contract.

Step 4: Checking for Political Donations & Lobbying Records

Tools & Databases Used:

📌 **Federal Election Commission (FEC - USA)** – Campaign finance data
📌 **UK Electoral Commission** – Political donations database
📌 **Lobbying Transparency Register (EU, USA, UK)** – Lobbying activity

Searching the UK Electoral Commission database shows:

✓☐ John Doe donated £50,000 to the ruling political party
✓☐ His previous company hired a lobbying firm to influence contract decisions

💡 **Major Red Flag**: The director's political contributions and lobbying activities suggest favoritism in awarding the contract.

Step 5: Property & Asset Search for Financial Links

Tools & Databases Used:

📌 **UK Land Registry** – Property records linked to individuals
📌 **Zillow (USA)** – Real estate ownership history
📌 **Panama Papers Database** – Offshore company ownership

A property search for John Doe reveals:

✓☐ He owns multiple high-value properties in London
✓☐ Some of these properties were purchased through an offshore company
✓☐ That offshore company is linked to other government officials

💡 **Final Red Flag**: Potential money laundering and corruption scheme uncovered.

Conclusion: Exposing a Corrupt Business Network

🔍 **Key Findings:**

✅ XYZ Solutions Ltd. was a shell company with no real operations

✅ The company's director had a history of fraud and financial crimes

✅ The company received a large government contract without competition

✅ Political donations and lobbying efforts influenced the contract decision

✅ The director laundered money through offshore property purchases

📌 **Outcome**: The investigation exposed a corrupt network, leading to media coverage, legal scrutiny, and a formal government inquiry.

Lessons Learned: Using Government Data for OSINT

✓☐ Corporate databases help track hidden ownership structures
✓☐ Legal and court records reveal past financial crimes
✓☐ Public contract databases expose conflicts of interest
✓☐ Political donation and lobbying records uncover influence operations

✓☐ Property records help trace hidden assets and potential money laundering

8. Deep & Dark Web Search Techniques

The deep and dark web contain vast amounts of information that standard search engines do not index. The deep web consists of databases, private forums, and hidden content accessible only through direct queries or credentials, while the dark web requires specialized tools like Tor or I2P to access anonymous sites. OSINT analysts use deep web search engines such as Ahmia, DarkSearch, and OnionLand to uncover hidden marketplaces, leaked databases, and discussions on underground forums. Techniques like leveraging site-specific queries, monitoring dark web threat intelligence platforms, and analyzing breached data dumps can provide critical insights into cyber threats, illicit activities, and hidden intelligence. However, ethical and legal considerations must always be prioritized when exploring these less-regulated corners of the internet.

8.1 Understanding the Deep Web vs. Dark Web

When most people think of the internet, they imagine search engines like Google, Bing, and Yahoo indexing websites for easy access. However, what we see on traditional search engines represents only a tiny fraction of the internet. Beneath the surface lies a vast digital space known as the Deep Web and a more secretive and often misunderstood area called the Dark Web.

For OSINT investigators, understanding these hidden layers is crucial for gathering intelligence, tracking illicit activities, and uncovering valuable data not indexed by standard search engines.

In this chapter, we'll explore:

✅ The differences between the Surface Web, Deep Web, and Dark Web

✅ How and why data is hidden from traditional search engines

✅ Legal and ethical considerations when accessing hidden web content

1. The Three Layers of the Web

◆ **Surface Web (Publicly Indexed Web)**

📌 The Surface Web includes all websites indexed by search engines like Google and Bing. This consists of:

✓□ News websites, blogs, social media profiles
✓□ E-commerce platforms like Amazon and eBay
✓□ Public forums and business websites

💡 **Example**: If you search for "latest cybersecurity trends" on Google, the results you see are part of the Surface Web.

◆ **Deep Web (Unindexed, Restricted Content)**

📌 The Deep Web consists of webpages not indexed by search engines but still accessible with proper credentials. This includes:

✓□ Online banking portals
✓□ Subscription-based news websites
✓□ Private databases, academic journals, and legal records
✓□ Corporate intranet systems and government databases

💡 **Example**: Logging into your email or a university research portal takes you into the Deep Web, as these pages require authentication.

◆ **Dark Web (Anonymized, Encrypted Content)**

📌 The Dark Web is a small subset of the Deep Web that requires special tools like Tor (The Onion Router) to access. It is often associated with:

✓□ Anonymous marketplaces (both legal and illegal)
✓□ Encrypted communication forums for journalists and activists
✓□ Cybercriminal networks, hacking forums, and darknet markets

💡 **Example**: A whistleblower leaking sensitive documents might use a Dark Web forum to remain anonymous.

2. Why the Deep Web Exists: The Limits of Search Engines

Search engines do not index everything for several reasons:

◆ Content Requires Authentication

◆ Private emails, banking sites, and corporate databases require logins, preventing search engines from accessing them.

◆ Paywalls & Subscription-Only Content

◆ News sites, research journals, and streaming services restrict access to paid users only.

◆ Noindex & Robots.txt Protocols

◆ Website administrators can prevent search engines from crawling certain pages using robots.txt or meta tags.

◆ Database-Driven Content

◆ Many websites generate content dynamically, meaning search engines cannot store or index it properly.

💡 **Example**: Searching for court cases in a government database often requires specific queries within the website itself—Google cannot access this data directly.

3. How to Access Deep Web Content for OSINT

While Google won't find Deep Web data, OSINT investigators can use direct access points like:

◆ Government & Legal Databases

📌 **PACER (US Court Records)** – Access to federal legal cases
📌 **UK Companies House** – Business registration and ownership records
📌 **SEC EDGAR** – Corporate filings and financial reports

◆ Academic & Research Databases

📌 **Google Scholar** – Scientific papers and legal articles

📌 **PubMed** – Medical research and case studies
📌 **World Bank Open Data** – Global economic and development reports

◆ **Specialized Search Engines for Deep Web**

📌 **Carrot2** – Clusters deep web results into categories
📌 **Pipl** – Searches for people across databases
📌 **Wayback Machine (Archive.org)** – Retrieves deleted or altered web content

💡 **Example**: A journalist investigating a politician's business dealings might use Companies House and SEC EDGAR to find historical business filings that Google does not index.

4. Introduction to the Dark Web: Myths vs. Reality

The Dark Web is not inherently illegal, but it is home to both legitimate and illicit activities.

◆ **Legal Uses of the Dark Web**

✓ Secure communication for journalists, activists, and whistleblowers
✓ Anonymous browsing in censorship-heavy countries
✓ Privacy-focused marketplaces for legitimate goods and services

◆ **Illegal Uses of the Dark Web**

✗ Darknet markets selling drugs, weapons, and counterfeit goods

✗ Hacking forums for buying and selling stolen data

✗ Fraudulent services like fake passports and identity theft

💡 **Example**: The infamous Silk Road was a Dark Web marketplace used to sell illegal drugs before being shut down by the FBI in 2013.

5. How to Access the Dark Web Safely

Accessing the Dark Web requires specialized tools and precautions:

◆ **Tor Browser (The Onion Router)**

✓☐ Routes traffic through multiple encrypted layers, making users harder to track.

✓☐ Allows access to .onion websites, which are not available on standard browsers.

◆ Dark Web Search Engines

📌 **DuckDuckGo (Tor Version)** – A privacy-focused search engine that works on Tor

📌 **Ahmia.fi** – Indexes .onion sites

📌 **OnionLinks** – Lists verified .onion directories

◆ Safety Tips for Dark Web Investigations

✓☐ Use a VPN + Tor for extra security

✓☐ Never enter personal information on Dark Web sites

✓☐ Avoid downloading files from unknown sources

✓☐ Use disposable email addresses for any interactions

💡 **Example**: A cybersecurity analyst investigating a stolen data marketplace might use Ahmia.fi to search for darknet forums discussing the breach.

6. Legal & Ethical Considerations for OSINT Investigators

Before accessing the Deep Web or Dark Web, consider the legal implications:

◆ What's Legal?

✓☐ Accessing public records and legal databases

✓☐ Using the Tor network for anonymous browsing

✓☐ Collecting intelligence from open-source forums

◆ What's Illegal?

✗ Buying or selling stolen data

✗ Hacking private databases

✗ Participating in cybercrime activities

💡 Tip: Always document your OSINT process and stay within ethical and legal boundaries to avoid legal risks.

7. Conclusion: Leveraging the Hidden Web for OSINT

🔍 Key Takeaways:

✅ The Surface Web is what search engines index, but it's only a small part of the internet.

✅ The Deep Web includes password-protected databases, academic papers, and government records.

✅ The Dark Web requires Tor for access and hosts both legitimate and illegal activities.

✅ OSINT investigators can legally use government databases, academic resources, and specialized search tools to gather intelligence.

✅ Caution is essential when accessing the Dark Web—avoid illegal marketplaces and protect your identity.

8.2 Searching Unindexed Pages on the Deep Web

Most people rely on Google, Bing, and Yahoo for online searches, but these search engines only index a small portion of the internet. The vast majority of online data exists in the Deep Web—content that is unindexed and inaccessible through standard search engines.

For OSINT investigators, uncovering valuable intelligence often requires going beyond Google and using specialized methods to search databases, archives, government portals, and hidden web pages that do not appear in traditional search results.

In this chapter, we'll explore:

✅ Why search engines don't index the Deep Web

✅ Advanced techniques for uncovering unindexed data

✅ Specialized tools for Deep Web searches

✅ Real-world OSINT applications of Deep Web searching

1. Why Search Engines Don't Index the Deep Web

Traditional search engines use crawlers (also called spiders or bots) to index web pages. However, many types of online content remain hidden from these crawlers, including:

◆ Password-Protected & Restricted Content

✓□ Banking & financial accounts
✓□ Corporate intranets & private forums
✓□ Medical records & legal case files

◆ Dynamic & Database-Driven Content

✓□ Search engines can't query databases, so records inside government, legal, or academic databases remain hidden.
✓□ Example: Searching for a company's financial filings requires direct access to a corporate registry, not Google.

◆ Noindex & Robots.txt Protections

✓□ Website administrators can block search engines from indexing content using robots.txt files or "noindex" tags.

💡 **Example**: A government database containing court records may prevent Google from indexing its pages, requiring users to search directly inside the website.

2. How to Search the Deep Web Effectively

While Google won't find Deep Web content, investigators can manually query databases, use alternative search engines, and apply OSINT techniques to extract hidden information.

◆ 1. Searching Government & Legal Databases

📌 **PACER (USA)** – Federal and district court case records
📌 **Companies House (UK)** – Business ownership and corporate filings

📌 **SEC EDGAR (USA)** – Public company financial disclosures

💡 **Example**: Investigating a business partner? Search SEC EDGAR for financial filings or Companies House for corporate connections.

◆ **2. Searching Academic & Research Databases**

📌 **Google Scholar** – Academic research, legal cases, and patents
📌 **PubMed** – Medical and scientific research papers
📌 **IEEE Xplore** – Engineering and technology publications

💡 **Example**: Need historical research on cybersecurity trends? Google Scholar can uncover peer-reviewed studies that standard search engines miss.

◆ **3. Searching Business & Corporate Filings**

📌 **OpenCorporates** – Global company data and financial reports
📌 **Offshore Leaks Database** – Exposes offshore companies and tax havens
📌 **SEC EDGAR** – Investigate publicly traded companies

💡 **Example**: Searching OpenCorporates for a business owner might reveal hidden offshore companies and international financial ties.

◆ **4. Searching Unindexed News Archives & Historical Records**

📌 **Wayback Machine (Archive.org)** – Retrieve deleted web pages
📌 **ProPublica's Nonprofit Explorer** – Investigate charities and donations
📌 **Factiva & LexisNexis** – Subscription-only historical news archives

💡 **Example**: Want to see a deleted website from 2015? Wayback Machine can show you snapshots of old pages that no longer exist.

3. Advanced Deep Web Search Techniques

To extract intelligence from unindexed sources, OSINT investigators must adapt their search methods:

◆ **1. Using Site-Specific Search Queries**

Many Deep Web databases have an internal search feature that allows users to query specific records manually.

💡 **Example**: Searching "fraud case" in PACER will return a list of federal court cases related to fraud.

◆ 2. Using Google to Search Unindexed Content

While search engines don't index entire Deep Web databases, they sometimes index public summaries, metadata, or cached versions.

Google Dorking Example

☞ site:sec.gov "XYZ Corporation" filetype:pdf
📌 Finds financial reports related to XYZ Corporation inside the SEC database.

☞ site:archive.org "deleted news article" "company name"
📌 Retrieves archived pages of deleted articles about a company.

◆ 3. Searching Forum & Private Data Leaks

Sometimes, hidden data leaks can be found in forum discussions, breach dumps, or specialized leak sites.

📌 **Have I Been Pwned?** – Checks if an email or username was exposed in a data breach
📌 **BreachForums (Deep Web)** – Sometimes contains leaked corporate data
📌 **Hunchly OSINT Search** – Monitors discussions for leaked information

💡 **Example**: Searching Have I Been Pwned for an email address can reveal if it was part of a past data breach, helping track compromised accounts.

4. Specialized Search Engines for Deep Web Content

Since Google and Bing can't search the Deep Web, OSINT professionals rely on specialized search engines that focus on specific datasets.

◆ Alternative Deep Web Search Engines

✦ **Carrot2** – Clusters deep web results into categories
✦ **Pipl** – People search engine for emails, usernames, and phone numbers
✦ **Wayback Machine** – Archives historical versions of websites

◆ **Investigative Search Engines**

✦ **OSINT Framework** – A structured collection of OSINT tools
✦ **IntelTechniques Search Tool** – Finds people across deep web sources
✦ **Shodan** – Searches internet-connected devices (cameras, servers, databases)

💡 **Example**: Searching Shodan for open databases can reveal exposed corporate data that should be private.

5. Real-World OSINT Applications of Deep Web Searching

🗂️ Case Study 1: Investigating a Suspicious Business

Scenario: A journalist suspects that XYZ Corporation is a shell company used for financial fraud.

✅ **Step 1**: Searches OpenCorporates for the company's registration
✅ **Step 2**: Uses SEC EDGAR to find missing financial filings
✅ **Step 3**: Queries Wayback Machine for deleted corporate web pages
✅ **Step 4:** Runs a Google Dork search for leaked internal PDFs

✦ **Outcome**: The journalist discovers that XYZ Corporation's directors were linked to a previous fraud scheme.

🗂️ Case Study 2: Identifying a Target's Online Activity

Scenario: An OSINT investigator is tracking a high-profile cybercriminal operating under a pseudonym.

✅ **Step 1:** Runs a Pipl search for usernames and emails
✅ **Step 2**: Checks Have I Been Pwned? for past breaches
✅ **Step 3**: Searches Shodan for open databases linked to their known IP
✅ **Step 4**: Monitors dark web forums for username mentions

📌 **Outcome**: The investigator finds a leaked database entry containing the cybercriminal's real email, leading to further tracking.

6. Conclusion: Unlocking Hidden Information with Deep Web Searches

🔍 **Key Takeaways:**

✅ Traditional search engines only index a small fraction of the internet

✅ Government, business, and academic databases hold valuable intelligence

✅ Advanced search techniques, including Google Dorking, help extract unindexed data

✅ Specialized search engines like Pipl, Shodan, and OpenCorporates are key tools

✅ Real-world OSINT investigations rely heavily on Deep Web searches

8.3 Using Tor & Onion Search Engines for OSINT

The Dark Web is often portrayed as a lawless digital underworld, but in reality, it's a small, encrypted part of the internet that offers both legitimate and illicit content. While the Surface Web is indexed by Google and the Deep Web consists of private databases and restricted content, the Dark Web requires special tools like Tor to access.

For OSINT investigators, the Dark Web can provide valuable intelligence on cybercrime, leaked data, underground marketplaces, and hidden forums. However, navigating it requires specialized search engines, anonymity tools, and strict operational security (OpSec) to avoid exposing your identity.

In this chapter, we will explore:

✅ How Tor works and why it's essential for Dark Web access

✅ Onion search engines and how to find hidden Dark Web sites

✅ OSINT use cases for Dark Web investigations

✅ Safety measures and legal considerations when conducting Dark Web OSINT

1. How Tor Works: The Gateway to the Dark Web

The Tor network (The Onion Router) enables anonymous access to websites ending in .onion, which are not indexed by standard search engines and are inaccessible via regular browsers like Chrome or Firefox.

◆ How Tor Protects Anonymity

Tor routes internet traffic through multiple encrypted relays, making it extremely difficult to trace a user's location.

Tor Process:

1☐ Your data is encrypted multiple times

2☐ It is routed through several Tor nodes (relays)

3☐ Each node removes one layer of encryption, knowing only the next destination

4☐ Your request exits through an "exit node", appearing as if it originated from there

💡 **Example**: If an OSINT investigator accesses a Dark Web marketplace, their real IP address remains hidden behind multiple relays.

◆ Downloading and Using the Tor Browser

To access the Dark Web safely, download the official Tor Browser:

🔗 https://www.torproject.org

Once installed, simply launch Tor and enter a .onion URL in the browser to access hidden websites.

💡 **Tip**: Always use a VPN in combination with Tor for additional security.

2. Onion Search Engines: Finding Hidden Websites

Unlike Google, Dark Web search engines do not fully index .onion sites, making searches more challenging. However, specialized search engines can help locate underground forums, leaked data, and intelligence sources.

◆ Popular Onion Search Engines

📌 **Ahmia.fi** – One of the best search engines indexing .onion sites

📌 **DuckDuckGo (Tor Version)** – Privacy-focused search with some .onion results

📌 **OnionLand Search** – A Dark Web search engine focused on markets and forums

📌 **Torch** – One of the oldest and largest Dark Web search engines

💡 **Example**: Searching for "whistleblower forums" on Ahmia.fi might reveal hidden platforms used by journalists and activists.

◆ **How to Find Onion Links Without Search Engines**

Because Dark Web search engines are limited, investigators often rely on onion link directories:

📌 **The Hidden Wiki** – A directory of Dark Web sites (⚠️ Some links may lead to illegal content)

📌 **OnionLinks** – A regularly updated list of .onion domains

📌 **r/onions (Reddit)** – A community discussing and sharing .onion sites

💡 **Tip**: Many Dark Web sites frequently change URLs to avoid tracking. Always verify sources before investigating.

3. OSINT Use Cases for Dark Web Investigations

The Dark Web can provide valuable intelligence for various OSINT applications, including cybercrime investigations, corporate security, law enforcement, and financial fraud detection.

◆ **1. Investigating Data Breaches & Leaked Credentials**

Dark Web marketplaces and hacking forums often contain leaked databases, stolen credentials, and corporate documents.

Tools for Data Leak Investigations:

🔍 **Have I Been Pwned?** – Checks if emails and passwords were exposed in breaches

🔍 **IntelX** – Searches leaked databases and Dark Web archives

🔍 **DeHashed** – Allows searching for usernames, passwords, emails, and phone numbers

💡 **Example**: A company's cybersecurity team might use IntelX to check if employee credentials have been leaked in a data breach.

◆ 2. Tracking Criminal Marketplaces & Illicit Transactions

The Dark Web is home to black markets selling drugs, weapons, counterfeit money, and stolen data.

Investigation Methods:

✓☐ Monitoring Dark Web marketplaces for fraudulent goods
✓☐ Tracking cryptocurrency transactions linked to illicit purchases
✓☐ Analyzing forum discussions for emerging cyber threats

💡 **Example**: An OSINT analyst might monitor darknet markets for stolen corporate documents being sold.

◆ 3. Identifying Cyber Threats & Hacking Groups

Many hacking groups and cybercriminals communicate in hidden Dark Web forums.

Where to Look:

📌 **Exploit.in** – A forum where hackers discuss vulnerabilities and exploits
📌 **BreachForums** – A known site for sharing leaked data (⚠☐ Often taken down and rebranded)
📌 **Dread** – A Reddit-style forum discussing hacking, security, and darknet activities

💡 **Example**: A government cybersecurity agency might monitor Dark Web hacker forums to identify new malware threats before they spread.

◆ 4. Investigating Whistleblowing & Activist Sites

Not all Dark Web activity is criminal—many whistleblowers, journalists, and activists use .onion sites for secure communication.

🔍 **SecureDrop** – Used by journalists for whistleblower leaks
🔍 **ProPublica (Onion Version)** – A legitimate investigative journalism platform

🔍 **TorBox** – A secure and anonymous email service

💡 **Example**: A journalist covering government corruption might use SecureDrop to communicate with an anonymous source.

4. Safety & Legal Considerations for Dark Web OSINT

Since the Dark Web hosts both legal and illegal content, OSINT investigators must take precautions to avoid exposure to illegal material or tracking risks.

◆ Essential Security Measures

✓ **Use a VPN with Tor** – Prevents your ISP from detecting Tor usage

✓ **Disable JavaScript** – Reduces tracking and security risks

✓ **Never enter personal information** – Avoid signing up for accounts with real credentials

✓ **Use a dedicated OSINT machine** – Preferably a virtual machine or Tails OS for anonymity

✓ **Avoid downloading files** – Dark Web files may contain malware

💡 Tip: Running Tor inside a virtual machine (VM) adds an extra layer of security.

◆ Legal Considerations

While accessing the Dark Web is not illegal, engaging in criminal activities (e.g., buying stolen data, hacking services, or illicit materials) can lead to legal consequences.

🚫 DO NOT:

✕ Engage in illegal transactions

✕ Participate in hacking forums or exploit discussions

✕ Download or distribute illicit content

📌 Always document your OSINT investigations and follow local cybersecurity laws.

5. Conclusion: Unlocking Dark Web Intelligence for OSINT

Key Takeaways:

✓ Tor allows anonymous access to .onion sites and the Dark Web

✓ Onion search engines like Ahmia and Torch help locate hidden content

✓ OSINT investigators use the Dark Web to track data breaches, cybercrime, and intelligence leaks

✓ Strong security measures (VPN, Tails OS, VM) are critical for safe Dark Web investigations

✓ Legal and ethical guidelines must be followed when conducting OSINT research on the Dark Web

8.4 Finding & Analyzing Dark Web Marketplaces & Forums

Dark Web marketplaces and forums serve as hubs for illicit activities, including stolen data sales, hacking services, counterfeit goods, and cybercrime discussions. However, these platforms are also valuable sources of intelligence for OSINT investigators, law enforcement, corporate security teams, and cybersecurity professionals.

This chapter will cover:

✓ How to find and access Dark Web marketplaces and forums

✓ Analyzing marketplace structures and seller reputations

✓ Monitoring cybercriminal activities and emerging threats

✓ Ethical and legal considerations for Dark Web OSINT

⚠️ **Warning**: Accessing the Dark Web comes with risks, including exposure to illegal content, scams, and malware. Always follow strict OpSec (Operational Security) practices when conducting investigations.

1. Finding Dark Web Marketplaces & Forums

Unlike the Surface Web, where Google indexes most content, Dark Web marketplaces and forums are not easily searchable. Many of these sites operate in closed or invite-only networks, and their URLs frequently change to avoid law enforcement takedowns.

◆ How to Find Dark Web Marketplaces & Forums

Since standard search engines do not index .onion sites, here are alternative methods to locate them:

📌 Onion Search Engines

- **Ahmia.fi** – A rare search engine indexing .onion sites
- **OnionLand Search** – A Dark Web search tool focused on forums and markets
- **Phobos Search** – Another deep-search engine for Tor content

📌 Hidden Wiki & Dark Web Directories

- **The Hidden Wiki** – A frequently updated collection of .onion links
- **Dark.fail** – A marketplace and forum link directory (⚠️ Always verify links, as scams are common)
- **r/onions (Reddit)** – A subreddit that occasionally shares active .onion sites

📌 Underground Telegram & Discord Channels

- Many cybercriminals and fraudsters use Telegram and Discord to share updated .onion links for marketplaces and forums.
- OSINT investigators often monitor these groups for intelligence gathering.

💡 **Example**: A security analyst tracking stolen corporate credentials may start by searching for marketplace URLs on OnionLand, then verify marketplace activity through Telegram groups where cybercriminals discuss trades.

2. Analyzing Dark Web Marketplaces

Dark Web marketplaces often function similarly to e-commerce platforms like eBay or Amazon, with vendors, product listings, reviews, and transaction systems.

◆ Key Features of Dark Web Marketplaces

🔍 Key Takeaways:

✅ Tor allows anonymous access to .onion sites and the Dark Web

✅ Onion search engines like Ahmia and Torch help locate hidden content

✅ OSINT investigators use the Dark Web to track data breaches, cybercrime, and intelligence leaks

✅ Strong security measures (VPN, Tails OS, VM) are critical for safe Dark Web investigations

✅ Legal and ethical guidelines must be followed when conducting OSINT research on the Dark Web

8.4 Finding & Analyzing Dark Web Marketplaces & Forums

Dark Web marketplaces and forums serve as hubs for illicit activities, including stolen data sales, hacking services, counterfeit goods, and cybercrime discussions. However, these platforms are also valuable sources of intelligence for OSINT investigators, law enforcement, corporate security teams, and cybersecurity professionals.

This chapter will cover:

✅ How to find and access Dark Web marketplaces and forums

✅ Analyzing marketplace structures and seller reputations

✅ Monitoring cybercriminal activities and emerging threats

✅ Ethical and legal considerations for Dark Web OSINT

⚠️ **Warning**: Accessing the Dark Web comes with risks, including exposure to illegal content, scams, and malware. Always follow strict OpSec (Operational Security) practices when conducting investigations.

1. Finding Dark Web Marketplaces & Forums

Unlike the Surface Web, where Google indexes most content, Dark Web marketplaces and forums are not easily searchable. Many of these sites operate in closed or invite-only networks, and their URLs frequently change to avoid law enforcement takedowns.

◆ How to Find Dark Web Marketplaces & Forums

Since standard search engines do not index .onion sites, here are alternative methods to locate them:

📌 Onion Search Engines

- **Ahmia.fi** – A rare search engine indexing .onion sites
- **OnionLand Search** – A Dark Web search tool focused on forums and markets
- **Phobos Search** – Another deep-search engine for Tor content

📌 Hidden Wiki & Dark Web Directories

- **The Hidden Wiki** – A frequently updated collection of .onion links
- **Dark.fail** – A marketplace and forum link directory (⚠ Always verify links, as scams are common)
- **r/onions (Reddit)** – A subreddit that occasionally shares active .onion sites

📌 Underground Telegram & Discord Channels

- Many cybercriminals and fraudsters use Telegram and Discord to share updated .onion links for marketplaces and forums.
- OSINT investigators often monitor these groups for intelligence gathering.

💡 **Example**: A security analyst tracking stolen corporate credentials may start by searching for marketplace URLs on OnionLand, then verify marketplace activity through Telegram groups where cybercriminals discuss trades.

2. Analyzing Dark Web Marketplaces

Dark Web marketplaces often function similarly to e-commerce platforms like eBay or Amazon, with vendors, product listings, reviews, and transaction systems.

◆ Key Features of Dark Web Marketplaces

Most Darknet markets share the following characteristics:

✓ **Escrow System** – Buyers deposit cryptocurrency before the seller ships goods/services
✓ **User Reviews & Vendor Ratings** – Customers leave feedback on vendors
✓ **PGP Encryption for Communication** – Protects the identities of buyers and sellers
✓ **Bitcoin & Monero Payments** – Most markets use Monero (XMR) for increased anonymity

◆ **Types of Goods Sold on Dark Web Markets**

- **Stolen Credentials & Data Leaks** – Login details, credit cards, SSNs, passport scans
- **Hacking Services & Malware** – Botnets, ransomware, exploit kits
- **Drugs & Counterfeit Goods** – Narcotics, fake IDs, counterfeit money
- **Fraud & Financial Crime Tools** – Bank logs, cash-out services, scam guides

💡 **Example**: A security researcher monitoring data breaches might find corporate login credentials being sold on a Dark Web market.

3. Monitoring Dark Web Forums for OSINT

◆ **How Dark Web Forums Work**

Unlike marketplaces, Dark Web forums serve as discussion hubs for:

🔍 **Hacking Communities** – Discussions on zero-day exploits, malware development, and cyber attacks
🔍 **Fraudster Networks** – Scammers exchanging methods for carding, phishing, and identity theft
🔍 **Drug & Arms Trafficking** – Illicit trade discussions
🔍 **Leaked Data & Doxxing** – Forums where users publish stolen databases

◆ **Notable Dark Web Forums (Frequently Changing URLs)**

📌 **Dread** – The Reddit of the Dark Web, covering a wide range of topics
📌 **Exploit.in** – A well-known hacking forum for discussing cyber exploits

📌 **BreachForums** – Previously a marketplace for stolen data (often taken down and rebranded)

📌 **Rutor** – A Russian-language Dark Web forum used for cybercrime discussions

💡 **Example**: If a company suffers a data breach, an OSINT investigator might monitor Dread and BreachForums to determine if employee passwords or customer data have been leaked.

4. Extracting & Analyzing Dark Web Data for OSINT

Once access to a marketplace or forum is secured, investigators can extract intelligence for deeper analysis.

◆ **Techniques for Extracting OSINT from Dark Web Marketplaces**

✓ **Tracking Vendor Profiles** – Identifying sellers involved in fraudulent transactions

✓ **Analyzing User Reviews** – Understanding trends in cybercrime, fraud, and data leaks

✓ **Monitoring Cryptocurrency Transactions** – Tracing Bitcoin or Monero payments linked to illicit activities

◆ **Using OSINT Tools for Dark Web Analysis**

🔍 **BitcoinWhosWho** – Traces Bitcoin addresses used in Dark Web transactions

🔍 **Maltego** – Maps connections between cybercriminals, vendors, and stolen data

🔍 **Intelligence X** – Searches historical Dark Web data and leaked records

💡 **Example**: A law enforcement team tracking a cybercriminal might use Maltego to map connections between stolen data vendors on BreachForums and their Bitcoin wallets.

5. Ethical & Legal Considerations for Dark Web OSINT

While conducting OSINT on the Dark Web, investigators must follow strict ethical and legal guidelines to avoid crossing into illegal activities.

◆ **What OSINT Investigators SHOULD Do**

✅ Monitor cybercriminal activity without engaging in transactions

✅ Document intelligence gathering methods for legal purposes

✅ Use Tor and VPNs for operational security

✅ Follow local laws regarding cybersecurity investigations

◆ What Investigators SHOULD NOT Do

🚫 Never purchase illicit goods or services

🚫 Do not participate in hacking discussions or request illegal data

🚫 Avoid downloading files from unverified sources (Risk of malware)

⚠️ **Important**: Even passively browsing Dark Web marketplaces may raise red flags with law enforcement. Always document your OSINT methodology and use legitimate cybersecurity reasons for conducting investigations.

6. Conclusion: The Power & Risks of Dark Web OSINT

Dark Web marketplaces and forums provide valuable intelligence but come with significant risks. OSINT investigators must balance effective data gathering with strong security and ethical considerations.

🔍 Key Takeaways:

✅ Dark Web marketplaces function like underground e-commerce sites

✅ Forums contain discussions on hacking, fraud, and cyber threats

✅ OSINT tools like Maltego and Intelligence X can analyze Dark Web data

✅ Strict OpSec (VPN, Tor, Virtual Machines) is necessary for safety

✅ Legal and ethical boundaries must be followed at all times

8.5 Monitoring Dark Web Leaks & Breaches

The Dark Web serves as a major dumping ground for leaked databases, stolen credentials, and corporate breaches. Cybercriminals frequently sell, trade, or even release sensitive data for free, making it a goldmine for OSINT investigators, cybersecurity analysts, and threat intelligence professionals.

Monitoring these leaks is crucial for:

✅ Identifying stolen credentials before they are exploited

✅ Assessing the impact of a data breach on an organization

✅ Tracking cybercriminal activities and breach sources

✅ Notifying affected individuals and taking mitigation steps

However, investigating Dark Web leaks requires strong operational security (OpSec), specialized tools, and a clear ethical framework to ensure legal compliance.

1. Understanding Dark Web Data Leaks

◆ How Data Leaks End Up on the Dark Web

After a breach occurs, stolen data typically follows three main distribution stages:

1️⃣ **Private Sale** – Hackers first attempt to sell the data privately to the highest bidder.

2️⃣ **Dark Web Marketplace Listing** – If not sold privately, it may be listed for sale on Dark Web markets (e.g., BreachForums, Genesis Market).

3️⃣ **Public Leak** – If the data loses its value (e.g., passwords reset), it is dumped on hacking forums for free.

💡 **Example**: In 2023, a major hospital system breach resulted in medical records being sold on Genesis Market, later leaked on a Russian hacking forum after being exploited.

2. Where to Find Leaked Data on the Dark Web

Dark Web leaks are scattered across hacking forums, marketplaces, and leak sites. Some sources require registration, vetting, or cryptocurrency deposits, while others provide free, open access.

◆ Dark Web Sources for Data Leaks

📌 **BreachForums (successor to RaidForums)** – Popular marketplace for stolen databases.

✦ **Exploit.in** – Russian hacking forum known for breach discussions.

✦ **Genesis Market (often taken down & rebranded)** – Sold browser fingerprints and credentials.

✦ **Dread** – Reddit-style forum for cybercrime discussions.

✦ **KickAss Forum** – Known for leaked credentials and exploit sharing.

✦ **Telegram Channels** – Some hackers post real-time data leaks in Telegram groups.

💡 **Example**: If an OSINT investigator is tracking a recent financial institution breach, they may monitor BreachForums and Telegram groups where stolen bank logins are often traded.

◆ **Open-Source Leak Monitoring Tools (Surface Web & Dark Web)**

While the Dark Web is the primary hub for breaches, several tools and databases allow surface-level searches for leaked credentials:

🔍 **Have I Been Pwned (HIBP)** – Checks if an email or password has appeared in breaches.

🔍 **DeHashed** – Allows searching leaked data by username, email, or IP.

🔍 **IntelX** – Advanced search engine for leaked databases, including .onion sites.

🔍 **LeakLookUp** – Collects breach data for OSINT analysts.

💡 **Tip**: While these tools don't access full Dark Web dumps, they can help identify if certain data has been compromised before digging deeper.

3. How to Monitor Dark Web Leaks for OSINT Investigations

◆ **Step 1: Identify Key Data Points to Track**

Before searching for leaked data, define the critical assets to monitor, such as:

✓ **Email addresses & usernames** – Often used to check for credential leaks.

✓ **Corporate domains** – To see if company emails were exposed.

✓ **IP addresses** – Especially useful for tracking compromised infrastructure.

✓ **Customer or employee data** – To assess the severity of a breach.

💡 **Example**: A cybersecurity analyst monitoring a retail company's security might set alerts for corporate email domains appearing in new breaches.

◆ Step 2: Automate Leak Detection with OSINT Tools

Instead of manually searching Dark Web forums daily, leverage automated tools to monitor breaches in real time.

🔍 **DarkTracer** – Monitors Dark Web forums for stolen credentials and leaks.
🔍 **SOCRadar** – Provides breach alerts for corporate security teams.
🔍 **CyberSixgill** – Analyzes Dark Web intelligence and alerts on leaked data.
🔍 **ShadowDragon** – OSINT suite for tracking cyber threats.

💡 **Tip**: Many of these tools require paid access, but OSINT researchers can also use free community-driven alerts like Have I Been Pwned.

◆ Step 3: Investigate & Verify Leaks

Once a potential leak is identified, investigators should:

✓ **Validate the data** – Check if the breach is new or a re-upload of old data.
✓ **Analyze sample records** – Look for PII (Personal Identifiable Information) or credentials.
✓ **Trace the source** – Identify where the leak originated (internal vs. external breach).
✓ **Determine impact** – Assess if the leak includes passwords, SSNs, payment details, or sensitive business data.

💡 **Example**: A leaked healthcare database might contain patient records, posing legal risks under HIPAA regulations.

4. Case Study: Investigating a Leaked Database on the Dark Web

Scenario: A Fortune 500 Company Faces a Credential Leak

- A cybersecurity team receives an alert that company emails have appeared on BreachForums.

Step 1: Finding the Leak

- Using Have I Been Pwned, they confirm that over 5,000 corporate emails have been compromised.

- Searching BreachForums, they find a hacker selling employee credentials and internal documents.

Step 2: Verifying the Data

- They download a sample leak (without buying the full dump).
- By checking password hashes, they confirm that some credentials are still active.

Step 3: Assessing the Risk

- The breach includes admin accounts, which could allow attackers to access internal systems.
- Threat actors discuss using stolen credentials for phishing attacks.

Step 4: Mitigation Actions

✓☐ Immediately force password resets for affected employees.

✓☐ Deploy multi-factor authentication (MFA) to prevent credential stuffing attacks.

✓☐ Monitor Dark Web forums for further discussions about the breach.

✓☐ Engage law enforcement if financial or national security risks are involved.

5. Ethical & Legal Considerations in Dark Web Monitoring

Since many Dark Web activities are illegal, OSINT investigators must follow strict guidelines to ensure legal compliance and ethical integrity.

◆ What is Legal?

✓ Passive monitoring of leaked data for intelligence purposes.

✓ Documenting cybercriminal activities without engaging in transactions.

✓ Alerting affected organizations about data breaches.

◆ What is Illegal?

⊘ Buying, selling, or redistributing stolen data.

⊘ Engaging in hacking discussions or joining criminal networks.

⊘ Using breached credentials for unauthorized access.

💡 Tip: If conducting OSINT for a company, consult legal teams before investigating leaks to ensure compliance with cybersecurity and data privacy laws.

6. Conclusion: Dark Web Leak Monitoring as a Critical OSINT Skill

Tracking Dark Web leaks is an essential OSINT skill, allowing investigators to stay ahead of cyber threats and protect organizations from breaches.

🔍 Key Takeaways:

✅ Most stolen data goes through private sales, then marketplaces, and finally public leaks.

✅ Dark Web forums (BreachForums, Exploit.in) are major hubs for credential leaks.

✅ Automated tools (DeHashed, DarkTracer) help track breaches in real-time.

✅ OSINT investigators must verify and assess leaked data before taking action.

✅ Strict ethical and legal guidelines must be followed to avoid legal risks.

8.6 Case Study: Investigating Dark Web Content for OSINT

The Dark Web is a treasure trove of intelligence for OSINT investigators, law enforcement, cybersecurity professionals, and threat intelligence analysts. It houses cybercriminal forums, illicit marketplaces, hacking communities, and leaked databases, all of which can provide valuable insights into cyber threats, fraud networks, and underground activities.

This case study walks through a realistic Dark Web OSINT investigation, demonstrating how professionals can identify, analyze, and act on Dark Web intelligence while maintaining strong operational security (OpSec) and legal compliance.

1. Scenario: Tracking a Cybercriminal Selling Stolen Data

◆ **Background**

A financial institution's security team detects suspicious activity on employee accounts, suggesting a possible credential leak. OSINT analysts are tasked with investigating whether company data is being sold on the Dark Web.

◆ Objectives

✓☐ Identify if stolen credentials or sensitive company data are available on Dark Web marketplaces.
✓☐ Analyze seller profiles to track their activities and affiliations.
✓☐ Determine the origin of the data breach.
✓☐ Assess the potential impact and suggest mitigation strategies.

2. Step 1: Gathering Initial Intelligence

◆ Using Open-Source Tools to Check for Leaked Credentials

Before diving into the Dark Web, investigators start by using surface web OSINT tools to check for employee credentials in previous data breaches.

☐☐ Tools Used:

🔍 **Have I Been Pwned (HIBP)** – Checks if corporate email domains appear in known breaches.
🔍 **DeHashed & IntelX** – Searches usernames, passwords, and emails in leaked databases.
🔍 **LeakCheck** – Identifies compromised credentials.

💡 Findings:

✓☐ Several corporate emails appear in previous breaches, but none explain the recent activity.
✓☐ The team suspects new stolen data might be circulating on Dark Web forums.

3. Step 2: Locating the Stolen Data on the Dark Web

Since mainstream search engines do not index .onion sites, investigators turn to Dark Web search engines and directories.

◆ **Searching for the Breach on Dark Web Marketplaces**

□□ **Tools & Methods Used:**

🔍 **Ahmia.fi & OnionLand Search** – Index some .onion sites for leaked data.
🔍 **Dark.fail & The Hidden Wiki** – Provide updated links to active Dark Web markets.
🔍 **Telegram & Discord** – Criminal groups often share leaked data outside Tor.

💡 **Findings:**

✓□ A vendor on BreachForums claims to be selling corporate credentials and internal documents from the financial institution.
✓□ The listing includes a sample dataset, revealing that some login credentials are still active.

4. Step 3: Investigating the Seller & Their Reputation

Once the vendor is identified, analysts must assess their credibility and past activities.

◆ **Analyzing the Vendor's Profile**

📌 **Vendor Name**: "ShadowBrokerX"
📌 **Reputation**: 4.8/5 stars (indicating successful past sales)

📌 **Products Sold:**

- **Corporate login credentials** (banks, healthcare, and government agencies)
- **Fullz** (full identity profiles)

Malware tools

📌 **Languages Used**: English & Russian
📌 **Preferred Payment**: Monero (XMR) for increased anonymity
📌 **Activity History**: Operating for over 8 months, with verified sales on multiple forums

💡 **Findings:**

✓☐ "ShadowBrokerX" appears to be a high-volume seller specializing in corporate breaches.

✓☐ They use OPSEC measures, making direct tracking difficult.

✓☐ Other forum users confirm previous successful transactions, making the threat credible.

5. Step 4: Verifying the Breach Data

Investigators need to confirm if the data is legitimate, recent, and damaging before recommending a response.

◆ How Verification is Conducted

✓☐ **Checking Sample Data**: Some vendors provide small samples of leaked credentials.

✓☐ **Testing Old Passwords**: Analysts check if exposed passwords match historical company logins.

✓☐ **Cross-Referencing with Internal Logs**: The security team compares leaked user accounts with their internal database.

💡 Findings:

✓☐ The leaked data is recent and includes sensitive employee credentials.

✓☐ The breach likely resulted from a phishing attack or compromised admin account.

✓☐ Some accounts still have active credentials, requiring immediate action.

6. Step 5: Mitigation & Response

Once the breach is verified, the company's security team takes action to limit damage and prevent future incidents.

◆ Immediate Steps Taken

🏛 Forced password reset for all affected employees.

🏛 Implemented multi-factor authentication (MFA) to prevent unauthorized access.

🏛 Increased phishing awareness training for employees.

🏛 Engaged law enforcement to track the cybercriminal.

📍 Outcome: The company successfully prevented further account takeovers and secured its internal systems before cybercriminals could escalate their attacks.

7. Ethical & Legal Considerations

Dark Web investigations must be conducted legally and ethically. Investigators must:

✅ Document all findings carefully.

✅ Monitor criminal activities without engaging in transactions.

✅ Work within legal boundaries to avoid entrapment or hacking laws.

🚫 Illegal actions include:

✘ Buying stolen data.

✘ Impersonating cybercriminals.

✘ Accessing private systems without authorization.

8. Conclusion: Key Lessons from Dark Web Investigations

This case study highlights how OSINT investigators can track and verify data breaches on the Dark Web while maintaining strong security practices and legal compliance.

◆ Key Takeaways

✅ Dark Web forums & marketplaces are prime sources for stolen data.

✅ Tracking cybercriminal vendors can reveal their tactics & history.

✅ Leaked data should always be verified before taking action.

✅ Legal and ethical guidelines must be followed to avoid legal issues.

✅ A proactive security strategy, including MFA and phishing training, reduces risk.

9. Social Media Search Strategies

Social media platforms are goldmines of real-time information, making them essential for OSINT investigations. Each platform—Facebook, X (Twitter), LinkedIn, Instagram, TikTok, and others—has its own search functionalities, but advanced techniques can enhance intelligence gathering. Using platform-specific search operators, hashtags, geolocation filters, and reverse image searches, analysts can track digital footprints, uncover hidden connections, and monitor conversations. Tools like Maltego, OSINT Framework, and Who Posted What streamline social media data extraction. Additionally, archived and deleted content can often be retrieved via cached pages or third-party tools. By strategically leveraging these methods, OSINT practitioners can gain critical insights into individuals, organizations, and emerging events while remaining mindful of ethical and privacy considerations.

9.1 Social Media as a Search Engine for OSINT

Social media platforms are more than just places for sharing updates and memes—they function as real-time search engines that provide valuable OSINT (Open-Source Intelligence) data. With billions of users actively posting, commenting, and engaging, social media is a goldmine for investigators, analysts, and researchers looking to gather intelligence on individuals, groups, or events.

Unlike traditional search engines like Google, social media searches can provide:

✓ Real-time updates on events, trends, and breaking news.

✓ Direct insights into people's interests, connections, and locations.

✓ Unstructured data (videos, images, and comments) that is often not indexed by Google.

This chapter explores how to use social media as a search engine, the best techniques for extracting intelligence, and the tools that can enhance investigations.

1. Understanding Social Media Search Capabilities

Each social media platform has its own search engine with different capabilities and limitations.

◆ How Social Media Differs from Google

Feature	Google	Social Media
Indexing	Crawls & indexes most of the web	Limited indexing; private content is hidden
Real-time data	Delayed indexing	Instant updates from users
Content type	Websites, PDFs, structured text	Posts, images, videos, comments
User interactions	No direct user engagement	Comments, likes, shares, hashtags
Search depth	Broad searches	More personalized, niche searches

💡 **Key Takeaway**: While Google is great for broad searches, social media is superior for real-time investigations and tracking people or events.

2. Using Social Media Platforms as OSINT Search Engines

◆ Facebook Search Techniques

Facebook's search engine can retrieve posts, photos, check-ins, and user interactions—even from accounts that aren't friends.

🔍 Facebook Search Operators:

- **"Keyword" site:facebook.com** → Searches Facebook posts via Google.
- **"John Doe" AND "New York" site:facebook.com** → Finds profiles mentioning "John Doe" in New York.
- **"Live video" AND "protest" AND "Berlin"** → Searches for real-time live streams.

☐ Tools for Facebook OSINT:

✅ **Facebook Graph Search** (via third-party tools like Social Searcher)
✅ **WhoPostedWhat.com** (Historical post searches)
✅ **SearchIsBack.com** (Advanced people search)

💡 **Example**: An investigator tracking a protest can use Facebook Live search to find live-streamed videos from the scene.

◆ Twitter (X) as a Real-Time Intelligence Engine

Twitter is one of the best platforms for breaking news, crisis monitoring, and influencer tracking.

🔍 Twitter Advanced Search Operators:

- from:username → Finds tweets from a specific user.
- "keyword" since:2024-01-01 until:2024-02-01 → Searches tweets within a date range.
- #hashtag AND location:"Los Angeles" → Finds posts using a specific hashtag in Los Angeles.

☐ Tools for Twitter OSINT:

✅ **TweetDeck** (Live monitoring)
✅ **Twitonomy** (User analytics & mentions)
✅ **TweetBeaver** (Username & email searches)

💡 **Example**: A journalist investigating a cyberattack can search leaked data discussions using keywords like "database dump" or "breach".

◆ Instagram: Searching for Geotagged Content

Instagram is valuable for finding location-based intelligence, images, and influencer networks.

🔍 Instagram Search Strategies:

- **Location-based searches**: Search for geotagged posts by entering a location name.
- **Hashtag tracking:** Look for trends like #DataLeak, #CyberAttack.
- **Reverse image searching**: Use Google Reverse Image Search or PimEyes to trace an image's origin.

☐ Tools for Instagram OSINT:

✅ Picuki & Imginn (View profiles & stories anonymously)

✅ InstaDP (Extract profile pictures)

✅ PimEyes (Reverse image search)

💡 **Example**: An investigator tracking a criminal suspect can search Instagram check-ins to find potential locations they've visited.

◆ LinkedIn: Corporate & Employment Intelligence

LinkedIn is a goldmine for corporate OSINT, helping investigators map out employee networks, company structures, and insider threats.

🔍 LinkedIn Search Operators:

- **"Current position" AND "Company name"** → Finds employees in a company.
- **"CTO" AND "blockchain" site:linkedin.com** → Searches for blockchain-related CTOs.
- **"Past company" AND "leaked data"** → Finds discussions about data leaks.

☐ Tools for LinkedIn OSINT:

✅ Hunter.io (Find work emails from LinkedIn)

✅ RocketReach (Extract professional contacts)

✅ PeopleDataLabs (Enrich LinkedIn data with additional info)

💡 **Example**: A recruiter investigating a competitor's hiring trends can search for employees who recently changed jobs to identify recruitment patterns.

◆ TikTok & YouTube: Video Intelligence

Both platforms are useful for tracking viral trends, extremist propaganda, and deepfake videos.

🔍 YouTube & TikTok Search Tactics:

- **"Keyword" site:youtube.com** → Searches YouTube via Google.
- **"leak" AND "database" AND "hacker"** → Finds videos discussing data breaches.
- **TikTok Trends**: Use TikTok's Discover page to find trending content.

☐ **Tools for YouTube & TikTok OSINT:**

✅ **YouTube Data Viewer** (Extracts video metadata)
✅ **ShadowDragon VideoTrack** (Monitors influencer trends)
✅ TikTok OSINT tools like OSINT Techniques TikTok Scraper

💡 **Example**: A government agency tracking extremist recruitment videos can use YouTube search filters to find propaganda content.

3. Automating Social Media OSINT Searches

◆ Using APIs & Bots for Large-Scale Monitoring

Instead of manual searches, OSINT analysts use APIs and automation to track trends in real-time.

☐ **Automation Tools:**

✅ **Twint** – Scrapes Twitter without API restrictions.
✅ **FacePager** – Automates Facebook & Instagram data collection.
✅ **Maltego** – Maps relationships between social media profiles.

💡 **Example**: A journalist monitoring election disinformation can set up a Twitter bot that collects and analyzes posts containing fake news hashtags.

4. Ethical & Legal Considerations

When conducting OSINT on social media, investigators must:

✅ Respect platform terms of service (TOS).

✅ Avoid unauthorized data scraping or hacking.

✅ Verify information before acting on it (to prevent misinformation).

🚫 **Illegal Activities Include:**

✖ Impersonating someone to gain private data.

✖ Hacking or bypassing security controls.

✖ Posting doxxed (private) information.

💡 **Best Practice**: Use only publicly available information and follow ethical OSINT guidelines.

5. Conclusion: Mastering Social Media as an OSINT Search Engine

Social media is one of the most powerful tools for OSINT investigations, offering real-time insights, rich media content, and detailed user interactions.

🔍 **Key Takeaways:**

✅ Each social platform has unique search capabilities—knowing them gives an advantage.

✅ Using advanced search operators can refine results and improve efficiency.

✅ Automating searches through APIs and OSINT tools helps track trends at scale.

✅ Ethical and legal compliance must always be maintained when conducting investigations.

9.2 Facebook Search Techniques & Hidden Profile Data

Facebook remains one of the largest social media platforms, with billions of users sharing personal details, locations, photos, and connections. For OSINT (Open-Source Intelligence) investigators, Facebook is a goldmine of intelligence—but much of its data isn't easily searchable through basic queries.

Since Facebook has limited public search features and removed Graph Search in 2019, investigators need advanced techniques to uncover hidden profile data, track activities, and extract valuable intelligence.

This chapter explores how to conduct advanced Facebook searches using search operators, third-party tools, and strategic OSINT methods.

1. Understanding Facebook's Search Limitations

Facebook's search function is not as powerful as Google, and its privacy settings hide a lot of data from public view.

◆ What You Can Find with Basic Facebook Search

✅ Profiles & Pages (if set to public)

✅ Posts mentioning keywords

✅ Groups & discussions (public only)

✅ Photos & tagged locations

◆ What Facebook Hides or Restricts

✖ Private profiles & friends lists

✖ Historical post searches (limited visibility)

✖ Email & phone number lookups

✖ Advanced search filters removed after Graph Search was discontinued

💡 **Solution**: Use Google dorking, third-party tools, and URL manipulation to retrieve hidden data.

2. Using Google to Search Facebook More Effectively

Since Facebook's internal search is limited, Google dorking can help extract public data more effectively.

🔍 Google Search Operators for Facebook OSINT

Use these operators in Google search (not Facebook) to find hidden data:

Search Type	Google Dork Example	What It Finds
Profile Search	`site:facebook.com "John Doe"`	Public Facebook profiles
Keyword in Posts	`site:facebook.com "leaked data"`	Public posts mentioning "leaked data"
Posts by a User	`site:facebook.com inurl:posts "John Doe"`	Public posts by "John Doe"
Photos from a Profile	`site:facebook.com/photos "Jane Doe"`	Public photos of "Jane Doe"
Location-Based Search	`site:facebook.com "checked in at New York"`	People who checked in at a location
File Search	`site:facebook.com filetype:pdf OR filetype:doc`	Documents shared on Facebook

💡 Example:

An investigator looking for leaked corporate documents might search:

- site:facebook.com "confidential report" filetype:pdf

3. Extracting Hidden Profile Data Using Facebook URL Tricks

Even though Graph Search is gone, direct URL manipulation can reveal hidden data.

🔍 Finding a User's Unique Facebook ID

Every Facebook profile has a unique numeric ID, even if the user has a custom username.

◆ Steps to Find a Facebook ID:

- Go to the person's profile.
- Right-click and select View Page Source.
- Press CTRL + F and search for "profile_id" or "entity_id".
- The number next to it is their Facebook ID.

💡 **Example**: If the ID is 1000123456789, you can use it in the URLs below.

🔍 Revealing Hidden Profile Photos

Even if a user hides their tagged photos, you can access some of them using this URL:

- https://www.facebook.com/search/1000123456789/photos-tagged

📌 **Reveals photos where the person is tagged.**

🔍 Finding Public Friends Lists

Even if a user's friends list is hidden, you can sometimes view it:

- https://www.facebook.com/search/1000123456789/friends

📌 Shows mutual friends and sometimes hidden connections.

🔍 Checking Recent Check-Ins & Places Visited

If a user checks in at places, you can retrieve this data:

- https://www.facebook.com/search/1000123456789/places-visited

📌 **Useful for tracking locations.**

🔍 Finding Groups a User Has Joined

To see which groups a user is in (if public):

- https://www.facebook.com/search/1000123456789/groups

📌 Useful for analyzing interests and affiliations.

💡 **Example Use Case**: If an OSINT investigator is tracking a cybercriminal, they might check which hacking-related groups they've joined.

4. Searching Facebook Groups for Intelligence

Facebook Groups are often used for:

✓ Organized crime discussions

✓ Leaked data & dark web leaks

✓ Black market deals & hacking communities

✓ Political activism & extremism

🔍 Searching Public Facebook Groups via Google

To find public discussions in Facebook groups:

- site:facebook.com/groups "carding forum"
- site:facebook.com/groups "hacker tools"

📌 This will reveal group discussions related to cybercrime, leaks, and hacking.

💡 **Example**: A fraud investigator looking for credit card black markets might search:

- site:facebook.com/groups "CC dump" OR "carding site"

5. Extracting Metadata from Facebook Images

Facebook strips most metadata (EXIF data) from uploaded images. However:

✓ If the image is uploaded as a file attachment (not as a post), it might still contain metadata.

✓ If users link images from other sites, metadata can sometimes be extracted.

☐ Tools to Analyze Facebook Images:

✅ **ExifTool** – Extracts metadata from photos.
✅ **Google Reverse Image Search** – Finds similar photos on the web.
✅ **PimEyes** – Facial recognition tool to track images.

💡 **Use Case**: An OSINT analyst tracking a missing person can reverse search their Facebook images to see where else they appear online.

6. Automating Facebook OSINT with Third-Party Tools

While manual searches are effective, automation speeds up investigations.

☐ **Recommended Facebook OSINT Tools:**

✅ **Facebook UID Finder** – Extracts Facebook user IDs.
✅ **OSINT Combine Facebook Tool** – Finds Facebook user data.
✅ **IntelX** – Searches leaked Facebook data.
✅ **Maltego** – Maps relationships between Facebook profiles.

💡 **Example**: A journalist tracking a fake profile network can use Maltego to visualize connections between multiple Facebook accounts.

7. Ethical & Legal Considerations

OSINT investigators must follow ethical and legal boundaries when collecting Facebook data.

✅ **Do:**

✔ Use only publicly available data.

✔ Respect Facebook's Terms of Service.

✔ Verify information before making conclusions.

🚫 **Don't:**

✘ Use hacking, phishing, or unauthorized access.

✘ Scrape data in violation of Facebook's policies.

✘ Engage in doxxing or sharing private information.

8. Conclusion: Mastering Facebook OSINT

Facebook is a powerful OSINT tool, but its search restrictions require creative methods.

🔍 **Key Takeaways:**

✅ Google dorking helps find hidden Facebook data.

✅ Direct URL manipulation can uncover hidden profile details.

✅ Facebook Groups are a valuable resource for OSINT investigations.

✅ Reverse image searches & metadata tools help track Facebook photos.

✅ Automating searches with OSINT tools speeds up investigations.

9.3 Twitter Advanced Search: Hashtags, Mentions & Geo-Tracking

Twitter (now rebranded as X) is a real-time intelligence hub where people share opinions, news, location check-ins, and even sensitive information. Unlike other social media platforms, Twitter's default setting is public, making it a valuable resource for OSINT investigators tracking events, individuals, and trends.

This chapter explores advanced Twitter search techniques using hashtags, mentions, geo-tracking, and specialized tools to uncover hidden insights.

1. Understanding Twitter's Search Capabilities

🔍 What Twitter Allows You to Search

✓ Tweets (text, images, videos)

✓ Hashtags & trending topics

✓ User mentions (@username)

✓ Location-tagged tweets

✓ Conversations (replies, threads)

✓ Links to external content

🔍 Twitter Search Limitations

✗ Deleted tweets are not searchable.

✗ Some users have private (protected) accounts.

✗ Historical tweets may not appear in Twitter's search.

✗ Advanced searches require third-party tools for deeper analysis.

💡 **Solution**: Use Twitter's advanced search operators, OSINT tools, and automation scripts to overcome these limitations.

2. Using Twitter Advanced Search Operators

Twitter supports search operators to refine searches and extract specific information.

🔍 Essential Twitter Search Operators

Search Type	Operator Example	What It Finds
Keyword Search	`OSINT techniques`	Tweets mentioning "OSINT techniques"
Exact Phrase	`"data breach"`	Tweets containing "data breach" (exact match)
Hashtag Search	`#cybersecurity`	Tweets with the hashtag #cybersecurity
Mentions	`@elonmusk`	Tweets mentioning Elon Musk
From a User	`from:snowden`	Tweets from @snowden
To a User	`to:jack`	Tweets directed at @jack
Links Only	`filter:links`	Tweets containing links
No Links	`-filter:links`	Tweets without links
Images Only	`filter:images`	Tweets with images
Videos Only	`filter:videos`	Tweets with videos
Geo-Location	`geocode:37.7749,-122.4194,10km`	Tweets within 10km of San Francisco
Date-Specific Search	`since:2024-01-01 until:2024-02-01`	Tweets from January 2024
Language Filter	`lang:en`	Tweets in English

💡 **Example:**

To find tweets about data leaks in 2024, use:

- "data breach" OR "leak" since:2024-01-01 filter:links

3. Tracking Hashtags for OSINT Investigations

Hashtags help track trending topics, events, and movements in real time.

🔍 How to Search for Hashtags

Search hashtags directly in Twitter: #RussiaUkraineWar

Use Google:

- site:twitter.com "#CyberAttack"

Use tools like Trendsmap for live hashtag tracking.

💡 Example Use Case:

An OSINT analyst tracking hacktivist groups may monitor hashtags like:

- #OpIsrael #CyberWar #DDoSAttack

4. Finding Hidden Conversations Using Mentions & Replies

Mentions (@username) help track direct interactions and conversations.

🔍 How to Track Mentions & Conversations

To see all tweets mentioning a user:

- @wikileaks

To find tweets replying to a user:

- to:wikileaks

To find tweets from a user:

- from:wikileaks

💡 Example Use Case:

To track responses to a leaked government document, search:

- to:wikileaks "classified"

5. Geo-Tracking Tweets for Location-Based Intelligence

🔍 Searching Tweets by Location

Twitter allows geo-tagged searches using latitude, longitude, and radius.

◆ Format:

- geocode:LATITUDE,LONGITUDE,RADIUS

Example: Tweets from New York City (10km radius)

- geocode:40.7128,-74.0060,10km

🔍 Finding Location-Tagged Media

Tweets with images from a location:

- geocode:51.5074,-0.1278,5km filter:images

Tweets with videos from a location:

- geocode:48.8566,2.3522,5km filter:videos

💡 Example Use Case:

To track tweets from a protest in Washington D.C., search:

- geocode:38.9072,-77.0369,5km "protest" OR "demonstration"

6. Automating Twitter OSINT with Tools & APIs

Manual searches are effective but OSINT tools & automation improve efficiency.

🔍 Best OSINT Tools for Twitter Investigations

Tool	Features
Twint	Scrapes Twitter without API access
TweetDeck	Real-time monitoring of keywords & users
Trendsmap	Tracks hashtag trends by location
IntelX	Finds deleted tweets & leaked data
Social Bearing	Analyzes user engagement & activity
GeoSocial Footprint	Maps geo-tagged tweets

💡 Example Use Case:

An OSINT analyst tracking dark web operators on Twitter can use Twint to scrape historical tweets without an API key.

7. Ethical & Legal Considerations

Investigating Twitter data comes with responsibilities.

✅ Do:

✔ Use only publicly available tweets.

✔ Respect Twitter's terms of service.

✔ Verify tweets before making conclusions.

🚫 Don't:

✘ Attempt to access private (protected) tweets.

✘ Scrape Twitter in violation of Twitter API policies.

✘ Engage in harassment or doxxing.

8. Conclusion: Mastering Twitter OSINT

Twitter/X is a powerful real-time OSINT platform for tracking events, individuals, and trends.

⚲ Key Takeaways:

✅ Search operators refine OSINT searches.

✅ Hashtags & mentions uncover hidden conversations.

✅ Geo-tracking finds tweets from specific locations.

✅ Automation tools enhance investigations.

9.4 Instagram & TikTok Search Tricks for OSINT

Instagram and TikTok have become two of the most popular social media platforms, with billions of users sharing photos, videos, locations, and personal data. Unlike Twitter, these platforms are heavily visual, making them essential for OSINT investigations involving facial recognition, geolocation, and behavioral analysis.

Since Instagram and TikTok have limited built-in search tools, OSINT investigators need advanced search techniques, metadata analysis, and external tools to extract valuable intelligence.

1. Instagram OSINT: Finding Hidden Information

1.1 Understanding Instagram's Search Capabilities

✔ Public profiles, posts, and stories

✔ Hashtags & location tags

✔ User mentions & tagged content

✔ Reels & video metadata

✔ Comments & follower activity

⊘ Limitations:

✗ No advanced text search like Twitter.

✗ Private accounts hide posts and stories.

✗ Instagram restricts bulk data scraping.

💡 **Solution**: Use Google dorking, metadata tools, and OSINT platforms to access hidden data.

1.2 Using Google Dorking to Search Instagram

Instagram's internal search is limited, but Google dorking can extract more data.

🔍 Google Search Operators for Instagram OSINT

Search Type	Google Dork Example	What It Finds
Profiles by Name	`site:instagram.com "John Doe"`	Public Instagram profiles
Keyword in Captions	`site:instagram.com "data breach"`	Posts mentioning "data breach"
Location-Based Posts	`site:instagram.com "New York" inurl:locations`	Public posts tagged in New York
Hashtag Search	`site:instagram.com #hacker`	Posts with #hacker
Posts by a User	`site:instagram.com inurl:john_doe`	Public posts from @john_doe
Images from Instagram	`site:instagram.com filetype:jpg`	Direct image URLs from Instagram

💡 **Example**: To find Instagram posts about stolen credit cards, search:

- site:instagram.com "credit card dump" OR "carding"

1.3 Extracting Data from Instagram Posts & Stories

Even though Instagram removes EXIF metadata from uploaded photos, investigators can still gather intelligence using:

✓ Reverse Image Search (Google Lens, Yandex, PimEyes)

✓ Hashtag & Location Tracking

✓ Analyzing Post Timelines & Patterns

🔍 Finding User Mentions & Tagged Photos

Even if a target's profile is private, their tagged photos might still be visible if others have tagged them.

◆ Find a user's tagged posts:

- https://www.instagram.com/explore/tags/USERNAME/

💡 **Example**: If investigating a criminal using Instagram, check their tagged posts to see who interacts with them.

1.4 Searching Instagram Stories & Reels for OSINT

Instagram Stories & Reels disappear after 24 hours, but they can still be accessed using third-party tools.

✓ Tools to View Instagram Stories & Reels Anonymously:

✓ **StoriesIG** – View & download public stories.
✓ **InstaDP** – Download profile pictures & stories.
✓ **4K Stogram** – Automates Instagram media downloads.

💡 **Use Case**: If tracking a suspect's activity, regularly check and archive their stories before they disappear.

2. TikTok OSINT: Tracking Viral Content & Hidden Data

2.1 Understanding TikTok's OSINT Potential

✓ Real-time trends & viral videos

✓ Geo-tagged posts & user activity

✓ Hashtag analysis & content tracking

✓ User interactions & comment networks

✓ Video metadata & audio analysis

🚫 **Limitations:**

✗ No text-based advanced search.

✗ Private accounts hide videos & interactions.

✗ Some data is only available via TikTok's API.

💡 **Solution**: Use Google dorking, third-party scrapers, and metadata extraction tools to retrieve hidden data.

2.2 Using Google Dorking for TikTok Investigations

Search Type	Google Dork Example	What It Finds
Profiles by Name	site:tiktok.com "John Doe"	Public TikTok profiles
Keyword in Captions	site:tiktok.com "leaked database"	Videos mentioning "leaked database"
Hashtag Search	site:tiktok.com #hacker	Videos with #hacker
Videos by a User	site:tiktok.com @username	Public videos from @username
Geo-Tagged Videos	site:tiktok.com "New York" inurl:video	Videos tagged in New York

💡 **Example**: To find TikTok videos about cybercrime, search:

- site:tiktok.com "how to hack" OR "hacking tutorial"

2.3 Extracting Metadata from TikTok Videos

TikTok removes most metadata, but some details can still be found in the video itself.

🔍 What Can Be Extracted?

✓ Video date & time (from post timestamps)

✓ Audio metadata & original sounds

✓ Hashtags & captions for content trends

✓ User engagement (likes, shares, comments)

🔍 Tools to Analyze TikTok Content

✅ **TikTokScraper** – Extracts data from TikTok profiles.
✅ **PimEyes** – Reverse searches TikTok faces.
✅ **SnapTik** – Downloads TikTok videos without a watermark.

💡 **Example Use Case**: If investigating a fake influencer spreading disinformation, use TikTokScraper to extract engagement stats over time.

3. Geo-Tracking Instagram & TikTok Posts

Since Instagram and TikTok both allow location tagging, OSINT investigators can use this data to track movements and events.

🔍 Searching Location-Based Posts

Instagram Location Search:

- site:instagram.com "New York" inurl:locations

TikTok Geo-Tagged Videos:

- site:tiktok.com "Los Angeles" inurl:video

Tools for Geo-Tracking Social Media:

✅ **OSINT Combine Geo-Intel Tool** – Tracks social media posts by location.
✅ **Echosec** – Monitors social media activity in specific regions.
✅ **GeoSocial Footprint** – Maps user activity over time.

💡 **Use Case**: If tracking protests or conflicts, search geo-tagged Instagram and TikTok posts from the area.

4. Automating Instagram & TikTok OSINT with Tools

Since both platforms limit bulk searches, automation is key for large-scale investigations.

🔍 Best OSINT Tools for Instagram & TikTok

Tool	Platform	Features
Twitonomy	Instagram & TikTok	User analytics & activity tracking
Maltego	Instagram & TikTok	Maps social media connections
TikTokScraper	TikTok	Extracts profile & video data
4K Stogram	Instagram	Downloads Instagram photos/videos

💡 **Example Use Case**: To investigate a missing person, an OSINT investigator can use Maltego to analyze their Instagram & TikTok interactions.

5. Ethical & Legal Considerations

✅ Do:

✔ Use only publicly available data.

✔ Follow platform terms of service.

✔ Cross-reference data before drawing conclusions.

🚫 Don't:

✘ Attempt to access private accounts illegally.

✘ Scrape data in violation of API policies.

✘ Engage in doxxing or unauthorized tracking.

6. Conclusion: Mastering Instagram & TikTok OSINT

Instagram & TikTok contain valuable open-source intelligence, but their search restrictions require advanced methods.

🔍 Key Takeaways:

✅ Google dorking helps retrieve hidden posts.

✅ Reverse image search uncovers linked content.

✅ Geo-tracking finds posts from specific locations.

✅ Automation tools speed up investigations.

9.5 Finding Deleted & Archived Social Media Content

Social media users delete posts for various reasons—whether it's to hide past statements, cover up evidence, or simply clean up their profiles. However, deleted doesn't always mean gone. In OSINT (Open-Source Intelligence), retrieving deleted content can be crucial for tracking digital footprints, uncovering evidence, and verifying claims.

This chapter explores methods and tools for retrieving deleted, archived, or cached social media content across platforms like Instagram, TikTok, Facebook, Twitter, and YouTube.

1. Understanding How Social Media Deletion Works

When a user deletes a post, what actually happens?

✓ **Soft Deletion**: The content is no longer visible, but it may still exist in cached copies, archives, or backups.

✓ **Hard Deletion**: The content is removed permanently from the platform's database (rare, but possible).

✓ **Third-Party Copies**: Other users may have saved, reposted, or screenshotted the content.

💡 **OSINT Opportunity**: Even if content is deleted, traces may still exist in search engines, web archives, cached pages, and automated backups.

2. Google Cache & Search Engine Archives

Search engines like Google, Bing, and Yandex store temporary snapshots of web pages, which can be retrieved even after deletion.

🔍 How to View Cached Social Media Pages

✓ Google Cache:

Use the following URL format:

- cache:instagram.com/username
- cache:tiktok.com/@username

Alternatively, search:

- site:twitter.com/username "deleted tweet"

✓ Bing Cache:

Similar to Google, Bing also stores cached versions. Click the downward arrow next to a search result, then select Cached Page.

✓ Yandex Cache:

Yandex often retains cached images and videos for longer than Google.

💡 **Example Use Case**: If an Instagram influencer deletes a controversial post, you may still find it in Google Cache for a short time.

3. The Wayback Machine (Archive.org) & Social Media Archives

The Wayback Machine (Archive.org) is one of the most powerful tools for retrieving deleted content, storing snapshots of websites over time.

🔍 How to Find Deleted Social Media Posts on Archive.org

- Visit https://web.archive.org.
- Enter the URL of the social media profile or post.

- https://www.instagram.com/username
- https://twitter.com/username

- Browse the archived snapshots to see past versions.

💡 Example: If a politician deletes a controversial tweet, you may find older versions stored on Wayback Machine.

🚫 Limitations:

✘ Archive.org does not automatically save every post.

✘ Some sites block the Wayback Machine from archiving their content (e.g., Facebook).

Alternative Social Media Archives

✓ **archive.ph** – Saves permanent snapshots of web pages.

✓ **Politwoops** – Tracks deleted tweets from politicians.

✓ **Unddit** – Recovers deleted Reddit comments.

4. Screenshots, Reposts & Third-Party Archives

Even if official sources delete content, users often take screenshots, share copies, or discuss it elsewhere.

🔍 Where to Look for Reposted or Screenshotted Content

✓ **Reverse Image Search**: If a post was deleted, someone may have screenshotted it and shared it elsewhere. Use:

✅ **Google Lens** (Google Images)
✅ **Yandex Reverse Image Search** (Yandex Images)
✅ **PimEyes** (for facial recognition)

✓ Social Media Archives & Forums:

Some platforms specialize in tracking deleted content:

✅ **r/DataHoarder (Reddit)** – Users archive deleted social media posts.
✅ **Wayback Machine Twitter Bot (@wayback_exe)** – Tracks deleted tweets.
✅ **Telegram Groups** – Some groups track deleted Instagram and TikTok content.

💡 Example: If a TikTok influencer deletes a controversial video, search reverse image tools or Reddit archives to find saved copies.

5. Recovering Deleted YouTube, Instagram & TikTok Videos

5.1 Finding Deleted YouTube Videos

Even if a YouTube video is deleted, traces of it can still exist.

✔ Search YouTube's API for Video Titles:

Even if a video is deleted, the title and metadata may remain in YouTube's database.

✔ Find Video Links in Archive.org or Google Cache:

- site:youtube.com "deleted video"

✔ Use Third-Party Video Archives:

✅ **Yout.com** – Download cached copies of videos.
✅ **Huffduffer** – Saves podcast & video links.

💡 Example: If a whistleblower uploads a video and later deletes it, check Archive.org or video archives.

5.2 Finding Deleted Instagram & TikTok Videos

Instagram and TikTok do not store deleted videos publicly, but you can still recover them:

✔ Check Video Previews in Google Search:

- site:tiktok.com "@username" "deleted"

✔ Look for Reposts on Other Platforms:

✅ TikTok videos are often reposted on YouTube Shorts, Twitter, or Instagram Reels.

✅ Instagram videos may be shared on Reddit or Telegram.

✔ **Use Third-Party Video Downloaders:**

✅ **4K Video Downloader** – Downloads Instagram & TikTok videos.
✅ **SnapTik** – Saves TikTok videos before they disappear.

💡 **Example**: If a TikTok influencer deletes a viral video, search YouTube Shorts & Instagram Reels for reuploads.

6. Automation & Scripting for Tracking Deleted Content

Since deleted content is time-sensitive, automation is key for tracking changes.

6.1 Using OSINT Tools for Automated Archiving

✔ **twarc (Twitter Archiver)** – Automates Twitter data collection.

✔ **Wayback Machine CLI** – Automates website snapshots.

✔ **Instaloader** – Downloads Instagram posts & stories.

✔ **youtube-dl** – Saves YouTube videos before they are deleted.

💡 **Example**: If monitoring a target's social media activity, set up automated scripts to archive posts before they are removed.

7. Ethical & Legal Considerations

✅ **DO:**

✔ Only use publicly available data.

✔ Archive content before it's deleted (not after unauthorized access).

✔ Respect platform terms of service.

🚫 **DON'T:**

✗ Attempt to hack or gain unauthorized access to private data.

✗ Share personal or sensitive deleted content without ethical justification.

✗ Violate data protection laws (GDPR, CCPA, etc.).

8. Conclusion: Mastering Deleted Content Retrieval for OSINT

Deleted content is not always gone forever—traces can be found in cached pages, archives, search engine snapshots, third-party reposts, and automated backups.

🔍 **Key Takeaways:**

✅ Google Cache & Archive.org store past versions of web pages.

✅ Reverse image search finds reposted images & screenshots.

✅ Social media archives track deleted tweets, posts, and videos.

✅ Automation tools help archive data before it disappears.

9.6 Case Study: Identifying Fake Social Media Accounts Through Search

Fake social media accounts are used for a variety of purposes, including disinformation campaigns, fraud, impersonation, cyberstalking, and intelligence gathering. OSINT investigators often need to identify fake profiles to uncover networks of bot accounts, sock puppets, and coordinated influence operations.

In this case study, we'll walk through a realistic scenario where an OSINT analyst investigates a suspected fake Twitter (X) account using search techniques, metadata analysis, and cross-referencing tools.

1. The Investigation Begins: Spotting Suspicious Social Media Behavior

A cybersecurity researcher receives a tip about a Twitter account spreading false information about a recent data breach. The account, @DataLeaks_2025, claims to have insider knowledge but lacks credibility.

Red Flags of Fake Accounts:

✓ **Recent Creation Date** – The account was created in the past few months.

✓ **Low Engagement, High Activity** – Tweets often, but has few replies or likes.

✓ **Anonymous Profile Details** – No real name, no verifiable bio, and a generic profile picture.

✓ **Follower/Friend Pattern** – Follows many accounts but has few followers.

✓ **Copy-Paste Content** – Tweets are copied from other sources or heavily use hashtags.

💡 **OSINT Goal**: Investigate @DataLeaks_2025 to determine if it's a fake account and uncover its possible connections.

2. Reverse Searching Profile Images & Avatars

Step 1: Checking for Stolen Profile Pictures

Many fake accounts use stock images, AI-generated faces (Deepfake), or stolen profile pictures from real people.

✓ **Google Reverse Image Search** (Google Lens)

✓ **Yandex Reverse Image Search** (Yandex Images)

✓ **PimEyes** – Facial recognition for finding duplicate images.

✓ **TinEye** – Checks if an image exists elsewhere online.

💡 **Findings**: The profile picture of @DataLeaks_2025 appears in a stock photo website, suggesting it's not an authentic personal image.

3. Cross-Referencing Usernames & Email Handles

Step 2: Checking for Other Accounts Using the Same Username

People often reuse usernames across different platforms. Searching for @DataLeaks_2025 elsewhere can help uncover linked accounts.

✓ Google Search:

- "DataLeaks_2025" site:instagram.com
- "DataLeaks_2025" site:linkedin.com
- "DataLeaks_2025" site:github.com

✔ **Username Search Tools:**

✅ **WhatsMyName** – Finds accounts linked to a username.
✅ **Namechk** – Checks username availability across platforms.
✅ **Social Searcher** – Tracks social media activity.

💡 **Findings**: The username DataLeaks_2025 also appears on a Reddit account discussing hacking tools, suggesting a possible link.

4. Analyzing Metadata & Account Creation Details

Step 3: Checking Account Metadata

Social media accounts contain hidden metadata that can reveal useful clues.

✔ **Twitter/X OSINT Tools:**

✅ **Tinfoleak** – Extracts metadata from Twitter accounts.
✅ **Twitonomy** – Analyzes tweet patterns, mentions & geolocation.
✅ **TweetBeaver** – Checks if the account follows suspicious networks.

💡 **Findings**: @DataLeaks_2025 was created two months ago, tweets daily about hacking leaks, and follows other suspicious accounts with similar names.

5. Investigating Connections & Followers

Step 4: Looking at Who They Follow & Interact With

Fake accounts often operate in networks, following similar accounts to create the illusion of credibility.

✔ **Follower Analysis:**

✅ **Followerwonk** – Identifies unusual follower patterns.

✅ **Botometer** – Detects bots & fake Twitter accounts.

💡 **Findings**: The account mainly follows other fake-looking accounts that post similar content, suggesting a bot network.

6. Checking for Archived & Deleted Content

Step 5: Searching for Deleted Tweets or Past Versions

Even if an account deletes tweets or changes its bio, older versions may still exist.

✓ **Wayback Machine**: https://web.archive.org

✓ **Google Cache**: cache:twitter.com/DataLeaks_2025

✓ **Politwoops**: Tracks deleted tweets from politicians.

💡 **Findings**: The user previously claimed to work in cybersecurity but later deleted the tweet, raising credibility concerns.

7. Confirming a Fake Account: Key Findings

After applying OSINT techniques, the investigation concludes that @DataLeaks_2025 is likely a fake account due to:

✓ Stock photo profile picture (reverse image search).

✓ Username appears on hacking-related forums (cross-referencing).

✓ Newly created account with low engagement (metadata analysis).

✓ Bot-like activity & network of similar fake accounts (follower analysis).

✓ Deleted past tweets revealing inconsistent claims (archived content).

Possible Explanations:

1☐ A bot account created to spread disinformation.

2☐ A sock puppet account used by a real person to mislead others.

3☐ A fake account set up for phishing or social engineering.

8. Next Steps: How to Report or Track Fake Accounts

Option 1: Reporting the Account

✔ If the fake account is impersonating someone, spreading false information, or engaging in fraud, report it to the platform.

✔ Twitter, Facebook, and Instagram have reporting features for fake accounts.

Option 2: Monitoring for Further Activity

✔ Use OSINT automation tools (e.g., Python scripts, API monitoring) to track new activity.

✔ Archive content regularly using Wayback Machine & screenshots.

9. Ethical & Legal Considerations

✔ Always use publicly available information—do not attempt unauthorized access.

✔ Respect privacy laws (GDPR, CCPA) when investigating individuals.

✔ Use OSINT responsibly—don't engage in doxxing or harassment.

10. Conclusion: Mastering Fake Account Detection with OSINT

Fake social media accounts are widespread, but OSINT techniques allow investigators to uncover bot activity, sock puppets, and coordinated disinformation networks.

🔍 Key Takeaways:

✅ Reverse image search reveals stolen profile pictures.

✅ Username search connects accounts across platforms.

✅ Metadata analysis uncovers fake account behavior.

✅ Archived data provides past versions of profiles & deleted content.

✅ Follower patterns expose bot networks.

10. Automation & Scripting for Search

Manual searches can be time-consuming and inefficient, but automation and scripting can significantly enhance OSINT capabilities. By leveraging Python, Bash, or PowerShell, analysts can automate repetitive tasks such as data scraping, query generation, and result filtering. Tools like Selenium, Scrapy, and BeautifulSoup enable automated web searches, while APIs from Google, Bing, and social media platforms facilitate structured data extraction. Additionally, frameworks like SpiderFoot and Recon-ng streamline reconnaissance efforts by aggregating intelligence from multiple sources. By developing custom scripts and leveraging automation tools, OSINT practitioners can conduct large-scale searches, track evolving datasets, and uncover intelligence with greater speed and efficiency—all while ensuring compliance with ethical and legal boundaries.

10.1 Introduction to Search Automation & OSINT

Open-Source Intelligence (OSINT) investigations often require scanning multiple sources, collecting large datasets, and analyzing information efficiently. Manually searching through search engines, social media, databases, and forums can be time-consuming. Search automation allows investigators to speed up data collection, reduce errors, and enhance accuracy in intelligence gathering.

In this chapter, we introduce search automation techniques, including OSINT tools, scripting with Python, and APIs. By the end, you'll understand how to automate repetitive OSINT searches, extract valuable intelligence, and enhance your workflow.

1. The Benefits of OSINT Search Automation

Why Automate Search Processes?

✓ **Speed** – Automation can scan hundreds of sources in seconds, compared to manual searches.

✓ **Efficiency** – Reduces repetitive work, allowing analysts to focus on analysis rather than data collection.

✓ **Accuracy** – Scripts can eliminate human errors, ensuring consistent results across multiple searches.

✓ **Scalability** – Collects large datasets across multiple platforms, useful for tracking trends and patterns.

✓ **Anonymity & Safety** – Reduces manual exposure, especially when investigating dark web or sensitive topics.

Examples of Automated OSINT Use Cases

- Monitoring news, social media, and forums for emerging threats.
- Tracking leaked credentials and data breaches on the dark web.
- Gathering metadata and public records from multiple sources.
- Investigating online personas by scraping user profiles.
- Checking websites for exposed databases, login portals, and vulnerabilities.

💡 **Use Case**: A security researcher wants to track mentions of leaked corporate emails across Twitter, Pastebin, and breach databases. Instead of searching manually every day, they use a Python script with APIs to automate monitoring and receive alerts.

2. OSINT Tools for Automated Search

Before diving into coding, let's explore some existing OSINT automation tools that can simplify the process.

Search Engine Automation

✓ **Googler** – A command-line tool to run Google searches automatically.

✓ **SerpAPI** – An API that allows programmatic Google, Bing, and Yandex searches.

✓ **Scrapy** – A Python web scraping framework for automating custom search crawlers.

Social Media OSINT Tools

✓ **Twint** – Scrapes Twitter (X) without needing an API key.

✓ **Sherlock** – Finds usernames across hundreds of platforms.

✓ **Snscrape** – Extracts data from Twitter, Instagram, Reddit, and other social sites.

Dark Web & Data Leak Monitoring

✓ **OnionSearch** – Automates searches on Tor hidden services.

✓ **H8mail** – Finds leaked emails in breach databases.

✓ **Holehe** – Checks if an email is registered on social platforms.

💡 **Example**: A journalist investigating disinformation campaigns automates Twitter searches using Twint to track hashtags and mentions over time.

3. Automating OSINT with Python

Python is one of the most powerful languages for search automation. Below is a simple example of automating Google searches using the googlesearch-python library.

Step 1: Install the Required Library

- pip install googlesearch-python

Step 2: Run an Automated Google Search

from googlesearch import search

query = "site:pastebin.com leaked passwords"
results = search(query, num=5, stop=5, pause=2)

for result in results:
print(result)

🔍 This script searches Google for leaks on Pastebin and prints the first five results.

Expanding the Script: Save Results to a File

with open("osint_results.txt", "w") as file:
for result in results:
file.write(result + "\n")

💡 **Use Case**: A cybersecurity team automates Google dorking searches to find exposed documents daily and saves results for review.

4. Using APIs for OSINT Search Automation

APIs (Application Programming Interfaces) allow investigators to fetch data directly from search engines, social media, and databases without web scraping.

Example: Using SerpAPI to Automate Google Searches

Step 1: Get a Free SerpAPI Key

Sign up at https://serpapi.com/ and get an API key.

Step 2: Install the Python Library

- pip install google-search-results

Step 3: Automate Search with Python

```
from serpapi import GoogleSearch

params = {
    "q": "intitle:'index of' confidential",
    "api_key": "YOUR_SERPAPI_KEY"
}

search = GoogleSearch(params)
results = search.get_dict()

for result in results['organic_results']:
    print(result['link'])
```

🔍 This script automates a Google Dorking query to find open directories with confidential files.

💡 **Use Case**: A penetration tester automates Google searches for exposed FTP servers and files before a security audit.

5. Scraping Data for OSINT Investigations

Web scraping allows OSINT analysts to collect and store data from multiple sources. However, always check a website's robots.txt file to ensure compliance with ethical and legal guidelines.

✓ **OnionSearch** – Automates searches on Tor hidden services.

✓ **H8mail** – Finds leaked emails in breach databases.

✓ **Holehe** – Checks if an email is registered on social platforms.

💡 **Example**: A journalist investigating disinformation campaigns automates Twitter searches using Twint to track hashtags and mentions over time.

3. Automating OSINT with Python

Python is one of the most powerful languages for search automation. Below is a simple example of automating Google searches using the googlesearch-python library.

Step 1: Install the Required Library

- pip install googlesearch-python

Step 2: Run an Automated Google Search

```
from googlesearch import search

query = "site:pastebin.com leaked passwords"
results = search(query, num=5, stop=5, pause=2)

for result in results:
   print(result)
```

🔍 This script searches Google for leaks on Pastebin and prints the first five results.

Expanding the Script: Save Results to a File

```
with open("osint_results.txt", "w") as file:
   for result in results:
      file.write(result + "\n")
```

💡 **Use Case**: A cybersecurity team automates Google dorking searches to find exposed documents daily and saves results for review.

4. Using APIs for OSINT Search Automation

APIs (Application Programming Interfaces) allow investigators to fetch data directly from search engines, social media, and databases without web scraping.

Example: Using SerpAPI to Automate Google Searches

Step 1: Get a Free SerpAPI Key

Sign up at https://serpapi.com/ and get an API key.

Step 2: Install the Python Library

- pip install google-search-results

Step 3: Automate Search with Python

```
from serpapi import GoogleSearch

params = {
    "q": "intitle:'index of' confidential",
    "api_key": "YOUR_SERPAPI_KEY"
}

search = GoogleSearch(params)
results = search.get_dict()

for result in results['organic_results']:
    print(result['link'])
```

🔍 This script automates a Google Dorking query to find open directories with confidential files.

💡 **Use Case**: A penetration tester automates Google searches for exposed FTP servers and files before a security audit.

5. Scraping Data for OSINT Investigations

Web scraping allows OSINT analysts to collect and store data from multiple sources. However, always check a website's robots.txt file to ensure compliance with ethical and legal guidelines.

Simple Web Scraping with BeautifulSoup

```
import requests
from bs4 import BeautifulSoup

url = "https://example.com"
headers = {"User-Agent": "Mozilla/5.0"}

response = requests.get(url, headers=headers)
soup = BeautifulSoup(response.text, "html.parser")

for link in soup.find_all("a"):
    print(link.get("href"))
```

💡 **Use Case**: A researcher scrapes government archives for newly released declassified documents.

6. Automating Dark Web & Data Breach Monitoring

Using Tor & Onion Search Engines in Python

```
import requests

proxies = {
    "http": "socks5h://127.0.0.1:9050",
    "https": "socks5h://127.0.0.1:9050"
}

url = "http://onion-search-engine.onion"

response = requests.get(url, proxies=proxies)
print(response.text)
```

💡 **Use Case**: A security analyst monitors dark web forums for mentions of a company's leaked credentials.

7. Ethical & Legal Considerations in OSINT Automation

✓ **Respect Robots.txt**: Some websites prohibit scraping in their terms of service.

✓ **Avoid DDoS Attacks**: Scraping too frequently can overload a server, causing legal issues.

✓ **Anonymity & Privacy**: Use VPNs, proxies, and burner accounts when conducting sensitive OSINT searches.

✓ **Compliance**: Understand GDPR, CCPA, and data privacy laws before collecting personal data.

8. Conclusion: Mastering Search Automation for OSINT

Search automation is a powerful skill for OSINT analysts. Whether you're investigating threats, tracking disinformation, or monitoring data leaks, automating searches with Python, APIs, and OSINT tools can save time and improve accuracy.

Next Steps:

✅ Explore Python scripting for deeper automation.

✅ Experiment with OSINT APIs for Google, Twitter, and dark web searches.

✅ Learn how to store and analyze OSINT data effectively.

10.2 Using Google Custom Search for Advanced Queries

Google's default search interface provides powerful capabilities, but OSINT analysts often need more precision, control, and automation in their investigations. This is where Google Custom Search Engine (CSE) becomes invaluable. With CSE, you can:

✅ Focus searches on specific domains or datasets

✅ Apply advanced Google Dorking techniques efficiently

✅ Automate searches via APIs for large-scale OSINT operations

✅ Filter out irrelevant results for better intelligence gathering

In this chapter, we'll explore how to set up, configure, and use Google Custom Search Engine (CSE) to enhance OSINT investigations. By the end, you'll be able to build your own specialized OSINT search tools and automate queries for better intelligence collection.

1. What is Google Custom Search Engine (CSE)?

Google Custom Search Engine (CSE) is a search tool that allows users to create a customized version of Google Search, tailored to search specific websites, domains, or topics. This is especially useful for OSINT analysts who need to:

✓ Search only trusted intelligence sources (e.g., government, law enforcement, cybersecurity blogs)

✓ Exclude irrelevant results that clutter investigations

✓ Focus on deep indexing of specific sites (e.g., searching within Pastebin, GitHub, or government databases)

✓ Automate Google Dorking without manual input

2. Setting Up Your Own Google Custom Search Engine

To use CSE effectively, follow these steps to create your own Google-powered OSINT search engine:

Step 1: Create a Google Custom Search Engine

1☐ Go to Google CSE

2☐ Click "Get Started"

3☐ Under "Sites to Search", enter domains to focus on (e.g., site:pastebin.com, site:linkedin.com)

4☐ Click "Create", then go to Control Panel for customization

Step 2: Customize Your OSINT Search

In the CSE Control Panel, adjust the following settings:

✓ **Refine Results** – Set up filters and categories for better precision

✓ **Enable Advanced Search Operators** – Allow filetype:, site:, intitle: searches

✓ **Remove Ads** – If using for investigations, remove distractions

✓ **Enable JSON API** – Automate searches programmatically

3. Using Google Custom Search for OSINT Investigations

Example 1: Creating an OSINT Search Engine for Leaked Data

Suppose you want to track leaked data on sites like Pastebin, GitHub, and data breach forums. Your Google CSE should include:

- site:pastebin.com
- site:github.com
- site:raidforums.com
- site:twitter.com

💡 **Search Query:**

- site:pastebin.com "email password" OR "database leak"

🔍 **Use Case**: Investigators can quickly find leaked credentials, database dumps, and exposed API keys without manually browsing these sites.

Example 2: Searching Government and Legal Databases

A journalist investigating politicians' financial records or legal filings could create a CSE that searches:

- site:sec.gov
- site:opencorporates.com
- site:fec.gov
- site:justice.gov

💡 **Search Query:**

- site:sec.gov "fraud investigation"

🔍 **Use Case**: This helps filter financial misconduct records, corporate filings, and legal proceedings from official sources only.

Example 3: Investigating Social Media & Forums

For tracking social media discussions, disinformation campaigns, or extremist content, a Google CSE could focus on:

- site:facebook.com
- site:twitter.com
- site:reddit.com
- site:4chan.org
- site:tiktok.com

💡 **Search Query:**

- site:twitter.com "breaking news" OR "trending now"

🔍 **Use Case**: Analysts can monitor trends, track disinformation campaigns, and find deleted social media posts.

4. Automating Google Custom Search with APIs

For large-scale investigations, CSE supports API-based automation, allowing scripts to run queries and store results automatically.

Step 1: Get a Google CSE API Key

1️⃣ Go to Google Developers Console

2️⃣ Create a New Project

3️⃣ Enable Custom Search API

4️⃣ Get your API Key

Step 2: Install the Google Search API Library

pip install google-api-python-client

Step 3: Automate OSINT Search with Python

```
from googleapiclient.discovery import build

API_KEY = "YOUR_GOOGLE_CSE_API_KEY"
CSE_ID = "YOUR_CUSTOM_SEARCH_ENGINE_ID"

def google_custom_search(query):
    service = build("customsearch", "v1", developerKey=API_KEY)
    res = service.cse().list(q=query, cx=CSE_ID).execute()

    for item in res.get("items", []):
        print(f"Title: {item['title']}\nLink: {item['link']}\n")

# Example search for exposed documents
google_custom_search('filetype:xls "confidential" site:drive.google.com')
```

💡 **Use Case**: Automating Google Dorking to find exposed Excel files containing confidential data in Google Drive.

5. Google Custom Search vs. Regular Google Dorking

Feature	Google Search	Google Custom Search (CSE)
Searches all indexed web pages	☑	◌ (Limited to chosen sites)
Uses advanced operators (filetype, site, etc.)	☑	☑
API for automation	◌	☑
Focused results from specific domains	◌	☑
Removes irrelevant results	◌	☑

🚀 CSE is best for OSINT analysts who need highly focused, efficient searches without manually filtering through results.

6. Ethical & Legal Considerations for Google CSE in OSINT

✓ **Respect Google's Terms of Service** – Don't automate excessive searches without permission.

✓ **Avoid Unauthorized Data Access** – Never use CSE for hacking or illegal data retrieval.

✓ **Anonymity & OPSEC** – Use VPNs or Tor when conducting sensitive OSINT investigations.

✓ **Comply with GDPR & Data Privacy Laws** – Ensure searches align with ethical OSINT practices.

7. Conclusion: Powering OSINT Investigations with Custom Search

Google Custom Search is a powerful tool for OSINT professionals, allowing them to refine, automate, and scale intelligence gathering efficiently.

Next Steps:

✅ Set up your own OSINT CSE targeting leaked data, corporate records, or social media intelligence.

✅ Experiment with advanced search operators to extract hidden information.

✅ Integrate CSE API into Python scripts for automated intelligence gathering.

10.3 Python & APIs for Automating OSINT Searches

Open-source intelligence (OSINT) investigations often involve repetitive searches across multiple platforms, including Google, social media, people search engines, government databases, and the dark web. Manually running these searches can be time-consuming and inefficient.

🚀 *This is where Python and APIs come in. By leveraging scripting and automation, OSINT analysts can:*

✓ Run multiple search queries simultaneously

✓ Extract and structure search results automatically

✓ Monitor for new information in real time

✓ Reduce human errors in intelligence gathering

In this chapter, we'll explore:

✅ How to use APIs for OSINT searches

✅ Automating Google Dorking with Python

✅ Extracting social media data with APIs

✅ Monitoring leaks and breaches in real-time

1. Understanding APIs for OSINT

What is an API?

An Application Programming Interface (API) allows one system to communicate with another. Many search engines and platforms provide APIs to fetch search results programmatically instead of using a web browser.

Why Use APIs in OSINT?

✅ **Saves time** – Automate repetitive search queries
✅ **Access structured data** – API responses return machine-readable results (JSON, XML)
✅ **Avoid search personalization** – APIs bypass tracking and biased results
✅ **Monitor in real-time** – Set up automated alerts for new data

2. Automating Google Dorking with Python & API

Step 1: Get a Google Custom Search API Key

1️⃣ Go to Google Cloud Console

2️⃣ Create a New Project

3️⃣ Enable Custom Search API

4️⃣ Generate and copy your API Key

5️⃣ Create a Custom Search Engine (CSE) at Google CSE

Step 2: Install Google API Client

- pip install google-api-python-client

Step 3: Automate Google Searches with Python

```
from googleapiclient.discovery import build

API_KEY = "YOUR_GOOGLE_CSE_API_KEY"
CSE_ID = "YOUR_CUSTOM_SEARCH_ENGINE_ID"

def google_dorking(query):
    service = build("customsearch", "v1", developerKey=API_KEY)
    res = service.cse().list(q=query, cx=CSE_ID).execute()

    for item in res.get("items", []):
        print(f"Title: {item['title']}")
        print(f"URL: {item['link']}\n")

# Example: Finding Exposed PDFs with Sensitive Data
google_dorking('filetype:pdf "confidential" site:drive.google.com')
```

🔥 **Use Case**: This script automatically searches Google Drive for exposed PDFs containing sensitive data.

3. Automating Social Media OSINT with APIs

Social media platforms store a vast amount of intelligence, from personal details to criminal activity. Many platforms provide APIs to extract public data.

3.1 Twitter API for OSINT Monitoring

⬧ **Use Case**: Track hashtags, mentions, and geolocation data in real time.
⬧ **Example**: Monitor tweets mentioning a leaked database.

Step 1: Get Twitter API Access

1️⃣ Apply for a Twitter Developer Account at developer.twitter.com

2️⃣ Create an app and generate API keys

3️⃣ Install tweepy library

- pip install tweepy

Step 2: Automate Twitter Searches

```
import tweepy

# Twitter API Credentials
API_KEY = "YOUR_TWITTER_API_KEY"
API_SECRET = "YOUR_TWITTER_API_SECRET"
ACCESS_TOKEN = "YOUR_ACCESS_TOKEN"
ACCESS_SECRET = "YOUR_ACCESS_SECRET"

# Authenticate with Twitter API
auth = tweepy.OAuthHandler(API_KEY, API_SECRET)
auth.set_access_token(ACCESS_TOKEN, ACCESS_SECRET)
api = tweepy.API(auth)

# Search for Tweets Containing "Data Leak"
query = "data leak OR database breach"
tweets = tweepy.Cursor(api.search_tweets, q=query, lang="en").items(10)

for tweet in tweets:
    print(f"User: {tweet.user.screen_name}")
    print(f"Tweet: {tweet.text}\n")
```

🔥 **Use Case**: This script automatically collects tweets related to data leaks.

4. Automating Dark Web OSINT Searches

The dark web hosts illegal markets, hacker forums, and leaked data, but it's not indexed by standard search engines. Using Tor and Onion search engines, OSINT analysts can extract valuable intelligence.

4.1 Using Tor with Python for Anonymous Searching

Install the Tor client:

- sudo apt install tor

Install the requests library for browsing Tor hidden services:

- pip install requests[socks]

Example: Search for hacked databases on a dark web forum

import requests

proxies = {
 "http": "socks5h://127.0.0.1:9050",
 "https": "socks5h://127.0.0.1:9050",
}

url = "http://hackerforumxyz.onion/search?q=database+leak"

response = requests.get(url, proxies=proxies)
print(response.text)

🔥 **Use Case**: This script searches dark web forums anonymously using Tor.

5. Monitoring Data Breaches with OSINT APIs

Have I Been Pwned (HIBP) API allows OSINT analysts to check if emails, passwords, or accounts have been leaked.

5.1 Using Have I Been Pwned API to Check for Leaked Emails

1☐ Get an API key from https://haveibeenpwned.com/API/v3
2☐ Install requests

* pip install requests

3☐ Run the following script:

import requests

API_KEY = "YOUR_HIBP_API_KEY"
email = "target@example.com"

headers = {"hibp-api-key": API_KEY, "User-Agent": "OSINT-Search"}
url = f"https://haveibeenpwned.com/api/v3/breachedaccount/{email}"

```
response = requests.get(url, headers=headers)

if response.status_code == 200:
    print(f"Leaked Data for {email}: {response.json()}")
else:
    print("No leaks found.")
```

🔥 **Use Case**: Quickly check if an email address has been compromised.

6. Ethical & Legal Considerations for OSINT Automation

✓ **Comply with API Terms of Service** – Many platforms restrict excessive automation.

✓ **Do Not Access Private Data** – Only search publicly available information.

✓ **Maintain Anonymity** – Use VPNs or Tor for sensitive OSINT investigations.

✓ **Respect Privacy Laws** – Avoid violating GDPR, CCPA, or other data protection laws.

7. Conclusion: Automating OSINT for Efficiency

By leveraging Python and APIs, OSINT analysts can scale intelligence gathering, track threats in real time, and uncover hidden data more efficiently.

✓ Automate Google Dorking to find sensitive files

✓ Monitor Twitter for disinformation and data leaks

✓ Search the dark web using Tor

✓ Track email breaches with OSINT APIs

10.4 Scraping Search Results for Large-Scale Investigations

Search engines and websites store a massive amount of valuable intelligence, but manually searching and extracting data can be inefficient. OSINT analysts often need to:

✓ Collect data from multiple search engines at scale

✓ Bypass search engine restrictions to extract large datasets

✅ Automate searches across different platforms

✅ Monitor changes and updates to search results

⚠ Ethical & Legal Considerations

Before scraping, consider:

✓ **Respect robots.txt** – Many websites define scraping rules.

✓ **Avoid violating Terms of Service** – Google, Bing, and other search engines limit automated queries.

✓ **Use ethical OSINT practices** – Scraping should focus on publicly available data.

✓ **Anonymity & OPSEC** – Use VPNs, proxies, or Tor when conducting sensitive investigations.

1. Understanding Web Scraping for OSINT

What is Web Scraping?

Web scraping is the automated extraction of information from web pages using tools like:

- ♦ **BeautifulSoup** – Parses HTML content
- ♦ **Selenium** – Interacts with dynamic websites
- ♦ **Scrapy** – A powerful scraping framework
- ♦ **Requests** – Fetches webpage content

Why Scrape Search Engines for OSINT?

✓ **Extract search results for analysis** (Google, Bing, Yandex, etc.)

✓ Monitor keywords, leaks, and discussions in real-time

✓ Find exposed databases, credentials, and documents

2. Scraping Google Search Results with Python

2.1 Using Google Search API (Safer, but Limited)

Google provides an official API for search, but it limits free usage.

Step 1: Install the Required Library

- pip install google-api-python-client

Step 2: Fetch Search Results

from googleapiclient.discovery import build

API_KEY = "YOUR_GOOGLE_API_KEY"
CSE_ID = "YOUR_CUSTOM_SEARCH_ENGINE_ID"

def google_search(query):
* service = build("customsearch", "v1", developerKey=API_KEY)*
* results = service.cse().list(q=query, cx=CSE_ID).execute()*

* for item in results.get("items", []):*
*   print(f"Title: {item['title']}\nURL: {item['link']}\n")*

 # Example: Find exposed login pages
google_search('inurl:admin login site:.com')

🔥 **Use Case**: This script finds exposed admin login pages using Google Dorking.

2.2 Scraping Google Without an API (Using SerpAPI)

Since Google blocks automated scraping, SerpAPI is a paid service that provides structured Google results.

Step 1: Install SerpAPI

- pip install google-search-results

Step 2: Extract Google Search Results

from serpapi import GoogleSearch

API_KEY = "YOUR_SERPAPI_KEY"

```
def search_google(query):
    params = {
        "q": query,
        "api_key": API_KEY
    }
    search = GoogleSearch(params)
    results = search.get_dict()

    for result in results.get("organic_results", []):
        print(f"Title: {result['title']}\nURL: {result['link']}\n")

# Example: Find leaked PDF documents
search_google('filetype:pdf "confidential" site:gov')
```

🔥 **Use Case**: Automate finding leaked government documents in Google results.

3. Scraping Bing & Yandex for OSINT

Google is not the only source of intelligence. Bing and Yandex often reveal different data.

3.1 Scraping Bing with Python

Step 1: Install Bing Search API Library

* pip install requests

Step 2: Use Bing Search API

```
import requests

API_KEY = "YOUR_BING_API_KEY"
query = "intitle:index.of private files"
url = f"https://api.bing.microsoft.com/v7.0/search?q={query}"

headers = {"Ocp-Apim-Subscription-Key": API_KEY}
response = requests.get(url, headers=headers)
results = response.json()

for item in results["webPages"]["value"]:
    print(f"Title: {item['name']}\nURL: {item['url']}\n")
```

🔥 Use Case: Search for open directories exposing private files on Bing.

4. Scraping Social Media Search Results

4.1 Twitter Search Scraping (Without API Access)

If you don't have API access, Selenium can extract Twitter search results.

Step 1: Install Selenium

- pip install selenium

Step 2: Automate Twitter Search Extraction

```
from selenium import webdriver
from selenium.webdriver.common.by import By
from selenium.webdriver.common.keys import Keys
import time

driver = webdriver.Chrome()
driver.get("https://twitter.com/search?q=database%20leak&src=typed_query")

time.sleep(5)  # Wait for page to load

tweets = driver.find_elements(By.CSS_SELECTOR, "article div[lang]")
for tweet in tweets:
    print(tweet.text)

driver.quit()
```

🔥 Use Case: Extract tweets mentioning "database leaks" for analysis.

5. Large-Scale OSINT Data Collection with Scrapy

For large-scale investigations, Scrapy is a robust web scraping framework.

5.1 Install Scrapy

- pip install scrapy

5.2 Create a Scraper for Pastebin

import scrapy

```
class PastebinSpider(scrapy.Spider):
    name = "pastebin"
    start_urls = ["https://pastebin.com/archive"]

    def parse(self, response):
        for link in response.css("table.maintable a::attr(href)").getall():
            yield {"URL": f"https://pastebin.com{link}"}
```

🔥 **Use Case**: Monitor newly posted pastes on Pastebin for leaked credentials.

6. Bypassing Anti-Scraping Protections

Search engines and websites block automated scraping using:

✗ **CAPTCHAs** – Google often displays CAPTCHAs to bots.
✗ **IP Rate Limiting** – Too many requests from the same IP get blocked.
✗ **JavaScript Rendering** – Some sites load content dynamically.

How to Bypass These Restrictions

✓ **Use Proxies & VPNs** – Rotate IPs to avoid detection.

✓ **Use Headless Browsers** – Selenium can interact with JavaScript-heavy sites.

✓ **Time Delays & Randomization** – Avoid sending requests too quickly.

✓ **Use Residential Proxies** – Looks like real user traffic.

Example: Rotating Proxies in Python

import requests

```
proxies = {
    "http": "http://user:pass@proxy1.com:8000",
    "https": "http://user:pass@proxy2.com:8000",
}
```

```
response = requests.get("https://www.google.com", proxies=proxies)
print(response.text)
```

🔥 **Use Case**: Prevent IP bans while scraping search engines.

7. Conclusion: Scaling OSINT with Automated Scraping

By automating search result extraction, OSINT analysts can:

✅ Uncover hidden intelligence efficiently

✅ Monitor search results over time

✅ Extract large-scale data for analysis

✅ Improve the accuracy and speed of investigations

Next Steps:

🚀 Build an OSINT data pipeline to store search results in databases.

🚀 Use machine learning to analyze patterns in search results.

🚀 Apply scraping to real-world investigations for threat intelligence.

10.5 Monitoring Search Results for Real-Time Intelligence

OSINT (Open-Source Intelligence) investigations often require continuous monitoring of search results. Instead of running one-time searches, analysts can automate real-time alerts to track:

◆ Breaking news & emerging threats
◆ Data leaks & breaches
◆ Targeted individuals & organizations
◆ Social media trends & discussions
◆ Changes in search engine results

By automating search monitoring, analysts can stay ahead of the curve in cybersecurity, corporate intelligence, law enforcement, and investigative journalism.

1. Setting Up Google Alerts for Automated Search Monitoring

Google Alerts is a free, simple tool to monitor search queries over time.

1.1 Creating a Google Alert

1️⃣ Go to Google Alerts
2️⃣ Enter your search query (e.g., "data leak" site:pastebin.com)
3️⃣ Click Show Options and set:

- **Frequency**: "As-it-happens" or "Daily"
- **Sources**: News, Blogs, Web, etc.
- **Language** & Region filters

4️⃣ Enter your email and click "Create Alert"

🔥 **Use Case**: Monitor mentions of your organization or a target's name in search results.

2. Advanced Monitoring with Google Dorks & Operators

Google Alerts supports advanced search operators for targeted intelligence gathering.

2.1 Examples of Google Dorking for Search Monitoring

✅ Track leaked credentials

- "password" OR "username" OR "login" site:pastebin.com OR site:github.com

✅ Monitor newly uploaded confidential PDFs

- filetype:pdf "confidential" OR "internal use only" site:gov

✅ Detect exposed databases

- inurl:phpmyadmin OR inurl:admin/login site:.com

🔥 **Use Case**: Set up Google Alerts with these queries to get notified of new leaks or breaches.

3. Automating Search Monitoring with Python

For real-time, large-scale monitoring, Python can be used to automate search result extraction and send alerts when new information appears.

3.1 Using Google Search API for Continuous Monitoring

Step 1: Install Required Libraries

- pip install google-api-python-client

Step 2: Python Script for Monitoring Search Results

```
from googleapiclient.discovery import build
import time

API_KEY = "YOUR_GOOGLE_API_KEY"
CSE_ID = "YOUR_CUSTOM_SEARCH_ENGINE_ID"

def google_monitor(query):
    service = build("customsearch", "v1", developerKey=API_KEY)

    while True:
        results = service.cse().list(q=query, cx=CSE_ID).execute()
        for item in results.get("items", []):
            print(f"New Result: {item['title']}\nURL: {item['link']}\n")

        time.sleep(3600)  # Check every hour

# Example: Monitor for new breached databases
google_monitor('inurl:"wp-config.php" site:github.com')
```

🔥 **Use Case**: Automatically scan for new breached credentials on GitHub.

4. Real-Time Monitoring with Twitter & Social Media

4.1 Using Twitter API for Search Monitoring

Social media is faster than traditional search engines for breaking news and intelligence.

Step 1: Install Tweepy (Python Twitter API)

- pip install tweepy

Step 2: Python Script for Real-Time Twitter Monitoring

```
import tweepy

API_KEY = "YOUR_TWITTER_API_KEY"
API_SECRET = "YOUR_TWITTER_API_SECRET"
ACCESS_TOKEN = "YOUR_ACCESS_TOKEN"
ACCESS_SECRET = "YOUR_ACCESS_SECRET"

auth = tweepy.OAuthHandler(API_KEY, API_SECRET)
auth.set_access_token(ACCESS_TOKEN, ACCESS_SECRET)
api = tweepy.API(auth)

class TwitterStreamListener(tweepy.StreamListener):
    def on_status(self, status):
        print(f"New Tweet: {status.text}")

stream_listener = TwitterStreamListener()
stream = tweepy.Stream(auth=api.auth, listener=stream_listener)
stream.filter(track=["data breach", "leak", "ransomware"], languages=["en"])
```

🔥 **Use Case**: Detect leaks and cyberattacks as soon as they are mentioned on Twitter.

5. Automating Dark Web Search Monitoring

5.1 Monitoring Dark Web Leaks with Onion Search Engines

Dark web search engines like Ahmia, OnionSearch, and Dark.fail can be monitored for OSINT.

Step 1: Install Tor Requests Library

- pip install requests[socks]

Step 2: Python Script for Monitoring Dark Web

import requests

TOR_PROXY = "socks5h://127.0.0.1:9050"
search_query = "database leak"

url = f"http://ahmia.fi/search/?q={search_query}"

session = requests.Session()
session.proxies = {"http": TOR_PROXY, "https": TOR_PROXY}
response = session.get(url)

print(response.text)

🔥 **Use Case**: Monitor leaked credentials or illicit sales on dark web marketplaces.

6. Using RSS Feeds for Search Monitoring

6.1 Setting Up RSS Feeds for OSINT

Many search engines, news sites, and social media platforms support RSS feeds for updates.

Examples of Useful RSS Feeds for OSINT

- ◈ **Google News Alerts** – https://news.google.com/rss/search?q=cyberattack
- ◈ **Pastebin Leaks** – https://pastebin.com/archive/rss
- ◈ **Reddit Discussions** – https://www.reddit.com/r/osint/.rss

🔥 **Use Case**: Use an RSS reader like Feedly or automate RSS monitoring with Python.

7. Automating Alerts & Notifications

Real-time OSINT monitoring is most effective when paired with alerts.

7.1 Sending Alerts via Email (Python)

import smtplib

```
def send_email(subject, message):
    sender = "youremail@gmail.com"
    receiver = "alertrecipient@gmail.com"
    password = "YOUR_EMAIL_PASSWORD"

    email_body = f"Subject: {subject}\n\n{message}"

    with smtplib.SMTP("smtp.gmail.com", 587) as server:
        server.starttls()
        server.login(sender, password)
        server.sendmail(sender, receiver, email_body)

send_email("New OSINT Alert", "A new leaked database has been found.")
```

🔥 **Use Case**: Send email alerts when new intelligence appears in search results.

8. Conclusion: Scaling OSINT with Automated Search Monitoring

By implementing real-time monitoring techniques, OSINT analysts can:

✓ Detect threats before they escalate

✓ Monitor data leaks, social media, and dark web markets

✓ Automate intelligence gathering for faster decision-making

✓ Improve cybersecurity, investigations, and corporate security

10.6 Ethical & Legal Issues in Automated Search OSINT

Open-source intelligence (OSINT) is a powerful tool for uncovering valuable information, but its use raises critical ethical and legal questions. Automating OSINT searches, especially using scripts, web scraping, and monitoring tools, introduces complex risks related to:

♦ Privacy laws & data protection regulations
♦ Terms of service violations (Google, Twitter, etc.)
♦ Unintentional surveillance & mass data collection

- ◆ Cybercrime laws & unauthorized access
- ◆ Misinformation & ethical responsibilities

As an OSINT analyst, it's crucial to understand the legal boundaries and follow ethical best practices to avoid legal consequences and ethical dilemmas.

1. Understanding Legal Boundaries in OSINT Automation

Different countries have varying laws on data collection, web scraping, and monitoring.

1.1 Key Legal Areas Affecting Automated OSINT Searches

📜 1. Privacy Laws (GDPR, CCPA, etc.)

- The General Data Protection Regulation (GDPR) in the EU and the California Consumer Privacy Act (CCPA) in the U.S. restrict the collection and processing of personal data.
- OSINT analysts must be cautious when collecting personally identifiable information (PII).

📜 2. Terms of Service (ToS) Violations

- Websites like Google, Facebook, LinkedIn, and Twitter have strict ToS policies prohibiting automated data collection (scraping, bot searches, API abuse, etc.).
- Bypassing ToS with automation can lead to legal action or account bans.

📜 3. Computer Fraud and Abuse Act (CFAA) – U.S.

- The CFAA criminalizes "unauthorized access" to computer systems, including scraping private databases or bypassing access controls.
- **Example**: Scraping hidden LinkedIn profiles using automation could be considered unauthorized access.

📜 4. European E-Privacy Directive

- This law protects metadata and online communications, making automated monitoring of emails, cookies, or metadata legally complex.

📜 5. Anti-Cybercrime Laws (Hacking, Unauthorized Access, etc.)

- Many countries have laws against searching for exposed credentials or database breaches.
- **Example**: Searching for leaked credentials using Google Dorks could be interpreted as "intent to commit cybercrime."

🔥 **Key Takeaway**: Always check local laws, website ToS, and data protection rules before automating OSINT searches.

2. Ethical Challenges in Automated OSINT

Even if something is legal, it may still be ethically questionable. OSINT automation must be used responsibly to avoid harm.

2.1 Ethical Issues in OSINT Automation

⚠️ 1. Privacy Violations & Mass Surveillance

- Automated OSINT tools can be misused for mass data collection, leading to privacy breaches.
- **Example**: Continuously scraping social media profiles of non-public figures could be considered stalking or harassment.

⚠️ 2. Weaponizing OSINT for Malicious Purposes

- OSINT tools can be used for doxxing, cyberstalking, or corporate espionage.
- **Example**: Automating a script to track activists or journalists could be an abuse of OSINT techniques.

⚠️ 3. Misinformation & False Positives

- Automated search monitoring may pick up false information that, if misinterpreted, could cause reputational damage.
- Analysts should always verify sources manually before acting on automated results.

⚠️ 4. Ethical Scraping vs. Malicious Scraping

- Web scraping can be ethical when used for public interest research, but scraping private or sensitive data is a gray area.

- **Best Practice**: Respect robots.txt files and use APIs where available.

⚠️ 5. Consent & Transparency Issues

- **Collecting data without consent**—especially from individuals—raises ethical concerns.
- **Example**: Tracking employees or individuals without informing them can violate ethical OSINT guidelines.

🔥 **Key Takeaway**: Ethical OSINT practitioners set boundaries, focus on public data, and ensure they are not causing harm with their automation techniques.

3. Best Practices for Legal & Ethical OSINT Automation

To stay compliant and ethical, follow these best practices:

✅ 1. Follow Website Terms of Service

- Before automating searches, check the website's ToS for restrictions on scraping and API usage.
- **Example**: Instead of scraping Twitter, use the Twitter API legally.

✅ 2. Use Publicly Available & Open Data Sources

- Focus on public records, government data, and open-access databases.
- **Example**: Monitoring government business filings is legal, but scraping private HR records is not.

✅ 3. Avoid Collecting Personally Identifiable Information (PII)

- Do not collect names, addresses, emails, or phone numbers unless legally permitted.
- **Example**: Extracting metadata from leaked PDFs is fine, but publishing private emails from that metadata is illegal.

✅ 4. Use APIs Instead of Web Scraping

- Many platforms provide legal API access (Google, Twitter, OpenCorporates, etc.).

- **Example**: Use the Google Custom Search API instead of scraping Google search results.

✅ 5. Implement Rate-Limiting & Responsible Automation

- Avoid spamming search engines or causing server overloads.
- **Example**: Set a 1-minute delay between automated queries to prevent abuse.

✅ 6. Verify Data & Avoid Spreading Misinformation

- Cross-check multiple sources before relying on automated search results.
- **Example**: A Twitter bot falsely detecting "data breaches" could lead to panic or misinformation.

✅ 7. Document & Justify OSINT Activities

- Keep logs and reports to justify why data was collected and how it was used.
- **Example**: If conducting OSINT for an investigation, document why automation was necessary.

✅ 8. Seek Legal Advice if Uncertain

If unsure about a method's legality, consult a legal expert before proceeding.

4. Real-World Examples of OSINT Automation Gone Wrong

📷 1. Clearview AI's Illegal Facial Recognition Scraping

Clearview AI scraped billions of social media images without consent, leading to global lawsuits.

📷 2. Cambridge Analytica & Data Harvesting Scandal

Facebook data was scraped without user consent and used for political influence, violating privacy laws.

📷 3. Automated Doxxing Bots on Telegram

OSINT tools were misused to automatically expose personal data on Telegram, causing serious privacy risks.

🔥 **Lesson**: OSINT automation should be handled with caution to avoid legal repercussions.

Conclusion: Balancing Automation, Ethics & Legality in OSINT

Automated search techniques enhance OSINT investigations, but they must be used responsibly. To ensure compliance:

✅ Understand local laws & privacy regulations

✅ Respect website ToS & avoid unauthorized access

✅ Use ethical OSINT practices & public data sources

✅ Validate & verify automated search results

✅ Avoid misuse for surveillance, doxxing, or misinformation

By following ethical and legal guidelines, OSINT analysts can use automation responsibly while avoiding legal trouble or ethical pitfalls.

11. Anonymity & Safe Searching for OSINT

Conducting OSINT investigations requires maintaining operational security (OPSEC) to avoid exposing one's identity, triggering alerts, or leaving digital footprints. Using VPNs, Tor, and secure proxies helps anonymize searches and mask IP addresses, preventing tracking by websites or adversaries. Private search engines like Startpage and DuckDuckGo reduce exposure to personalized tracking, while browser isolation tools like Tails OS and Whonix enhance security. Additionally, using virtual machines and disposable email addresses helps prevent linkability between searches and personal accounts. By implementing strong anonymity practices, OSINT analysts can gather intelligence effectively while minimizing risks of detection, legal issues, or unintended attribution.

11.1 The Risks of Search Engine Tracking in OSINT Investigations

Every time you perform an OSINT investigation using Google, Bing, or other search engines, you leave a digital footprint. These platforms track who you are, what you search for, and even where you're searching from. This tracking can create serious risks for OSINT practitioners, journalists, cybersecurity experts, and investigators.

Key Risks of Search Engine Tracking in OSINT:

◆ **Exposure of Your Identity** – Your searches can be linked back to you.
◆ **Search Personalization Bias** – Results may be skewed based on your past activity.
◆ **Compromised Operational Security (OPSEC)** – Targets may detect your investigations.
◆ **Legal & Privacy Concerns** – Your search activity may be logged, subpoenaed, or monitored.
◆ **Algorithm Manipulation** – Search engines may alter results based on tracking data.

Understanding these risks is critical for anyone conducting sensitive or anonymous OSINT investigations. Let's break down how search engine tracking works, what dangers it poses, and how to mitigate them.

1. How Search Engines Track Users

Search engines gather extensive data on users in multiple ways, including:

1.1 IP Address Logging

- Your IP address is recorded every time you perform a search.
- This reveals your approximate location, ISP, and device information.
- **Risk**: If you search for a target, your real IP could be logged.

1.2 Browser Fingerprinting

- Search engines collect data on your browser type, extensions, fonts, screen resolution, and more.
- Even with VPNs or incognito mode, fingerprinting can uniquely identify you.

1.3 Cookies & Tracking Scripts

- Persistent cookies track your searches over time.
- Third-party tracking scripts (Google Analytics, Facebook Pixel, etc.) track your activity across multiple websites.

1.4 Search History & Account Tracking

- If logged into Google, Bing, or Yahoo, your search history is linked to your account.
- Even after logging out, Google and other platforms may still track you.

1.5 Location-Based Search Tracking

- Even with location settings disabled, search engines infer your location via IP address, GPS, Wi-Fi networks, and cell towers.
- If an OSINT analyst repeatedly searches about a specific company, person, or place, it may reveal their interest in that target.

🔍 Example:

If you are investigating a criminal organization and using your personal Google account, your searches may be flagged, logged, or even monitored by authorities.

2. Risks of Search Engine Tracking in OSINT

2.1 Exposure of Your Identity & Intentions

- If you are not using OPSEC measures, your searches may reveal your identity to search engines, law enforcement, or even your target.
- **Example**: A journalist investigating corruption may become a target if their searches are traced.

2.2 Search Personalization Bias

- Google customizes results based on your previous searches, location, and profile data.
- This means you may not see the same results as someone searching from a different location or account.
- **Risk**: Investigators may miss critical data due to filtered search results.

2.3 Law Enforcement & Government Monitoring

- Search engine data can be subpoenaed, monitored, or shared with intelligence agencies.
- Example: Governments can demand search histories via National Security Letters (NSLs) or court orders.

2.4 Corporate Tracking & Data Sales

- Search engines sell user data to advertisers, which may expose OSINT professionals to malvertising, phishing, or surveillance campaigns.
- **Example**: Searching for breach data or hacking tools may trigger ads related to cybersecurity, alerting companies.

2.5 Detection by Search Engine Algorithms

- Excessive advanced search queries (Google Dorking, metadata searches, etc.) can flag an OSINT investigator as suspicious.
- Google, Bing, and Yandex may temporarily block your searches or show CAPTCHA challenges.
- **Example**: Using multiple Google Dorks in rapid succession may result in a 403 Forbidden error or temporary ban.

3. How to Minimize Search Engine Tracking Risks

To protect anonymity and improve search accuracy, OSINT professionals should implement the following countermeasures:

3.1 Use a VPN or Proxy

✅ VPNs (Virtual Private Networks) hide your real IP address.

✅ Proxies provide extra layers of anonymity, but free proxies can be unreliable.

✅ Tor Browser is useful for anonymized searching but may be blocked by some websites.

⚠ **Warning**: Google and Bing may flag VPN or Tor-based searches as suspicious. Using multiple VPN exit nodes can help.

3.2 Use Private Search Engines

- **DuckDuckGo** – No logs, no tracking, Google-level search results.
- **Startpage** – Google results without tracking.
- **Searx** – Open-source, customizable meta-search engine.

🚀 **Tip**: Instead of searching directly on Google, use Startpage.com, which fetches Google results anonymously.

3.3 Disable Search Engine Personalization

- Use Incognito Mode or Private Browsing.
- Clear cookies and cache regularly.
- Opt out of Google's personalized search settings in account preferences.

3.4 Use Different Browsers for OSINT & Personal Use

- Use one browser (e.g., Firefox) for OSINT and another (e.g., Chrome) for personal browsing.
- Use browser isolation to prevent cross-tracking.

3.5 Block Tracking & Fingerprinting

- Use browser extensions like Privacy Badger, uBlock Origin, and NoScript.

♦ Enable anti-fingerprinting settings in Firefox (about:config -> resistFingerprinting = true).

3.6 Rotate Search Engines & Locations

♦ Avoid using Google exclusively—alternate between Bing, Yandex, DuckDuckGo, and others.
♦ Change your VPN server location regularly to simulate different users.

3.7 Monitor & Control Your Digital Footprint

♦ Regularly review your Google My Activity page to delete search history.
♦ Use MyPermissions or Jumbo Privacy to manage what data Google, Bing, and Yahoo store about you.

4. Case Study: How Poor OPSEC Exposed an OSINT Investigator

● **Scenario**: A private investigator was researching a high-profile target using Google and LinkedIn without hiding their identity.

● **What Happened?**

- The investigator's search history was logged by Google.
- Their LinkedIn profile was automatically suggested to the target due to repeated profile visits.
- The target became aware of the investigation and took countermeasures, removing sensitive information from the internet.

🔥 **Lesson Learned**: Failing to use private search engines, VPNs, and OPSEC best practices can expose an OSINT operation before it even begins.

Conclusion: Search Engines are a Double-Edged Sword

Search engines are powerful OSINT tools, but they also track investigators, creating serious privacy and security risks. To conduct safe and effective OSINT investigations, always:

✅ Use VPNs, proxies, and privacy-focused search engines.

✅ Disable tracking, cookies, and personalization settings.

✅ Avoid linking searches to personal accounts or devices.

✅ Rotate search engines, devices, and browser profiles to reduce traceability.

By following these best practices, OSINT professionals can reduce their digital footprint, improve their search accuracy, and protect their investigations from exposure.

11.2 How to Avoid Fingerprinting & Search Bias

Every time you perform an OSINT search, your browser, device, and search engine settings leave behind a unique fingerprint that can be used to track you. Even if you use incognito mode, a VPN, or a privacy-focused search engine, fingerprinting techniques can still identify and bias your search results.

Fingerprinting is one of the biggest threats to OSINT practitioners because it can:

◆ Expose your real identity even when using anonymous tools.
◆ Skew search results based on your past behavior and location.
◆ Allow search engines and websites to detect and block your activities.

In this chapter, we'll explore how fingerprinting works, how it affects OSINT investigations, and how to bypass search bias to get clean, unbiased results.

1. Understanding Browser Fingerprinting in OSINT

1.1 What is Browser Fingerprinting?

Browser fingerprinting is a method used by search engines, websites, and advertisers to track users without cookies. Instead of relying on IP addresses or stored cookies, fingerprinting collects detailed data about your browser and device to create a unique identifier.

1.2 What Data is Collected in Fingerprinting?

Fingerprinting works by analyzing multiple unique factors from your setup, including:

- **Browser Information** – Type (Chrome, Firefox, Edge), version, and settings.
- **Operating System** – Windows, macOS, Linux, mobile, etc.
- **Screen Resolution & Color Depth** – Your display settings.
- **Installed Fonts & Plugins** – Unique combinations of fonts and extensions.
- **Time Zone & Language Settings** – Regional settings that can pinpoint location.
- **WebGL & Canvas Fingerprinting** – Tracks unique graphics rendering data.

Each of these elements, when combined, creates a unique fingerprint that can track you across multiple searches, even if you're using a VPN or private browsing.

1.3 How Fingerprinting Affects OSINT Investigations

OSINT professionals and researchers face two major risks from fingerprinting:

1. **Loss of Anonymity** – If a search engine or website detects that the same fingerprint is performing repeated searches on a specific target, it could flag or track the investigation.

2. **Search Bias** – Search engines may personalize results based on fingerprinted data, hiding certain information or showing only what the algorithm believes you want to see.

Example: If you're investigating a person or company while logged into a Google account, your results will be biased toward your past searches, location, and profile data.

2. How Search Engines Personalize & Bias Search Results

Search engines like Google, Bing, and Yandex do not provide neutral results. Instead, they personalize and filter search results based on:

- **Your Location** – Search engines prioritize local results.
- **Your Search History** – Past searches influence future results.
- **Your Click Behavior** – What you click on affects what is shown in future searches.
- **Your Device & Browser** – Mobile vs. desktop searches return different results.
- **Your Google Account (if logged in)** – Personalized search is enabled by default.

2.1 Why Search Bias is a Problem for OSINT

- **Misses Important Data** – Personalized search hides alternative perspectives.

◆ **Prevents True Anonymity** – If Google knows who you are, your search results are no longer neutral.

◆ **Alters Investigative Outcomes** – Different users may get different results for the same query.

Example: Searching for "cybercrime forums" in the U.S. will show very different results than searching from Russia or China, even with the same keywords.

3. How to Avoid Fingerprinting & Search Bias

To bypass tracking, OSINT investigators need to control their digital footprint. Below are practical steps to reduce fingerprinting and search bias.

3.1 Use Privacy-Focused Browsers

◆ **Firefox (with Enhanced Privacy Settings)** – Best mainstream privacy browser.

◆ **Brave Browser** – Blocks fingerprinting and ads by default.

◆ **Tor Browser** – Excellent for anonymity but slow and flagged on some sites.

✅ Firefox Tweaks for OSINT

Disable WebRTC – Prevents IP leaks even when using a VPN.

- Type about:config in the Firefox address bar.
- Search for media.peerconnection.enabled and set it to false.

Enable Anti-Fingerprinting Mode

- Type about:config and search for privacy.resistFingerprinting.
- Set it to true.

Disable Telemetry (Tracking by Mozilla)

- Go to Settings → Privacy & Security → Disable all telemetry options.

3.2 Use Search Engines That Do Not Track You

Instead of Google, try:

- **Startpage** – Provides Google results without tracking.
- **DuckDuckGo** – No personalized tracking, but still limited for OSINT.
- **Searx** – Open-source search engine with multiple search sources.
- **Brave Search** – Independent search engine with no Google tracking.

🚀 **Pro Tip**: Use multiple search engines for the same query to compare unbiased results.

3.3 Use VPNs & Proxies to Mask IP Addresses

- **VPNs (NordVPN, ProtonVPN, Mullvad)** – Encrypt and anonymize traffic.
- **Tor Network** – Provides the best anonymity but can slow down searches.
- **Proxy Chains** – Rotates IP addresses for multiple search requests.

✅ **Best Practice**: Switch VPN locations periodically to prevent tracking.

3.4 Spoof Browser Fingerprinting with Extensions

Use browser extensions to mask your fingerprint:

- **CanvasBlocker** – Prevents Canvas fingerprinting.
- **Chameleon (for Firefox)** – Randomizes browser fingerprints.
- **User-Agent Switcher** – Changes browser identity to evade tracking.

🚀 **Pro Tip**: Combine fingerprint spoofing with a VPN for stronger anonymity.

3.5 Search in Incognito Mode (But With Caution)

Incognito mode prevents cookies but does NOT block fingerprinting.

- Use incognito mode only with other privacy tools (VPN, Startpage, Brave).
- Manually clear cache and cookies after each search session.

🚀 **Pro Tip:** Open multiple incognito windows with different VPN locations to compare search variations.

3.6 Avoid Search Bias by Changing Your Query Structure

◆ **Use different wording & synonyms** – e.g., instead of "data breach," try "leaked database."

◆ **Search in different languages** – Some results are hidden in English but visible in other languages.

◆ **Change the order of search terms** – A simple word swap can bypass search bias.

Example:

- "CEO email leaks site:pastebin.com" (may be blocked)
- "Company executive emails exposed filetype:txt" (may return different results)

🔎 **Pro Tip:** Rotate search queries across different search engines to avoid being flagged for repeated searches.

Conclusion: Stay Invisible, Stay Unbiased

OSINT professionals must actively fight against search engine tracking and bias. By using privacy-focused browsers, alternative search engines, VPNs, and fingerprinting countermeasures, you can maintain anonymity and get cleaner, more accurate search results.

◆ **Key Takeaways:**

✔ Use privacy-focused search engines (Startpage, Searx, Brave).

✔ Disable fingerprinting in Firefox or use anti-tracking extensions.

✔ Rotate VPN locations and use multiple browsers for OSINT.

✔ Change search query structures to avoid algorithmic bias.

By implementing these strategies, OSINT investigators can bypass search engine manipulation, protect their anonymity, and access more reliable intelligence.

11.3 Using VPNs, Proxies & Tor for Anonymous Searching

In OSINT investigations, maintaining anonymity is crucial. Whether you're searching for sensitive information, tracking a person of interest, or investigating cyber threats, exposing your real identity can lead to detection, retaliation, or even legal consequences.

Search engines, websites, and online services actively log your IP address, browser details, location, and search history. Without proper anonymity measures, you risk:

- ◆ **Being tracked by the target** – Your queries may alert individuals or organizations.
- ◆ **Search bias** – Your results may be tailored based on your location and past searches.
- ◆ **Legal & ethical concerns** – Some investigations require extra privacy precautions.

This chapter explores VPNs, proxies, and Tor, three powerful tools for anonymous OSINT searching. Each has strengths and weaknesses, and understanding when and how to use them is key to staying undetected.

1. Understanding VPNs: Encrypting & Masking Your Connection

1.1 What is a VPN?

A Virtual Private Network (VPN) creates a secure, encrypted tunnel between your device and a remote server. This hides your real IP address and makes your online activities appear as if they originate from another location.

1.2 How VPNs Improve OSINT Anonymity

✓ **Hides Your Real IP Address** – Websites and search engines see only the VPN server's IP.
✓ **Encrypts Your Internet Traffic** – Prevents ISPs and network admins from logging activity.
✓ **Bypasses Geo-Restrictions** – Lets you access region-specific search results and content.
✓ **Reduces Tracking Risks** – Makes it harder for targets to detect your investigations.

1.3 Best VPNs for OSINT Investigations

- ◆ **ProtonVPN** – Strong privacy policies, no logs, and free plan available.
- ◆ **Mullvad** – Excellent anonymity, allows cash payments for accounts.
- ◆ **NordVPN** – Large server network, double VPN option for extra security.
- ◆ **IVPN** – Privacy-focused, no-logs policy, and supports multi-hop connections.

🚀 **Pro Tip**: Always choose a no-logs VPN based in a country with strong privacy laws (not the US, UK, or Australia).

2. Using Proxies for OSINT Searches

2.1 What is a Proxy?

A proxy server acts as an intermediary between your device and the internet. Instead of connecting directly to a website, your request goes through the proxy, which changes your IP address.

2.2 Differences Between VPNs & Proxies

Feature	VPN	Proxy
Encryption	☑ Yes	✕ No
Hides IP Address	☑ Yes	☑ Yes
Anonymity Level	◍ Strong	Moderate
Speed	Slower	◍ Faster
Best Use Case	Secure browsing & OSINT	Quick IP masking & automation

2.3 Types of Proxies for OSINT

◆ **HTTP Proxies** – Used for specific web-based searches but do not encrypt data.
◆ **SOCKS5 Proxies** – More secure, works for all internet traffic, including search engines.
◆ **Residential Proxies** – Appear as normal user connections, less likely to be blocked.

🔧 **Pro Tip**: Use rotating proxies (like those from Smartproxy or Oxylabs) for large-scale data gathering and scraping.

3. Using Tor for High-Anonymity Searches

3.1 What is Tor?

Tor (The Onion Router) is a decentralized, multi-layered network that routes your traffic through multiple encrypted relays before reaching the final destination.

3.2 Why Use Tor for OSINT?

✓ **Strongest anonymity** – Each relay encrypts and changes your IP.

✅ **Access to the dark web** – Allows searches on .onion sites.
✅ **No centralized logging** – Unlike VPNs, Tor does not rely on a single provider.

3.3 How to Use Tor Safely for OSINT

◆ **Download the Official Tor Browser** – Avoid third-party versions.
◆ **Disable JavaScript & Plugins** – Prevents tracking and browser fingerprinting.
◆ **Do Not Log Into Personal Accounts** – Never use personal emails or logins over Tor.
◆ **Combine Tor with a VPN for Extra Security** – Connect to a VPN before opening Tor.

🖋 **Pro Tip**: For high-risk investigations, use Tails OS, a secure, bootable operating system that forces all traffic through Tor.

4. Combining VPNs, Proxies & Tor for Maximum Anonymity

Each of these tools has advantages and disadvantages. To achieve maximum anonymity, OSINT professionals often combine multiple methods.

4.1 VPN + Proxy

◆ **Best for**: Automating searches, bypassing simple blocks, and scraping data.
◆ **How**: Connect to a VPN, then use a proxy for specific search tasks.

4.2 VPN + Tor (Tor over VPN)

◆ **Best for**: Hiding Tor usage from ISPs and accessing dark web searches securely.
◆ **How**: Connect to a VPN first, then open the Tor Browser.

4.3 Proxy + Tor

◆ **Best for**: Masking your entry into the Tor network.
◆ **How**: Set up a proxy before connecting to Tor.

🖋 **Pro Tip**: Do not use free proxies or free VPNs—they often log your data and sell it.

5. Best Practices for Anonymous Searching in OSINT

✅ Use a Dedicated Machine for OSINT Searches

- Preferably a virtual machine (VM) or a separate burner laptop.
- Consider using Tails OS or Whonix for added anonymity.

✅ Change Your Digital Fingerprint

- Use Firefox with anti-tracking settings or a privacy-focused browser.
- Use tools like CanvasBlocker and User-Agent Switchers to prevent fingerprinting.

✅ Use Multiple Search Engines

- Google personalizes searches; try Startpage, DuckDuckGo, Searx, or Brave Search.
- Use Bing, Yandex, and Baidu for non-Western results.

✅ Avoid Logging Into Any Accounts

- Never sign into Google, Facebook, or other personal accounts while performing OSINT searches.

✅ Monitor Your Own IP Address

- Check what websites see using tools like ipleak.net or browserleaks.com.

✅ Rotate VPN Servers & IPs Regularly

- Avoid using the same VPN server for long-term investigations.
- Conclusion: Stay Hidden, Stay Safe

Anonymity is not just a luxury—it's a necessity for OSINT professionals. Using VPNs, proxies, and Tor correctly can protect your identity, prevent detection, and improve search results.

◆ Key Takeaways:

✅ VPNs offer strong encryption and IP masking but require trust in the provider.

✅ Proxies are fast and lightweight but lack encryption.

✓ Tor provides the highest anonymity but is slower and flagged on some sites.

✓ Combining tools (VPN + Tor, Proxy + Tor) provides stronger anonymity.

✓ Use privacy browsers, search engine alternatives, and fingerprint evasion tools.

By implementing these strategies, OSINT investigators can conduct anonymous searches with minimal risk.

11.4 Private Browsers & Search Engines for Secure OSINT

When conducting OSINT investigations, privacy is just as important as the accuracy of the data you collect. Traditional browsers like Google Chrome, Microsoft Edge, and Safari actively track user behavior, log search queries, and personalize search results—all of which can compromise your anonymity.

Additionally, mainstream search engines such as Google and Bing store your IP address, cookies, and search history, making it easy for them to profile and track your online activities. This creates two major risks for OSINT professionals:

Exposure of your identity – Your target may detect your searches.

Search engine bias – Personalized search results can limit the intelligence you collect.

This chapter explores private browsers and search engines that help OSINT analysts stay anonymous, bypass censorship, and access unbiased information.

1. Choosing the Right Private Browser for OSINT

1.1 Why Mainstream Browsers Are a Risk

Most popular browsers collect vast amounts of data for advertising and user tracking. Even in "Incognito Mode" or "Private Browsing," they still store IP addresses, DNS requests, and browsing patterns.

● **Browsers to Avoid for OSINT:**

- **Google Chrome** – Heavy tracking, syncs searches to Google.
- **Microsoft Edge** – Connected to Windows telemetry and Microsoft services.

- **Safari** – Logs user data and reports browsing activity to Apple.

1.2 Best Privacy-Focused Browsers for OSINT

✅ Firefox (Hardened for Privacy)

- Open-source, customizable, and privacy-friendly.
- Can be modified to block tracking, fingerprinting, and telemetry.

Enhance privacy with:

- **uBlock Origin** (blocks ads and trackers).
- **NoScript** (prevents malicious scripts from running).
- **CanvasBlocker** (prevents fingerprinting).

✅ Tor Browser (For Maximum Anonymity)

- Routes traffic through multiple encrypted relays.
- Prevents websites from tracking or logging user activity.
- Accesses .onion sites on the dark web.

Best for: High-anonymity OSINT searches where extreme privacy is needed.

✅ Brave Browser

- Built-in ad and tracker blocking.
- Supports Tor integration in private windows.

Best for: General OSINT research without full Tor anonymity.

✅ LibreWolf

- Hardened, privacy-focused fork of Firefox.
- No telemetry, no Google Safe Browsing, no auto-updates.

Best for: Researchers needing an ultra-private Firefox alternative.

📎 **Pro Tip**: Use a separate browser profile or dedicated browser for OSINT research to keep investigative searches isolated from personal activity.

2. Using Private Search Engines for OSINT

2.1 Why Google is a Problem for OSINT

While Google is powerful, it comes with serious privacy risks:

- Tracks and logs search queries tied to IP addresses.
- Personalizes search results, biasing investigations.
- Censors results, especially in politically sensitive topics.
- Filters out certain datasets that may be useful for OSINT.

2.2 Best Private Search Engines for OSINT Investigations

✅ Startpage (Google Results Without Tracking)

- Uses Google search index but removes tracking.
- Provides unbiased results without Google's personalization.
- Offers anonymous search via a proxy browsing feature.

Best for: Getting Google-quality results while staying private.

✅ DuckDuckGo

- Does not track or store searches.
- Provides uncensored results from multiple sources.
- Lacks advanced Google operators but useful for general OSINT.

Best for: Quick anonymous searches without tracking.

✅ Searx (Self-Hosted Meta-Search Engine)

- Aggregates results from multiple search engines.
- Can be self-hosted for complete control.
- Customizable to filter sources and focus on OSINT.

Best for: Researchers who want to control their search sources.

✅ Brave Search

- Independent index (not relying on Google or Bing).
- No ads, tracking, or bias in results.

Best for: OSINT analysts wanting non-Google search independence.

🖋 **Pro Tip**: Rotate between different search engines to reduce bias and get comprehensive results.

3. Combining Browsers & Search Engines for Maximum Privacy

For maximum privacy, use a private browser and a private search engine together.

- ◆ **Basic Privacy Setup**: Brave Browser + Startpage
- ◆ **Advanced Privacy Setup**: Firefox (hardened) + Searx
- ◆ **High-Anonymity Setup**: Tor Browser + DuckDuckGo

🖋 **Pro Tip**: Change your user agent and clear cookies between searches to prevent fingerprinting.

4. Practical Techniques for Anonymous Searching

- ✿ **Use Private Mode** – Always browse in a private/incognito session.
- ✿ **Disable JavaScript** – Many tracking scripts rely on JavaScript to collect data.
- ✿ **Use a VPN** – Always combine private browsing with a VPN to hide your IP.
- ✿ **Rotate Search Engines** – Different engines index different content.
- ✿ **Check Search Result Variations** – Compare results from Google, Bing, Startpage, and Yandex for different perspectives.

5. Avoiding Search Engine Fingerprinting

Even when using private search engines, websites can fingerprint your browser based on:

- Screen resolution
- Installed plugins

- Fonts and system settings
- Browser headers

5.1 How to Prevent Fingerprinting in OSINT Investigations

✅ **Use Tor Browser** – Its uniform fingerprint makes users harder to track.

✅ **Modify User Agent** – Tools like User-Agent Switcher can disguise your browser.

✅ **Block WebRTC** – This prevents your real IP from leaking.

✅ **Use Privacy Extensions** – CanvasBlocker, Trace, and uBlock Origin help reduce fingerprinting risks.

🚀 **Pro Tip**: Test your fingerprint using coveryourtracks.eff.org to see how unique your browser appears.

6. Case Study: Using Private Search Tools for a Real OSINT Investigation

A cybercrime investigator was searching for leaked credentials related to a high-profile data breach. Using Google and Chrome, they found limited results because:

- Google filtered out hacked data references.
- Their search results were biased by their location and previous queries.

How They Used Private Tools to Improve OSINT Results:

1☐ Switched to a privacy-focused browser (LibreWolf) with a VPN.

2☐ Used Startpage instead of Google to avoid tracking.

3☐ Cross-checked results with Searx and DuckDuckGo for additional findings.

4☐ Used Tor Browser to access dark web search engines for deeper intelligence.

🔍 Results:

- Found unindexed breach data that was missing from Google.
- Avoided search tracking and profiling.
- Collected unbiased and unrestricted intelligence.

Conclusion: Search Smarter, Stay Hidden

◆ **Key Takeaways:**

✅ Mainstream browsers and search engines track your activity—avoid them!

✅ Use privacy-focused browsers like Firefox (hardened), Brave, Tor, or LibreWolf.

✅ Switch to private search engines like Startpage, Searx, DuckDuckGo, or Brave Search.

✅ Prevent fingerprinting using extensions, private mode, and Tor when necessary.

✅ Combine multiple search engines to avoid bias and access diverse datasets.

By implementing these tools and techniques, OSINT analysts can conduct safer, more effective searches while minimizing exposure and tracking risks.

11.5 Best Practices for Protecting Your Digital Footprint

Every online action—whether a search query, website visit, or social media post—leaves behind a digital footprint. For OSINT professionals, this footprint can be a serious vulnerability if not managed properly. Tracking mechanisms, including cookies, browser fingerprinting, IP logging, and search history profiling, can compromise anonymity, expose investigative activities, and even tip off targets.

In this chapter, we'll explore practical steps to reduce digital exposure, covering everything from anonymous browsing techniques to operational security (OPSEC) strategies that help you remain undetected during investigations.

1. Understanding Your Digital Footprint

Your digital footprint consists of all the data traces you leave while using the internet. This includes:

- **Active footprint** – Information you intentionally share (e.g., social media posts, online forms).
- **Passive footprint** – Information collected without your awareness (e.g., IP address, browser settings, cookies, metadata).

1.1 How Your Digital Footprint is Tracked

- **IP Addresses** – Websites log your IP, revealing location and ISP.

- **Cookies & Tracking Scripts** – Sites track browsing behavior and link searches to your profile.
- **Browser Fingerprinting** – Unique settings (OS, fonts, screen size, plugins) make you identifiable.
- **Search Engine Logs** – Google and Bing store your queries and personalize results.
- **Social Media Activity** – Posts, likes, and comments can reveal patterns about you.

⬜ **Risk for OSINT Analysts**: If you are conducting an investigation on a target, your digital traces could be tracked back to you, compromising anonymity and security.

🎯 **Goal**: Minimize both active and passive footprints while conducting searches and investigations.

2. Best Browsing Practices for Reducing Your Footprint

2.1 Use Privacy-Focused Browsers

✅ Best Choices:

- **Tor Browser** – Fully anonymized browsing with multi-hop encryption.
- **LibreWolf** – A hardened, telemetry-free version of Firefox.
- **Brave Browser** – Built-in tracker blocking with an optional Tor mode.

⬧ Avoid Chrome, Edge, and Safari, as they actively track user data.

2.2 Disable Tracking & Fingerprinting

- Block cookies – Use extensions like uBlock Origin or Privacy Badger.
- Prevent fingerprinting – Use CanvasBlocker or Trace.
- Clear browser history & cache regularly.

2.3 Use a VPN or Tor for Anonymity

⬧ **VPN (Virtual Private Network)** – Hides your IP address by routing traffic through a secure server.

⬧ **Tor (The Onion Router)** – Provides multi-layered encryption for full anonymity.

Best VPNs for OSINT:

✅ **ProtonVPN** (No logs, high security)
✅ **Mullvad** (Privacy-focused, anonymous payments)
✅ **NordVPN** (Wide server network)

🚀 **Pro Tip**: Combine Tor + VPN for an extra layer of protection.

3. Search Engine Privacy: How to Search Anonymously

3.1 Avoid Google's Tracking

Google logs every search query, links it to your identity, and personalizes results. Instead:

✅ Use private search engines:

- **Startpage** (Google results without tracking)
- **DuckDuckGo** (No logs, no filter bubbles)
- **Searx** (Self-hosted meta-search engine)
- **Brave Search** (Independent index, no tracking)

🚀 **Pro Tip**: Compare search results across multiple engines to avoid bias.

3.2 Use Incognito Mode & Clear Search History

- Always search in private mode to avoid search history logging.
- Clear cookies & cache after every session.

4. Secure Communication & Device Hygiene

4.1 Use Secure Email & Messaging Apps

✗ Avoid Gmail, Yahoo, and Outlook (heavily monitored).

✅ Best Private Email Services:

- **ProtonMail** – Encrypted, no logs.
- **Tutanota** – Open-source, anonymous.

- **Skiff** – Zero-knowledge encryption.

✅ Best Encrypted Messaging Apps:

- **Signal** (Highly secure, self-destructing messages).
- **Session** (Decentralized, Tor-based messaging).
- **Matrix/Element** (Open-source, encrypted).

4.2 Device Security & Clean Investigative Workspaces

- Use a separate device for OSINT investigations (e.g., a burner laptop).
- Run OSINT tools on a virtual machine to avoid exposing your personal system.
- Disable location tracking on all devices.

🚀 **Pro Tip**: Consider Tails OS or Qubes OS for highly secure, anonymous investigations.

5. Protecting Your Social Media Presence

5.1 Lock Down Personal Accounts

◆ Review privacy settings and restrict profile visibility.

◆ Limit personal information – Remove birthdates, locations, job history.

◆ Use a burner account for OSINT research instead of personal profiles.

5.2 Avoid OSINT Cross-Contamination

✗ Never search for your OSINT targets from your personal accounts.

✅ Use a separate identity for investigations.

✅ Spoof metadata in images and documents before sharing them.

🚀 **Pro Tip**: Use Fake Name Generator or Privacy.com to create anonymous profiles and payments.

6. Case Study: How an Investigator Got Caught Due to a Poor Digital Footprint

A cybersecurity journalist was investigating data leaks on the dark web. While using Google Chrome without a VPN, they:

1☐ Visited breached forums from their real IP.

2☐ Used their regular Gmail account to contact a source.

3☐ Accessed a leaked database using their personal machine.

🔍 What Happened?

- Their IP address was logged on dark web forums.
- Google linked their searches to their personal profile.
- A threat actor traced their online behavior and sent them a phishing attack.

🚀 Lessons Learned:

✅ Use a VPN/Tor when investigating.

✅ Create separate burner accounts for OSINT.

✅ Never mix personal and investigative activities.

7. Summary: Key Takeaways for OSINT Professionals

✅ Use a privacy-focused browser (Tor, LibreWolf, Brave).

✅ Search with private search engines (Startpage, Searx, DuckDuckGo).

✅ Protect your IP using a VPN or Tor.

✅ Secure your communications with encrypted email and messaging.

✅ Use separate devices and burner accounts for investigations.

✅ Regularly clear cookies, cache, and browsing history.

✅ Minimize personal exposure on social media.

By following these best practices, OSINT analysts can reduce digital exposure, maintain anonymity, and conduct safer investigations without risking identity leaks or detection.

11.6 Case Study: Conducting OSINT While Maintaining OPSEC

Operational Security (OPSEC) is critical for OSINT practitioners. Whether investigating cybercriminals, tracking financial fraud, or analyzing geopolitical threats, failing to protect your digital footprint can compromise your identity, tip off your targets, or even put you at risk.

This case study walks through a realistic OSINT investigation, demonstrating how to gather intelligence while maintaining strong OPSEC.

Case Study Overview: Investigating a Suspicious Business Network

Scenario:

An OSINT analyst is tasked with investigating a network of suspicious businesses suspected of laundering money. These businesses have vague online profiles, but their owners appear linked through social media, corporate filings, and dark web activity.

The analyst must uncover:

- Company ownership structures
- Connections between businesses
- Hidden online activity
- Possible links to cybercrime

Challenges:

✗ The businesses have minimal online presence.

✗ Some entities operate on the dark web.

✗ Investigating without OPSEC could expose the analyst's identity.

🎯 **Objective**: Conduct the OSINT investigation without leaving traces or alerting the targets.

Step 1: Establishing a Secure Research Environment

1.1 Setting Up a Clean Investigation Workspace

The analyst avoids using their personal machine and instead:

✅ Uses a dedicated OSINT laptop (no personal logins, fresh OS installation).

✅ Runs a Virtual Machine (VM) with Tails OS for added security.

✅ Ensures all default telemetry (tracking) is disabled in the OS.

🚀 Why?

A clean environment ensures that investigations do not leak personal data, and any malicious content encountered won't infect the primary device.

1.2 Using a VPN & Tor for Anonymity

✅ VPN + Tor combination is used for anonymous browsing.

✅ The analyst switches VPN servers regularly to avoid tracking patterns.

✅ All traffic is routed through Tor when accessing the dark web.

🚀 Why?

Using VPNs and Tor prevents IP tracking by search engines, websites, and threat actors monitoring network traffic.

Step 2: Gathering Initial Intelligence Without Leaving a Footprint

2.1 Searching for Business Information Anonymously

The analyst begins by searching for the business names using privacy-focused search engines:

✅ **Startpage** (Google results without tracking)
✅ **Searx** (Self-hosted, open-source search)
✅ **DuckDuckGo** (Minimal tracking, no filter bubbles)

🚀 Why?

These search engines avoid logging queries and prevent Google from tracking the analyst's searches.

2.2 Extracting Metadata from Public Documents

The analyst looks for PDFs, DOCX files, and images related to the businesses using Google Dorking:

🔍 site:examplecompany.com filetype:pdf

🔍 intitle:confidential OR intitle:internal site:examplecompany.com

☐ **OPSEC Measure**: The analyst downloads files using a burner identity on a sandboxed machine to avoid exposure.

🚀 Why?

Metadata from documents can reveal hidden authors, edit history, and internal IP addresses—crucial for tracking business networks.

Step 3: Investigating Social Media While Remaining Undetected

3.1 Creating a Burner Account for OSINT

Instead of using a personal social media profile, the analyst:

✅ Creates a fake persona with a unique email & phone number.

✅ Uses a virtual phone number (not tied to their real identity).

✅ Accesses social media through a VPN and privacy browser.

🚀 Why?

Using a burner identity prevents accidental exposure, as many platforms notify users when someone views their profile.

3.2 Uncovering Connections Between Business Owners

The analyst:

- Uses Facebook Graph Search techniques to find mutual connections.
- Runs reverse image searches on LinkedIn profile pictures.
- Cross-references Twitter handles with forum activity using Google search operators.

🚀 Key Finding:

The business owners were linked through old social media interactions—something they had tried to scrub from public view.

🔲 **OPSEC Measure**: The analyst does not log in to any social media accounts on their real device.

Step 4: Exploring the Dark Web Securely

4.1 Using Onion Search Engines

To check for mentions of the business on dark web forums, the analyst uses:

✅ **Ahmia.fi** (Dark web search engine for indexed .onion sites)
✅ **Dark.fail** (Live links to known dark web marketplaces)

4.2 Avoiding Honey Pots & Traps

🚀 Best OPSEC Practices:

✅ Accessing only publicly available content (no login-required sites).

✅ Using disposable burner credentials if account creation is necessary.

✅ NEVER clicking links or downloading files without verifying safety.

🔎 Key Finding:

The business network had been mentioned on a darknet financial fraud forum, confirming their connection to illicit activity.

Step 5: Verifying & Cross-Referencing Intelligence

The analyst compiles all OSINT findings and verifies them using:

✅ Corporate & government databases for official business registration details.

✅ Archived versions of websites (Wayback Machine) to track historical changes.

✅ Leaked database searches (HaveIBeenPwned, DeHashed) to check for compromised emails.

🚀 Key Finding:

The businesses shared an IP address linked to a past money laundering investigation.

Step 6: Safeguarding the OSINT Investigation & Exfiltrating Data

6.1 Secure Data Storage & Documentation

- Findings are stored on encrypted external drives.
- Reports are generated using a secure offline system (not uploaded to cloud storage).

6.2 Destroying Traces After Investigation

After concluding the investigation, the analyst:

✅ Clears all cookies, caches, and logs from their OSINT environment.

✅ Destroys the virtual machine used for dark web research.

✅ Wipes the burner email and social media accounts used during the investigation.

Final Takeaways: Key OPSEC Lessons from This Case Study

1️⃣ Always Separate Personal & OSINT Identities

◆ Use burner accounts, virtual numbers, and separate devices.

2️⃣ Use Anonymization Tools

◆ VPNs, Tor, and secure browsers protect against tracking.

3️ Be Cautious with Dark Web Research

♦ Never log in with real credentials or download files blindly.

4️ Verify Information Across Multiple Sources

♦ Cross-check findings with corporate databases, social media, and archives.

5️ Destroy Traces After Investigations

♦ Securely delete logs, caches, and temporary accounts.

Conclusion: Why OPSEC is Critical for OSINT Analysts

Maintaining strong OPSEC is non-negotiable for OSINT investigations. Even a single mistake—such as logging into a personal email while researching a target—can lead to serious consequences, including compromised anonymity or exposure to cyber threats.

By following proper security protocols, analysts can conduct investigations effectively while staying undetected—ensuring both safety and the integrity of their work.

12. Case Studies: Real-World Search Challenges

Real-world OSINT investigations often present unique challenges that require creative problem-solving and adaptability. This chapter explores case studies where advanced search techniques played a crucial role in uncovering intelligence. Examples include tracking cybercriminals through metadata analysis, uncovering hidden connections using social media pivoting, and retrieving deleted web content via archived records. Other cases highlight how analysts have used Google Dorking to find exposed databases or leveraged deep web searches to identify threat actors. Each case study demonstrates the practical application of search mastery techniques, providing valuable lessons on overcoming obstacles, verifying information, and refining methodologies to extract actionable intelligence from open sources.

12.1 Finding a Missing Person Using Search Techniques

Finding a missing person using Open Source Intelligence (OSINT) requires a combination of search engine mastery, social media tracking, metadata analysis, and cross-referencing data points. Whether assisting in law enforcement cases, humanitarian efforts, or private investigations, OSINT can help uncover crucial leads.

This chapter walks through a realistic case study, demonstrating how to use search techniques to locate a missing person while ensuring ethical and legal compliance.

Case Study: The Disappearance of Alex Carter

Scenario:

Alex Carter, a 22-year-old college student, went missing after leaving a bar late at night. His last known online activity was a social media post about meeting someone but with no location data attached. His phone is off, and traditional searches by authorities have yielded no immediate results.

Objective:

Use OSINT techniques to find clues about Alex's whereabouts.

Challenges:

✘ Alex's phone is turned off, making geolocation tracking impossible.

✘ His social media accounts are private.

✘ He was last seen in an unfamiliar area, limiting initial search options.

🔖 **Approach**: Use search engines, social media searches, and metadata analysis to trace Alex's last movements and identify potential contacts.

Step 1: Gathering Initial Search Clues

1.1 Search Engine Queries for News & Public Mentions

The first step is to check news reports, forums, and social media discussions. Using Google and alternative search engines, we run:

🔍 "Alex Carter" AND "missing" AND "college student"
🔍 site:reddit.com "Alex Carter" missing (Checking Reddit discussions)
🔍 intitle:"missing person" Alex Carter (Finding missing person reports)

🔖 Findings:

- A local news article mentions that Alex was last seen leaving a nightclub around 2 AM.
- A Reddit thread discusses his disappearance, with someone claiming to have seen him near a convenience store hours later.

☐ **Next Step**: Verify and expand on these findings using social media and location-based searches.

Step 2: Social Media Investigation

2.1 Searching for Publicly Available Social Media Posts

Although Alex's profiles are private, his friends or acquaintances may have posted about him.

Using OSINT techniques, we search for mentions of Alex Carter on:

✅ **Facebook** (Public posts, event check-ins, comments)

✅ **Twitter** (Mentions, hashtags, geotagged tweets)
✅ **Instagram** (Tagged photos, stories, locations)
✅ **TikTok** (Recent videos near the nightclub)

🔍 **Google Dorking:**

- site:facebook.com "Alex Carter" AND "last seen"
- site:twitter.com "Alex Carter" AND "help find"

🚀 **Findings:**

A friend tagged Alex in a photo at the nightclub just an hour before he went missing. The post had comments from strangers discussing the event.

☐ **Next Step**: Identify who was with Alex that night and look for metadata in photos.

Step 3: Extracting Metadata from Photos & Videos

3.1 Checking EXIF Data for Hidden Location Clues

A publicly posted photo shows Alex at the club.

The image is downloaded and analyzed using EXIF metadata extraction tools like:

- **ExifTool** (exiftool image.jpg)
- **Metadata2Go** (Online metadata viewer)

🚀 **Findings:**

- The photo was taken at 1:45 AM near the nightclub.
- The GPS coordinates were embedded, revealing the exact exit Alex used.
- The camera model and phone type confirm the uploader took the photo on an iPhone.

☐ **Next Step**: Cross-reference the location with security cameras and nearby digital footprints.

Step 4: Searching Publicly Available CCTV & Traffic Cameras

4.1 Checking Open Public Camera Feeds

Some cities provide public access to:

✅ Traffic cams

✅ Business security feeds

✅ Live streaming sites (EarthCam, Insecam, YouTube feeds)

🔍 **Search Queries:**

- site:earthcam.com [City Name] nightlife camera
- site:youtube.com "[City Name] live street cam"
- inurl:view.shtml "[City Name] traffic camera"

🚀 **Findings:**

A nearby security camera captured someone matching Alex's description walking toward a gas station at 2:05 AM.

☐ **Next Step**: Check gas station check-ins, purchases, and eyewitness reports.

Step 5: Analyzing Financial & Phone Data (If Available)

If Alex's bank transactions are accessible (with family or law enforcement assistance), checking recent purchases can reveal his movements.

5.1 Searching for Digital Transactions & Check-ins

✅ Google Location History (If not disabled)

✅ Apple Find My iPhone (With family access)

✅ Credit/Debit card transactions

🚀 **Findings:**

- Alex's last known transaction was a $10 purchase at a gas station at 2:07 AM.
- The receipt includes a partial license plate of a car outside.

☐ **Next Step**: Identify the car owner and where it went next.

Step 6: Reverse Searching the Vehicle & Individuals

6.1 Running a Reverse Image Search on the Vehicle

A blurry photo of the car from a security cam screenshot is enhanced and reverse-searched using:

✓ Google Lens

✓ Yandex Reverse Image Search

🚀 **Findings:**

The vehicle belongs to a known rideshare driver who often operates in the area.

6.2 Finding the Driver's Online Footprint

Using OSINT searches, the driver's name and records are found through:

✓ **People search engines** (Spokeo, Pipl, TruthFinder)
✓ **Public legal databases** (court records, arrest records)

🚀 **Findings:**

The driver was previously accused of misconduct but was never charged.

☐ **Next Step**: Provide law enforcement with this lead.

Final Outcome: Locating Alex Carter

🔒 **Key Breakthrough:**

- The car's plate was tracked, leading to a hotel booking under Alex's name.
- Law enforcement checked the room and found Alex alive but disoriented.
- He had been drugged and abandoned, likely by someone he met that night.

✓ **Success**: Alex was found within 48 hours, largely due to OSINT techniques.

Key OSINT Techniques Used in This Investigation

1 Search Engine Mastery

◆ Google Dorking to find missing person mentions & hidden web content.

2 Social Media Tracking

◆ Finding tagged posts, mentions, and geotagged content.

3 Metadata Analysis

◆ Extracting GPS coordinates from photos & videos.

4 Surveillance Footage Searches

◆ Accessing public CCTV feeds, street cams, and YouTube live cams.

5 Financial & Digital Trail Analysis

◆ Checking bank transactions, check-ins, and online activity.

6 Reverse Image & License Plate Searches

◆ Identifying vehicles & potential suspects through Yandex, Google Lens, and databases.

Conclusion: The Power of OSINT in Finding Missing Persons

OSINT techniques can reveal hidden clues that traditional investigations may overlook. Search engines, social media, metadata, and public records can be powerful tools when used responsibly.

However, ethical and legal considerations must always be followed, ensuring data is gathered without violating privacy laws.

12.2 Tracking a Cybercriminal Through Search Engine Data

Search engines are powerful tools not only for everyday research but also for tracking cybercriminals. While many threat actors attempt to remain anonymous, they often leave behind digital footprints—whether in cached pages, metadata, exposed databases, or old forum posts. By leveraging OSINT (Open-Source Intelligence) search techniques, investigators can piece together a criminal's online identity, uncover hidden connections, and track their activities.

This chapter presents a real-world-inspired case study, demonstrating how search engine techniques can be used to trace a cybercriminal, identify their online infrastructure, and ultimately aid in an investigation.

Case Study: Unmasking "ShadowPhantom"—A Notorious Cybercriminal

Scenario:

"ShadowPhantom" is a black-hat hacker specializing in selling stolen credentials and malware. He operates mainly on dark web forums, but fragments of his activity have leaked onto the surface web. Law enforcement agencies suspect that ShadowPhantom is responsible for a recent data breach affecting thousands of victims.

Objective:

Use search engines and OSINT techniques to uncover ShadowPhantom's real identity and online infrastructure.

Challenges:

✗ ShadowPhantom uses aliases and fake identities.

✗ He frequently deletes accounts and changes usernames.

✗ His activities are mainly on the deep and dark web, making direct searches difficult.

🚀 **Approach:**

- Google Dorking & advanced search operators
- Tracking usernames, emails, and leaked credentials
- Reverse searching website infrastructure & domains

- Monitoring discussions in hacker forums

Step 1: Identifying Searchable Clues

Before diving into search techniques, we gather initial data:

- The hacker's known alias: "ShadowPhantom"
- A possible email linked to his activity: phantomx99@mail.com
- Mentions of a website he may have used to sell stolen credentials
- Our goal is to expand on these initial clues using OSINT search techniques.

Step 2: Google Dorking & Advanced Search Queries

We start by checking for cached pages, indexed discussions, and leaked data using Google Dorking techniques:

🔍 Searching for mentions of the alias:

- "ShadowPhantom" AND ("hacker" OR "breach" OR "malware")
- site:pastebin.com OR site:github.com OR site:reddit.com

✅ Findings:

- Mentions of ShadowPhantom in old forum posts on Reddit and Pastebin.
- A cached Pastebin page listing stolen credentials from a recent breach.
- A defunct GitHub repository possibly linked to malware scripts.

☐ **Next Step: Extract further details from these sources.**

Step 3: Tracking Usernames & Alias Pivoting

3.1 Reverse Searching the Alias Across Platforms

Even if a cybercriminal uses an alias, they may reuse variations across different sites.

🔍 Tools used:

✅ **Dehashed** (for searching username/email in breached databases)

✅ **WhatsMyName** (to find social media profiles linked to usernames)
✅ **Namechk** (checking username availability across platforms)

🚀 **Findings:**

- ShadowPhantom used a similar name "PhantomX99" on an old hacker forum.
- This username was linked to a Telegram account and a Dark Web marketplace profile.

☐ **Next Step: Identify associated emails, IPs, or forum discussions.**

Step 4: Searching for Email & Domain Connections

The leaked email phantomx99@mail.com could be linked to other accounts, websites, or breaches.

🔍 **Searching for email associations:**

- "phantomx99@mail.com"   site:pastebin.com   OR   site:github.com   OR   site:linkedin.com

✅ **Findings:**

- The email appears in multiple data breaches.
- It was used to register a domain (possibly a hacking site).

4.1 Reverse Searching the Domain

We use Whois lookup and reverse DNS tools to find connections:

🔍 **Searching for linked websites:**

- ViewDNS.info (to check subdomains)
- SecurityTrails (to find historical records of the domain)

🚀 **Findings:**

- The domain was linked to a hosting provider in Eastern Europe.
- Other connected sites were selling stolen credentials.

☐ **Next Step: Uncover hidden infrastructure.**

Step 5: Investigating Dark Web Activity

Since ShadowPhantom operates in the dark web, we use specialized dark web search engines:

🔍 **Using Dark Web Search Tools:**

✅ **Ahmia.fi** (Dark web search engine)
✅ **OnionLand Search**
✅ **Recon** (Dark web intelligence tool)

🚀 **Findings:**

- ShadowPhantom was active on a dark web forum selling ransomware tools.
- A discussion thread contained his PGP key, which can be used for further tracking.

☐ **Next Step: Check for related IP addresses and leaked credentials.**

Step 6: Tracking IP & Hosting Details

Even though cybercriminals use VPNs and proxies, they sometimes make mistakes, such as:

- Logging into a forum without anonymization.
- Reusing a traceable hosting provider.

🔍 **Using IP Analysis Tools:**

✅ **Shodan.io** (to find exposed services and devices)
✅ **Censys.io** (to track open ports & vulnerabilities)

🚀 **Findings:**

- One of ShadowPhantom's old sites was briefly hosted on a misconfigured VPS, exposing a real IP.
- The IP was linked to a specific city.

☐ **Next Step: Check for possible real-world identity matches.**

Final Outcome: Identifying the Cybercriminal

By connecting all digital footprints, investigators were able to:

✓ Find ShadowPhantom's old username & forum posts.

✓ Link his activities to a leaked email & domain registration.

✓ Discover a hosting provider exposing an IP location.

✓ Track down Telegram and Dark Web conversations leading to a suspect.

🔎 ShadowPhantom was ultimately identified as a known cybercriminal in Eastern Europe, leading to his arrest and dismantling of his malware operations.

Key OSINT Techniques Used in Cybercriminal Tracking

1☐ Google Dorking & Advanced Operators

♦ Finding cached pages, leaks, and hidden discussions.

2☐ Username & Alias Pivoting

♦ Tracking username variations across forums and platforms.

3☐ Email & Domain Investigations

♦ Searching for breached credentials, Whois data, and subdomains.

4☐ Dark Web Search Techniques

♦ Using Onion search engines & intelligence tools to track cybercriminal forums.

5☐ IP & Hosting Infrastructure Analysis

◆ Identifying mistakes in anonymization, leading to real-world clues.

Conclusion: The Power of Search Engines in Cybercrime Investigations
While cybercriminals attempt to hide behind anonymity, OSINT search techniques can reveal critical links that expose their activities. By using search engines strategically, investigators can track aliases, discover leaked data, and ultimately trace real-world identities.

12.3 Investigating a Disinformation Campaign via Google Dorking

Disinformation campaigns—whether state-sponsored, politically motivated, or financially driven—have become a powerful weapon in the digital age. These campaigns use false narratives, manipulated media, and coordinated online activity to mislead the public. While social media is often the primary battlefield, search engines play a crucial role in amplifying misleading content.

With Google Dorking and advanced search techniques, OSINT analysts can:

- Identify fake news networks and bot-driven amplification
- Trace the origins of disinformation narratives
- Uncover linked websites, sockpuppet accounts, and coordinated activity
- Find deleted or hidden content that exposes campaign organizers

This chapter presents a real-world-inspired case study on how Google Dorking techniques can be used to investigate a disinformation campaign, uncover hidden networks, and track those responsible.

Case Study: Exposing "Operation Echo"

Scenario:

A viral conspiracy theory has been spreading rapidly online, falsely claiming that a global health organization is fabricating disease outbreak statistics for financial gain. This campaign, dubbed "Operation Echo," appears to be coordinated across news blogs, social media accounts, and SEO-optimized websites.

A cybersecurity research group has tasked an OSINT investigator with uncovering who is behind the campaign, where the disinformation originates, and how it spreads.

Objective:

Use Google Dorking & OSINT techniques to:

- Identify the source websites & key players spreading the false narrative.
- Uncover connections between seemingly independent sites.
- Track sockpuppet accounts, automated bots, and duplicate content.
- Reveal hidden metadata and backlinks linking the network together.

Challenges:

✗ The campaign uses multiple domains and fake news sites.

✗ The actors frequently delete and rehost content.

✗ The disinformation is boosted through bot networks and SEO manipulation.

🚀 Approach:

- Google Dorking & advanced search operators
- Tracking duplicate content & linked domains
- Extracting metadata & identifying sockpuppet authors
- Analyzing backlink networks & SEO strategies

Step 1: Identifying Disinformation Websites Using Google Dorking

Since the false narrative has gone viral, we start by searching for keyword patterns commonly found in the articles.

🔍 Google Dorking Query for Identifying Disinformation Articles:

- "global health organization" AND ("fabricating" OR "faking" OR "scam") site:*.news OR site:*.info OR site:*.blog

✅ Findings:

- Multiple low-quality news sites (e.g., health-truth.info, realnewsnow.blog).

- Some articles are word-for-word identical, indicating automated reposting.
- The same misleading claim appears across different domains.

☐ Next Step: Identify ownership & connections between these sites.

Step 2: Tracking Website Ownership & Related Domains

2.1 Investigating Website Ownership

Even though disinformation websites often use privacy-protected WHOIS registrations, OSINT techniques can still reveal patterns.

🔍 Tools Used:

✅ **Whois lookup** (who.is, ViewDNS.info) – Checks domain registration details.
✅ **SecurityTrails & BuiltWith** – Finds historical records & hosting infrastructure.

🚀 Findings:

- All identified sites are hosted on the same server in a specific country.
- Whois records show that multiple sites were registered by the same entity.

2.2 Reverse Searching Related Domains

By analyzing IP addresses and hosting records, we can find other websites controlled by the same network.

🔍 Google Dorking for Finding Related Domains:

- ip:192.168.1.1

✅ Findings:

- Several other sites promoting conspiracy theories are hosted on the same server.
- The same template, article structure, and author names appear across multiple sites.

☐ Next Step: Search for patterns in article content.

Step 3: Finding Duplicate & Syndicated Content

Disinformation campaigns often use automated article syndication—copying the same misleading content across multiple sites to increase credibility.

🔍 Google Dorking Query to Find Duplicated Articles:

- "This global health organization is manipulating statistics"

✅ Findings:

- The same exact phrase appears on dozens of sites, confirming automation.
- Some articles include slightly rewritten versions, possibly using AI tools.

☐ Next Step: Track authors and sockpuppet identities.

Step 4: Identifying Fake Authors & Sockpuppet Accounts

Fake news websites often create fake authors with reused profile pictures and pseudonyms.

🔍 Google Dorking Query to Find More Articles by an Author:

- "John Doe" site:health-truth.info OR site:realnewsnow.blog

✅ Findings:

- The same author "John Doe" appears on multiple disinformation sites.
- A reverse image search of his profile picture reveals it is a stock photo.

☐ Next Step: Analyze SEO tactics & backlink networks.

Step 5: Analyzing SEO Manipulation & Backlinks

Disinformation networks use SEO tactics to make fake news rank higher in search results.

🔍 Google Dorking to Find Backlink Networks:

- link:health-truth.info

✅ Findings:

- A web of low-quality blogs is linking back to the main site.
- Some backlinks come from fake comment sections & forum spam.
- Certain backlinks come from expired domains repurposed for spreading disinformation.

☐ Next Step: Investigate social media amplification & bot activity.

Step 6: Tracking Social Media Amplification

The disinformation campaign is gaining traction through social media shares, automated retweets, and bot activity.

🔍 Google Dorking for Finding Social Media Mentions:

- "global health organization fake statistics" site:twitter.com OR site:facebook.com OR site:t.me

✅ Findings:

- Many accounts sharing the article were created recently and post identical messages.
- Certain hashtags are being spammed by multiple bot accounts.

6.1 Reverse Searching Social Media Profiles

- Many of the Twitter accounts have random usernames and use stolen profile pictures.
- Some are linked to other conspiracy campaigns, showing a coordinated disinformation effort.

Final Outcome: Mapping the Disinformation Network

By using Google Dorking & OSINT techniques, analysts successfully:

✅ Identified the main disinformation websites.

✓ Uncovered a network of linked domains & fake authors.

✓ Found SEO manipulation & backlink strategies.

✓ Tracked social media bots boosting the false narrative.

✓ Connected the campaign to a known disinformation group.

🚨 The findings were reported to fact-checking organizations, helping debunk the campaign before it spread further.

Key OSINT Techniques for Investigating Disinformation

1️ Google Dorking & Advanced Operators

◆ Finding hidden articles, metadata, and related domains.

2️ Reverse Searching Domains & IPs

◆ Exposing networks of related fake news sites.

3️ Detecting Content Syndication

◆ Identifying duplicate or AI-generated propaganda.

4️ Tracking Fake Authors & Sockpuppet Accounts

◆ Discovering reused stock photos & duplicate identities.

5️ SEO & Backlink Analysis

◆ Uncovering manipulative ranking strategies.

6️ Social Media Investigation

◆ Identifying bot activity & disinformation amplification.

Conclusion: The Power of OSINT in Fighting Disinformation

Disinformation thrives on manipulation and deception, but Google Dorking and OSINT techniques provide investigators with powerful tools to uncover hidden networks, debunk false narratives, and expose those responsible.

12.4 Exposing Fake News & Fraudulent Websites Through Search

The internet has become a breeding ground for fake news, scam websites, and fraudulent content, making it harder than ever to distinguish truth from deception. Fraudulent websites can take many forms—fake news outlets, phishing sites, impersonation scams, and misinformation campaigns—all designed to manipulate public perception, steal sensitive information, or promote an agenda.

Fortunately, OSINT analysts and investigators can use search engines, Google Dorking, metadata analysis, and backlink tracking to expose these deceptive practices. This chapter explores how search techniques can identify fake news, detect scam websites, and trace their origins.

Case Study: Investigating a Fake News Network

Scenario:

A viral news story claims that a high-profile political figure was secretly arrested and is being held in an undisclosed location. Major media outlets have not reported this, but multiple websites and social media accounts are spreading the claim.

A fact-checking organization has asked an OSINT analyst to determine:

- Who is behind the fake news?
- Where the misinformation originated from.
- How the story is being distributed and amplified.

Step 1: Identifying Fake News Websites

The first step in debunking fake news is to locate all the websites spreading the false narrative.

1.1 Google Dorking for Fake News Sources

Fake news articles often use similar phrases, sensational headlines, and clickbait wording.

🔍 **Google Dorking Query to Find Related Articles:**

- "high-profile political figure arrested" OR "secret detention" OR "government cover-up" site:*.info OR site:*.blog OR site:*.news

✅ Findings:

- Multiple websites are publishing nearly identical articles.
- Some sites do not have an "About Us" or contact page, a common sign of fake news.
- The same author names and bylines appear across different domains.

Step 2: Investigating Website Ownership & Hosting Details

Fake news websites often operate under different domains but share ownership or hosting infrastructure.

2.1 Whois Lookup & Domain History

Using Whois lookup tools (who.is, ViewDNS.info, SecurityTrails) can reveal who registered the domain and if the site has changed hands.

✅ Findings:

- Most of the fake news sites use privacy-protected domain registration.
- Some sites were created recently, suggesting they were made just for this campaign.

2.2 Finding Other Websites Under the Same Owner

If the owner is not hidden, the same registrant may have other fraudulent websites.

🔍 **Google Dorking to Find Related Domains:**

- inurl:whois.domaintools.com "Registrant Name"

✅ Findings:

- The same person or entity owns multiple fake news domains.
- The sites have identical layouts and publishing schedules, proving coordination.

Step 3: Detecting Plagiarized & AI-Generated Content

Fake news websites often copy articles from legitimate sources or use AI-generated text to produce misleading content.

3.1 Reverse Searching Content

To check if the article was copied, an investigator can take a sentence from the fake news article and reverse search it.

🔍 Google Dorking Query to Find Duplicate Content:

- "High-profile political figure secretly detained in an unknown location"

✅ Findings:

- The exact same article appears on multiple domains, confirming syndication.
- Some articles have minor wording changes, a sign of AI-generated content.

3.2 Checking for AI-Generated Fake News

If a website generates a large volume of fake news, chances are some of it was created with AI.

☐ **AI detection tools** (GPTZero, OpenAI Classifier, or AI-generated text detectors) can help confirm this.

Step 4: Tracking Fake News Backlinks & SEO Manipulation

Fake news networks use SEO strategies and backlink manipulation to increase their visibility on search engines.

4.1 Checking Backlinks to Fake News Articles

Backlinks can reveal a web of interconnected fake news websites boosting each other.

🔍 Google Dorking Query to Track Backlinks:

- link:fakenewswebsite.info

✅ Findings:

- Multiple low-quality blog networks are linking to the fake news site.
- Some backlinks come from expired domains that were repurposed for disinformation.

4.2 Identifying PBNs (Private Blog Networks)

PBNs are interlinked websites used to artificially boost SEO rankings.

🔍 Google Dorking to Find Related Blogs:

- "Breaking news" OR "Shocking truth" site:*.blog OR site:*.info OR site:*.press

✅ Findings:

A network of similar blogs is sharing links, confirming an SEO manipulation effort.

Step 5: Investigating Social Media Amplification

Fake news spreads rapidly through Twitter, Facebook, Telegram, and TikTok using bot accounts, sockpuppets, and clickbait groups.

5.1 Finding Social Media Mentions

🔍 Google Dorking Query to Find Fake News on Social Media:

- "high-profile political figure arrested" site:twitter.com OR site:facebook.com OR site:t.me

✅ Findings:

- Dozens of recently created accounts are sharing identical links.
- Many accounts have no profile pictures or are using stolen images.

5.2 Identifying Bots & Sockpuppets

Fake news is often boosted by automated accounts and fake personas.

☐ **Tools for Bot Detection:**

- **Botometer** (for Twitter bot analysis).
- **Hoaxy** (to visualize how fake news spreads).

✅ Findings:

- The same fake accounts are used in other misinformation campaigns.

Step 6: Uncovering the Real Source Behind Fake News

By combining website analysis, backlink tracking, and social media investigation, OSINT analysts can trace fake news networks back to their source.

✅ Final Discoveries:

- The disinformation campaign was created by a single organization with multiple domains.
- The content was mass-produced using AI and amplified by bots.
- The campaign was linked to a known group spreading political misinformation.

⚖ The results were reported to fact-checking organizations, leading to mass takedowns of fake news sites and bot networks.

Key OSINT Techniques for Exposing Fake News

1☐ Google Dorking & Search Operators

◆ Identify fake articles & manipulated content.

2️⃣ Domain & Whois Analysis

♦ Track website ownership & related domains.

3️⃣ Reverse Searching for Duplicate Content

♦ Detect AI-generated or syndicated misinformation.

4️⃣ Backlink & SEO Analysis

♦ Identify manipulated ranking tactics.

5️⃣ Social Media Investigation

♦ Find bot activity & fake amplification.

Conclusion: The Role of OSINT in Fighting Fake News

Fake news and fraudulent websites are designed to manipulate public perception, deceive users, and spread disinformation. By using advanced search techniques, metadata analysis, and SEO tracking, OSINT analysts can expose deception, debunk misinformation, and hold fake news networks accountable.

12.5 Extracting Intelligence from a Public Data Breach

Data breaches expose vast amounts of sensitive personal and corporate information, including emails, passwords, financial records, and confidential communications. While malicious actors use this data for fraud, identity theft, and cybercrime, OSINT investigators can leverage public breaches for intelligence gathering, cyber investigations, and threat analysis.

In this chapter, we explore how to:

✅ Identify and verify publicly available breach data.

✅ Extract intelligence from leaked credentials, emails, and metadata.

☑ Use search engines and OSINT tools to correlate breached data with real-world investigations.

☑ Ethically and legally analyze breaches without engaging in illicit activities.

Case Study: Investigating a High-Profile Data Breach

Scenario:

A major corporation recently suffered a data breach, and part of the stolen database has surfaced on a public paste site. Cybersecurity researchers and journalists want to determine:

- What type of information was leaked?
- Who might be responsible for the breach?
- Whether the leaked data exposes employees, customers, or infrastructure vulnerabilities.

An OSINT investigator begins by searching for the breach data online, verifying its authenticity, and extracting useful intelligence.

Step 1: Locating Publicly Available Breach Data

Many breached databases are shared on paste sites, hacking forums, Telegram groups, and the dark web. Some breaches also get indexed by search engines before being taken down.

1.1 Google Dorking for Public Data Dumps

🔍 **Search Query to Find Publicly Leaked Data:**

- site:pastebin.com OR site:paste2.org OR site:ghostbin.com "company.com" OR "internal email"

☑ **Findings:**

- Multiple paste sites contain leaked email addresses and credentials.
- Some pastes have been deleted, but cached versions may still be accessible.

1.2 Searching for the Breach on Public Leak Databases

Several online services track public data breaches and provide search access:

☐ **Useful OSINT Tools:**

- **Have I Been Pwned (hibp.io)** – Check if an email or domain was exposed in a breach.
- **DeHashed (dehashed.com)** – Search leaked credentials and passwords.
- **IntelX (intelx.io)** – Indexes dark web leaks and public breach data.

✅ Findings:

- The breached data contains thousands of employee emails and hashed passwords.
- Some email addresses are tied to previous leaks, suggesting password reuse risks.

Step 2: Extracting & Analyzing Breached Data

Once potentially compromised data is found, an investigator must validate and extract relevant intelligence.

2.1 Checking the Structure of the Leak

Leaked databases are typically formatted as:

- Email:Password pairs
- Hashed passwords (e.g., MD5, SHA-256)
- Internal documents & server logs

🔍 OSINT Check: Is the Breach Authentic?

- Are the email addresses real & active?
- Does the breach contain plaintext passwords or hashes?
- Does it include internal communications, IP addresses, or confidential data?

✅ Findings:

- The breach contains internal memos and configuration files, proving its authenticity.
- Some credentials are still active, making employees vulnerable.

2.2 Extracting Metadata for Attribution

Analyzing metadata in leaked files can reveal more about the source of the breach.

☐ **Metadata Extraction Tools:**

- **ExifTool** – Extracts metadata from documents, images, and PDFs.
- **Strings (Linux Command)** – Extracts hidden text from files.
- **CyberChef** – Analyzes encoded or hashed data.

✅ Findings:

The leaked documents contain internal usernames, timestamps, and software versions, hinting at how the breach occurred.

Step 3: Correlating Breach Data with Other OSINT Sources

3.1 Mapping Leaked Emails to Social Media & Other Accounts

Leaked corporate emails can be used to find employees' online presence.

🔍 **Google Dorking Query to Find Social Media Profiles Linked to Emails:**

- "@company.com" site:linkedin.com OR site:twitter.com OR site:facebook.com

✅ Findings:

- Several employees used their corporate emails for personal social media accounts.
- Some accounts reveal additional personal information, including locations and workplace details.

3.2 Checking for Credential Reuse Across Breaches

If an email appears in multiple breaches, it indicates a password reuse risk.

☐ **Tools for Cross-Breach Analysis:**

- **DeHashed** – Finds reuse of the same credentials across different leaks.
- **Snusbase** – Checks for exposed usernames, emails, and passwords.

✅ Findings:

Some employees reused the same password across multiple accounts, increasing their risk of being hacked.

Step 4: Investigating the Breach Source & Attackers

4.1 Tracking Down the Attacker's Identity

Some hackers leave traces of their activity in data dumps, forums, or social media.

🔍 **Google Dorking to Find Mentions of the Leak on Hacking Forums:**

- "company.com database" site:raidforums.com OR site:breachforums.st OR site:exploit.in

✅ Findings:

- The breach was advertised for sale on a hacker forum.
- The seller used the same alias on multiple forums, leading to their other online activity.

4.2 Tracing the Attacker's Infrastructure

If the breach includes IP addresses, hosting providers, or command-and-control (C2) servers, an OSINT analyst can track them using:

☐ **Network Analysis Tools:**

- **Shodan.io** – Finds exposed servers & IoT devices.
- **Censys.io** – Tracks SSL certificates & host fingerprints.
- **VirusTotal** – Checks if leaked IPs appear in malware datasets.

✅ Findings:

- A server linked to the attack was previously flagged for phishing campaigns.
- The attacker used the same infrastructure for multiple breaches.

Step 5: Reporting & Mitigating the Breach

5.1 Notifying the Affected Organization

Once the breach is verified, ethical OSINT analysts responsibly report findings to security teams.

✅ Key Reporting Details:

- What data was compromised?
- Is the breach still active?
- How can affected individuals protect themselves?

5.2 Recommending Security Measures

To mitigate future breaches, investigators recommend:

✔ **Password Resets** – Force resets for compromised accounts.

✔ **Multi-Factor Authentication (MFA)** – Reduces password reuse risks.

✔ **Dark Web Monitoring** – Track further leak exposure.

Key OSINT Techniques for Breach Analysis

1️ Google Dorking & Search Operators

◆ Locate exposed databases & breached credentials.

2️ Metadata & File Analysis

◆ Extract timestamps, usernames, and hidden details.

3️⃣ Social Media & Credential Correlation

◆ Link breached data to real-world identities.

4️⃣ Network & Infrastructure Investigation

◆ Track attackers via hosting services & server logs.

Conclusion: The Role of OSINT in Data Breach Investigations

Public data breaches provide a goldmine of intelligence for OSINT analysts, cyber investigators, and security professionals. By leveraging search engines, metadata analysis, and breach correlation tools, investigators can identify threats, track attackers, and protect individuals from cyber risks.

12.6 Final OSINT Search Challenge: Applying All Techniques

Throughout this book, you've learned how to harness search engines, pivot between data points, extract intelligence from breaches, and track digital footprints. Now, it's time to apply all these skills in a realistic OSINT search challenge.

This final challenge will simulate an OSINT investigation, requiring you to:

✓ Identify a target's online presence using search operators and people search engines.

✓ Find hidden and exposed documents through advanced Google Dorking.

✓ Track a username across social media and deep web sources.

✓ Correlate leaked data with public information.

✓ Ensure anonymity while conducting searches.

Scenario: Investigating a Suspected Fraudster

You are tasked with investigating "Jonathan Mercer," an individual suspected of running an online investment scam. The goal is to verify his identity, uncover his digital footprint, and find any potential evidence of fraud.

You start with minimal information:

- **Name**: Jonathan Mercer
- **Email**: jonmercerinvestments@gmail.com
- **Website**: mercerfinancials.com
- **Social Media**: Unknown

Phase 1: Identifying the Target's Online Presence

1.1 Google Dorking for Basic Profile Information

Search Query to Find Public Mentions:

- "Jonathan Mercer" OR "Jon Mercer" site:linkedin.com OR site:facebook.com OR site:twitter.com

✅ Findings:

- A LinkedIn profile appears under "Jon Mercer," claiming to be a financial consultant.
- His Facebook page is private, but old posts suggest he previously worked in crypto trading.
- Twitter posts under the username @Mercer_Invest promote investment schemes.

1.2 Finding His Email in Data Breaches

Using Have I Been Pwned or DeHashed, we check if jonmercerinvestments@gmail.com appears in past breaches.

✅ Findings:

- The email was exposed in two breaches related to financial scams.
- One breach includes a password hash, which could be cracked to reveal reused passwords.

Phase 2: Extracting Hidden & Exposed Documents

2.1 Using Google Dorking to Find Business Documents

Search Query for PDF & DOC Files Related to His Business:

- site:mercerfinancials.com filetype:pdf OR filetype:doc "investment plan"

✅ Findings:

- A PDF document containing investment terms with inconsistent legal wording.
- A Word document listing supposed investors but includes fake names.

2.2 Checking Metadata for Hidden Clues

Using ExifTool or FOCA, we extract metadata from the documents.

✅ Findings:

- The author of the documents is different from "Jonathan Mercer," hinting that he may be using a fake identity.
- A timestamp suggests the document was edited two months before the website launched.

Phase 3: Tracking a Username Across Platforms

3.1 Reverse Searching His Twitter Handle (@Mercer_Invest)

Search Query to Find Mentions in Forums & News

- "@Mercer_Invest" site:bitcointalk.org OR site:reddit.com OR site:medium.com

✅ Findings:

- He posted on cryptocurrency forums, promoting questionable investments.
- Multiple users accused him of running a Ponzi scheme.

3.2 Pivoting Through His Email & Username on Dark Web Search Engines

Using IntelX and Ahmia, we check if his email or username appears in dark web leaks.

✅ Findings:

- His email appears in a fraud-related database on the dark web.
- The username "Mercer_Invest" is linked to a Telegram group selling stolen credit cards.

Phase 4: Correlating Leaked Data with Public Information

4.1 Cross-Referencing Financial Records & Business Registrations

Using OpenCorporates and SEC filings, we check if "Mercer Financials" is a legally registered business.

✅ Findings:

- The company is NOT registered with any financial authorities.
- The website uses a fake business address.

Phase 5: Ensuring Anonymity & Safe Searching

Since the target is linked to fraud and the dark web, we take precautions:

✔ Using a VPN and Tor for sensitive searches.

✔ Avoiding direct interactions with the target online.

✔ Using disposable accounts for logins.

Final Conclusion: Uncovering the Truth

After applying OSINT search techniques, we confirm:

✔ Jonathan Mercer is likely using a fake identity.

✔ His financial business is unregistered and has been flagged in fraud discussions.

✔ His email and username are linked to data breaches and the dark web.

✔ His investment documents contain metadata inconsistencies, indicating deception.

Challenge: Can You Replicate This Investigation?

Try applying these OSINT techniques to a real-world scenario:

🔍 Investigate a suspicious website using Google Dorking.
🔍 Find leaked business documents and extract metadata clues.
🔍 Track a username across multiple platforms to uncover hidden connections.
🔍 Correlate leaked data with public records for deeper insights.

With these skills, you can now conduct powerful OSINT investigations using search engines, metadata analysis, breach data, and anonymous techniques.

The internet is a vast ocean of information, but finding the right data efficiently requires more than just basic search skills. The **OSINT Search Mastery: Hacking Search Engines for Intelligence** is your ultimate guide to unlocking the hidden depths of online information using advanced search techniques. Whether you're an investigator, journalist, researcher, cybersecurity analyst, or simply an inquisitive mind, this book provides the tools and strategies to turn you into a true search expert.

Search engines are powerful, but most people only scratch the surface of what they can do. This book dives deep into Google Dorking, Boolean logic, advanced operators, metadata extraction, and alternative search engines to help you uncover information that others miss. By mastering these techniques, you'll be able to perform targeted searches, locate hidden web pages, retrieve deleted content, and extract valuable intelligence from the internet.

What You'll Learn in This Book

- **The Science of Search**: Understand how search engines work, including crawling, indexing, and ranking algorithms.
- **Google Dorking & Advanced Operators**: Learn to use Google like a pro, uncovering hidden files, databases, and confidential information.
- **Boolean Search Mastery**: Use AND, OR, NOT, and parentheses to refine searches for laser-focused results.
- **Alternative Search Engines**: Discover powerful OSINT-friendly search tools beyond Google, including Bing, Yandex, DuckDuckGo, and specialized intelligence databases.
- **Finding Deleted & Archived Content**: Retrieve lost web pages using the Wayback Machine, cached versions, and forensic search techniques.
- **Metadata & Filetype Investigations**: Extract hidden data from PDFs, Word documents, images, and more.
- **Dark Web Search Techniques**: Learn the basics of searching TOR and deep web sources safely and legally.
- **Ethical Considerations**: Stay within legal and ethical boundaries while conducting OSINT investigations.

With step-by-step examples, real-world case studies, and practical exercises, this book transforms the way you search the internet. Whether you're conducting background checks, investigating cyber threats, or uncovering hard-to-find data, The OSINT Search Mastery gives you the expertise to navigate the digital world with confidence.

Thank you for choosing The OSINT Search Mastery as part of your journey into Open-Source Intelligence. Your curiosity and dedication to learning are what make the OSINT community stronger, and we are honored to be a part of your growth in this field.

Search engines are the gateway to vast amounts of intelligence, but knowing how to extract meaningful information is what sets skilled OSINT practitioners apart. By applying the techniques in this book, you've taken a major step toward becoming an expert in digital investigations.

We encourage you to keep practicing, experimenting, and refining your search strategies. The world of OSINT is constantly evolving, and the most successful investigators are those who continue learning and adapting.

Your feedback, insights, and experiences help us improve and create even more valuable content for the OSINT community. If this book has helped you, we'd love to hear about it!

Keep searching, keep learning, and most importantly—stay ethical in your investigations. Thank you for being part of this journey!

Continue Your OSINT Education

Expand your skills with the rest of The OSINT Analyst Series:

- **OSINT Foundations**: The Beginner's Guide to Open-Source Intelligence
- **OSINT People Finder**: Advanced Techniques for Online Investigations
- **Social Media OSINT**: Tracking Digital Footprints
- **Image & Geolocation Intelligence**: Reverse Searching and Mapping
- **Domain, Website & Cyber Investigations with OSINT**
- **Email & Dark Web Investigations**: Tracking Leaks & Breaches
- **OSINT Threat Intel**: Investigating Hackers, Breaches, and Cyber Risks
- **Corporate OSINT**: Business Intelligence & Competitive Analysis
- **Investigating Disinformation & Fake News with OSINT**
- **OSINT for Deep & Dark Web**: Techniques for Cybercrime Investigations
- **OSINT Automation**: Python & APIs for Intelligence Gathering
- **OSINT Detective**: Digital Tools & Techniques for Criminal Investigations
- **Advanced OSINT Case Studies**: Real-World Investigations
- **The Ethical OSINT Investigator**: Privacy, Legal Risks & Best Practices

We look forward to seeing you in the next book!

Happy searching!